Praise for Melissa Harris-Perry's *Sister Citizen*

"With clarity and passion, Harris-Perry reveals the ways . . . myths rob Black women of political power."—Bobbi Booker, *Sunday Tribune*

"Harris-Perry offers fascinating observations of how black women are, at times, constricted by their mythology and asserts that their 'experiences act as a democratic litmus test for the nation.'"—Vanessa Bush, *Booklist*

"This is a broad, ambitious and important book that centers black women at the heart of American politics. Harris-Perry broadens our ideas of what counts as political, disrupts our ideas about what the study of American politics should look like, and restores our belief that resistance and struggle can change lives, communities and nations."—Cathy J. Cohen, author of *Boundaries of Blackness* and *Democracy Remixed*

"In this compelling book, dazzling in its breadth and depth, Melissa Harris-Perry deploys the quantitative tools of the political scientist as expertly as she displays the qualitative methods of the literary and cultural critic. *Sister Citizen* challenges readers to rethink the meaning of politics when it comes to the complex lives of African American women."—Beverly Guy-Sheftall, founding director, Spelman College Women's Research and Resource Center

"*Sister Citizen* lends empirical heft to the adage the "personal is political." Melissa Harris-Perry does an excellent job of weaving literature, social science, and personal accounts to produce a powerful work on black women's politics. Brilliant."—Lester K. Spence, author of *Stare in the Darkness: The Limits of Hip-hop and Black Politics*

"[Melissa Harris-Perry's] academic research is inspired by a desire to investigate the challenges facing contemporary black Americans and the creative ways that African Americans respond to these challenges."—*Great Neck Record*

"In *Sister Citizen,* Harris-Perry combines her skills as a social scientist, political observer, writer and griot to deftly illustrate how the social, economic, and political conditions of black women, particularly those on the margins, are the index for America at large."—Byron Williams, *Oakland Tribune*

"A feminist manifesto endeavoring to free sisters forever from the cruel and very limiting ways in which they continue to be pigeonholed."—Kam Williams, *Insight*

Sister Citizen

SISTER CITIZEN

Shame, Stereotypes, and Black Women in America

Melissa V. Harris-Perry

Yale

UNIVERSITY PRESS

New Haven and London

Published with assistance from the Mary Cady Tew Memorial Fund.

Yale University Press books may be purchased in quantity for educational, business, or
promotional use. For information, please e-mail sales.press@yale.edu (US office) or
sales@yaleup.co.uk (UK office).

The publisher gratefully acknowledges permission to reproduce the following: Elizabeth
Alexander, "Praise Song for the Day," from *Crave Radiance: New and Selected Poems,
1990–2010,* copyright © 2009 by Elizabeth Alexander, reprinted with the permission of
Graywolf Press, Minneapolis, Minnesota, www.graywolfpress.org; "No Mirrors in My
Nana's House," copyright © 1998 by Ysaye M. Barnwell, reprinted by permission of
Houghton Mifflin Harcourt Publishing Company; "Resisting the Shaming of Shug Avery"
from *The Color Purple,* copyright © 1982 by Alice Walker, reprinted by permission of
Harcourt, Inc.; excerpt from *Their Eyes Were Watching God,* by Zora Neale Hurston,
copyright 1937 by Harper & Row, Publishers, Inc.; renewed © 1965 by John C. Hurston
and Joel Hurston; reprinted by permission of HarperCollins Publishers; Kate Rushin,
"The Bridge Poem," reprinted by permission of the author.

Set in Bulmer type by Keystone Typesetting, Inc., Orwigsburg, Pennsylvania.
Printed in the United States of America by Sheridan Books, Inc.

The Library of Congress has cataloged the hardcover edition as follows:
Harris-Perry, Melissa V. (Melissa Victoria), 1973–
Sister citizen : shame, stereotypes, and Black women in America / Melissa V. Harris-Perry.
p. cm.
Includes bibliographical references and index.
ISBN 978-0-300-16541-8 (clothbound : alk. paper)
1. African American women—Politics and government. 2. African American women—
Psychology—Political aspects. 3. Stereotypes (Social psychology)—United States.
4. African American women—Social conditions. I. Title.
E185.86.H375 2011
305.48'896073—dc22
2011015860

ISBN 978-0-300-18818-9 (pbk.)

A catalogue record for this book is available from the British Library.

10 9 8 7 6 5 4 3 2 1

For James, who is my Tea Cake ...
except the part where she shoots him
For Blair, who is my Charlotte ...
except the part where she dies young
For Parker, who is my everything ... and always will be

Contents

Acknowledgments

It has taken me an excruciatingly long time to write this book. I had my first glimmer of insight about the themes explored here more than ten years ago. The past decade has been full of dizzying success, failure, joy, loss, passion, betrayal, and change. I have put down and picked up this manuscript a thousand times. I have loved and hated it in rapid succession. I have defended it fiercely and thought of abandoning it entirely. I have never been alone as I have alternately sprinted and limped to the finish line of this project. I have been accompanied by an astonishingly loyal group of scholars, friends, students, loved ones, and critics who have pushed, prodded, and poked in an effort to get this book out of me and onto the page.

I owe so much to all the teachers who believed in me along the way. Mrs. Erickson introduced me to the love of literature in eighth grade. Allen Ramsier gave me permission to take the path less traveled. Maya Angelou held my hand through the sometime difficult years of college and launched me into an academic career. John Brehm and John Aldrich made sure I made it to the finish line. Thank you to Gary Dorrien, Katie Cannon, and my fellow travelers at Union Theological Seminary who renewed my love of experiencing the classroom as a student. I will be satisfied if I give my students even a fraction of what you each gave me.

I am grateful to my colleagues whom I first met during my years at the University of Chicago. Tracey Meares remains my friend, supporter, and inspiration as a black woman in the academy. Jacqueline Stewart's humor, insight, and kindness are beyond compare. As my senior colleague, Michael Dawson always ensured I had the resources and time to write. As my unyielding mentor, Cathy Cohen always made sure I had something about which to write. My interest in the politics of recognition is a direct result of having an office on the same hall with Patchen Markell for seven years. During those same years Jacob Levy planted my persistent skepticism with the assumptions of political science. Healthy competition with Daniel Drezner provided the impetus for taking my ideas beyond the academy and into the public realm. The Workshop on Race and the Reproduction of Racial Ideologies challenged and critiqued my work and forced me to think through new approaches and questions. John Cacioppo's Social Psychology Workshop is where I first encountered the research on shame that fundamentally shaped this project.

At the University of Chicago I was surrounded by fantastic graduate students. They are now successful professionals and scholars in their own right. These men and women went out into neighborhoods to distribute surveys, they helped me cull extant literature, they searched archives, and they helped me clarify complicated ideas. Thanks to Stephanie Allen, Elizabeth Todd, Tehama Lopez, Quincy Mills, Ezekiel Dixon-Roman, Pam Cook, Chris Deis, Rovana Popoff, Bill Clark, Tanji Gilliam, Sujatha Fernandes, and all the other brilliant students who contributed to my research over these years. I can never repay the debt I owe to Bethany Albertson, whose careful and responsive research assistance buoyed me for years and whose friendship continues to light my path. Erica Czaja's research support carried this project the last leg of the journey.

I am incredibly grateful to the undergraduate and graduate students at Princeton University who inspired and supported this book project in many ways. Megan Francis's diligence, intellect, and undeniable snark made my darkest moments in Princeton bearable. Emery Whalen, Farrell Harding, Abena Mackall, Cindy Hong, Kyle Hotchkiss-Carone, and Molly Alacron are just a few of the magnificent students who inspired, directed, and supported my work during the past five years. Many thanks to Gayle Brodsky, whose competence and diligence are the only reason I survived three years as director of undergraduate studies. Thanks are due to Nicole Shelton for walking the canal with me and for reading the psychology chapters and to Daphne Brooks for her careful reading of the introduction. Thanks also to Melvin McCray, whose encouragement, partnership, and energy led to great collaborations in teaching and research. No one was more important to my years at Princeton than Yolanda Pierce. We shared The Kitchen Table, cheered on each other's daughters, drank a thousand gallons of coffee, complained endlessly, and celebrated unceasingly. Thank you for reminding me why we show up to do this work.

I am profoundly thankful to Professor Henry Louis Gates. He gave me a regular platform for my public writing, invited me to deliver the Du Bois lectures, and has treated me to some of the best dinners of my life. Even when we have disagreed, he has always supported my work and cleared a path for me to walk. Elizabeth Alexander and Kimberle Crenshaw are the sister professors whose kindness, support, intellect, and friendship still take my breath away. Thanks to Jonathan Metzl, who believed in the project when it was little more than an idea. Thank you to Lisa Gaines McDonald, who conducted my focus groups. And many thanks to the American Academy of University Women, whose fellowship supported this project in its early phases. Thanks to Marc Lamont Hill for being my friend and writing partner. Thanks to all my African American colleagues in professional political science who have shared the often rough journey from graduate school to tenure and beyond.

Beyond the walls of the universities, I am grateful to the communities that embraced my family and me. Thank you to all the students at Kenwood Academy High School whom I have had the chance to teach and mentor. Thank you to my church family at First UU in Hyde Park. Thanks to Peter Dunham, who made sure I had a comfortable home. Thank you to Tibbie Samios for being a second mom to my daughter on more occasions than I can count. Thanks to Wendy Wintle, who always made sure I had a flight to get me where I was going and a car to get me home. Many thanks to Jane Altman, who protected me when I was most vulnerable, and to Geraldine Holt, who has been my constant advocate for years.

I owe a deep debt to Farai Chideya. Through her NPR show, she gave me my first regular public platform to discuss race and politics. She generously shared her microphone and launched me in a new direction. Richard Kim, my long-suffering editor at the *Nation*, has endured more bad writing, missed deadlines, and lame excuses than I care to admit. Whatever success I have enjoyed is a result of his willingness to clean it up, cheer me on, and push me to produce. I am grateful to Rachel Maddow, who believed in me enough to share her show with me and whose careful, conscientious, self-deprecating, and exceptional work is a constant inspiration. I am grateful to the many audiences with whom I have shared pieces of this project during the past several years. When I wanted to give up, your belief that I was "onto something" kept me going. Many of you will never know how important your well-timed email or hug at the end of a conference or note of thanks was to keeping me on this project. Thanks to the twenty-thousand-plus people who hang out with me on Twitter, read my posts as I complain about deadlines, and cheer me on, 140 characters at a time.

Thank you to the men and women who shared their perspectives in my focus groups, responded to my surveys, and wrote their stories so that I could learn from them. Thank you to all the African American women scholars whose work laid the foundation for my own. I would have been lost in the wilderness without their insights, research, and dedication to pursuing and presenting our stories. Thank you to the courageous women of New Orleans, who demanded their citizenship and rebuilt their city.

I will never forget the first meal I shared with Kathleen Anderson. She is much more than a literary agent. She has become my friend, advocate, constant champion, and insightful adviser. I would never have made it this far without her. Thanks to William Frucht for fighting for this project's home at Yale University Press and to Laura Jones Dooley for editing the messy manuscript with such care and passion. And the book is so much more beautiful because of Meg McVey's determination and expertise in tracking down the images.

Then there is my family. Many thanks to Dani Parker-Robinson for remaining my beloved cousin. Unspeakable gratitude to my eldest sister, Rolisa Tutwyler, who taught me how to be a courageous black woman. Thank you to my nieces and nephews, Catherine, Christina, Claudia, McKinley, Max, and Elise, for inspiring me and making me laugh. Many thanks to James and Corlis Perry, who have embraced me as their own. Thanks to my father, William Harris, Sr., who is my first professorial role model and who keeps surprising me with his love. Thank you to my mother, Diana Gray, who saved me over and over and over again, who has helped raise my daughter at every turn, who read the manuscript at least four times, and whose model of independence, smarts, and commitment to family I try hard to emulate.

Thank you, Blair Kelley. You are my best, most constant, unyielding friend. I know you hate the analogy, but you truly are the Charlotte to my Wilbur. When I think I can't go on, when I think I have nothing to offer, when I think everyone is out to get me, you always remind me that I am "some pig." You have literally saved my life by convincing me that I am "terrific" and "radiant." E. B. White writes of Charlotte, "It is not often that someone comes along who is a true friend and a good writer. Charlotte was both." Blair, you are my true friend and you are the visionary author of the life I now live. I love you . . . fiercely.

Thank you to my husband, James. I am still in awe of what you have done in my life. You changed everything when I no longer believed such change was possible. Thank you for giving me room to write, for giving me courage to move on, for making all the meals when I am working on deadline, for rubbing my shoulders when I am hunched over the computer, for laughing at my jokes, for being a father to my daughter, a son to my mother, and for taking us all in. You teach me every day what love is.

Finally, thank you to my daughter, Parker, who yielded many weekends, evenings, and hours to this book. Your humor, joy, intelligence, beauty, and astonishing embrace of life are inspiration for me. You make me proud, and I hope in your adulthood that this book will make you proud, too. I am finally done. Let's go ride our bikes.

"The Hurricane"

From *Their Eyes Were Watching God*

ZORA NEALE HURSTON

Zora Neale Hurston was criticized both by her contemporaries and by subsequent generations of scholars for being a romantic elitist disconnected from the substantive concerns of black Americans. Dismissed as disengaged storytelling in an era that produced serious political commentary about race, Hurston's work was consigned to a footnote of the Harlem Renaissance. But if we read Hurston carefully, we find important political lessons embedded in the story of a black woman's search for self. Throughout Their Eyes Were Watching God, *Hurston reveals how the politics of race and gender intersect the challenges of self-exploration. Together these forces become a storm, a literal hurricane, in the life of Hurston's main character, Janie Mae Crawford.*

It woke up old Okechobee and the monster began to roll in his bed. Began to roll and complain like a peevish world on a grumble. The folks in the quarters and the people in the big houses further around the shore heard the big lake and wondered. The people felt uncomfortable but safe because there were the seawalls to chain the senseless monster in his bed. The folks let the people do the thinking. If the castle thought themselves secure, the cabins needn't worry.

Their decision was already made as always. Chink up your cracks, shiver in your wet beds and wait on the mercy of the Lord. The bossman might have the thing stopped before morning anyway. It is so easy to be hopeful in the day time when you can see the things you wish on. But it was night, it stayed night. Night was striding across nothingness with the whole round world in his hands.

A big burst of thunder and lightning that trampled over the roof of the house. So Tea Cake and Motor stopped playing. Motor looked up in his angel-looking way and said, "Big Massa draw him chair upstairs."

"Ah'm glad y'all stop dat crap-shootin' even if it wasn't for money," Janie said. "Ole Massa is doin' His work right now. Us oughta keep quiet."

They huddled closer and stared at the door. They just didn't use another part of their bodies, and they didn't look at anything but the door. The time was past for asking the white folks what to look for through that door. Six eyes were questioning *God*.

Through the screaming wind they heard things crashing and things hurtling and dashing with unbelievable velocity. A baby rabbit, terror ridden, squirmed through a hole in the floor and squatted off there in the shadows against the wall, seeming to know that nobody wanted its flesh at such a time. And the lake got madder and madder with only its dikes between them and him.

In a little wind-lull, Tea Cake touched Janie and said, "Ah reckon you wish now you had of stayed in yo' big house 'way from such as dis, don't yuh?"

"Naw."

"Naw?"

"Yeah, naw. People don't die till dey time come nohow, don't keer where you at. Ah'm wid mah husband in uh storm, dat's all."

"Thanky, Ma'am. But 'sposing you wuz to die, now. You wouldn't git mad at me for draggin' yuh heah?"

"Naw. We been tuhgether round two years. If you kin see de light at daybreak, you don't keer if you die at dusk. It's so many people never seen de light at all. Ah wuz fumblin' round and God opened de door."

Introduction

So the beginning of this was a woman and she had come back from burying the dead. Not the dead of sick and ailing with friends at the pillow and the feet. She had come back from the sodden and the bloated; the sudden dead, their eyes flung wide open in judgment.

—Zora Neale Hurston, *Their Eyes Were Watching God*

I f you ask most people what they think of when they hear the word *politics,* they are likely to give a definition that includes voters, parties, elections, public policy, and processes of contestation and representation. But formal participation in government is only one part of a more encompassing effort to be recognized within the nation. The struggle for recognition is the nexus of human identity and national identity, where much of the most important work of politics occurs. African American women fully embody this struggle. By studying the lives of black women, we gain important insight into how citizens yearn for and work toward recognition.

To understand black women's politics, we must explore their often unspoken experiences of hurt, rejection, faith, and search for identity. Zora Neale Hurston's *Their Eyes Were Watching God* takes on the task of understanding the heart of a woman and thereby exposes meaningful political truths about hierarchy, oppression, and liberation. The goal of this book is a similar exploration. It is therefore not the kind of book you might expect from a political scientist. This book is not about black women who hold elected office or about the choices African American women make in the voting booth. It is not about black women's community organizing, protest activities, or policy choices. Rather, this book makes the claim that the internal, psychological, emotional, and personal experiences of black women are inherently political.

They are political because black women in America have always had to wrestle with derogatory assumptions about their character and identity. These assumptions shape the social world that black women must accommodate or resist in an effort to preserve their authentic selves and to secure recognition as citizens. This is less a book about what black women do to become first-class American citizens than one about how they feel while they are in that struggle.

A good place to start this exploration of black women's internal politics is with the extraordinary 1937 novel *Their Eyes Were Watching God,* by the anthropologist, essayist, folklorist, and playwright Zora Neale Hurston. It does not seem like an overtly political text, but in many ways it is emblematic of the racial and gender politics that we observe in contemporary American politics. Hurston's protagonist, Janie Mae Crawford, is a black woman living in the rural South in the years after World War I. It is a classic heroic tale in which Janie confronts the distorted expectations of others and discovers her authentic self.[1] Because Janie's journey forces her to grapple with limiting gender and race roles that constrain her, *Their Eyes Were Watching God* is more than a tale of achieving self-knowledge; it is a narrative that actively questions issues of power, prejudice, and human fulfillment.[2] Hurston takes Janie on a quest for self-understanding, a quest that is expressed in her efforts to find an authentic, loving relationship

in an unpredictable and threatening world where her black womanhood makes her vulnerable to people and systems that seek to trans-
form her into a beast of burden.[3] As a young woman she learns that
her assigned role is to serve as a mule, carrying the weight of racial
prejudice and gendered inequality. "So de white man throw down the
load and tell de nigger man tuh pick it up. He pick it up because he
have to, but he don't tote it. He hand it to his womenfolks. De nigger
woman is de mule uh de world so fur as Ah can see."[4] Janie's journey
is a political one because it is motivated by her refusal to accept this
role.[5]

As she seeks personal freedom, Janie struggles to be recognized
by her grandmother, her husbands, and her community for all of
who she is and not only for the things that her embodied black
womanhood represents. She survives a loveless marriage, arranged
while she was still a child, and then a privileged but brutal existence
with her status-conscious second husband. Ultimately she discovers
a sensual, mutually fulfilling love affair with the much younger Tea
Cake. Although framed by love, this story is about more than romance. Janie must discard the limiting roles that others seek to have
her fulfill. She refuses to be the world's mule but learns how much
she enjoys physical labor of her own choosing. She discovers that
even if she was offered a position at the top of a hierarchy, she prefers
egalitarian interactions. Janie learns to express her own wit and
intelligence, even if her ideas disappoint or scandalize others. In the
end she learns that she must preserve herself even if doing so is
painful. These lessons are as much about the collective struggles of
black women seeking their own freedom as they are about an individual black woman's quest to find fulfillment.

As the text draws to its climax, Hurston places Janie at the center of a storm. Janie and Tea Cake are living in a town in the Florida Everglades; their life is marked by poverty and hard work but also by companionship and community. In their second season there, they listen as Native Americans predict a major storm, and watch as they begin to leave for higher ground. Soon others evacuate too, but Janie, Tea Cake, and their friend Motor Boat are among those who decide to stay and ride out the storm. That night and the next day, the storm builds.

> They huddled closer and stared at the door. They didn't use another part of their bodies, and they didn't look at anything but the door. The time was past for asking the white folks what to look for through that door. Six eyes were questioning *God.* . . . The wind came back with triple fury, and put out the light for the last time. They sat in company with the others in other shanties, their eyes straining against crude walls and their souls asking if He meant to measure their puny might against His. They seemed to be staring at the dark, but their eyes were watching God.[6]

Finally the dikes of Lake Okeechobee burst and the waters begin to overtake the town. Janie and Tea Cake try to flee. They must swim past drowned animals, dead bodies, and massive destruction. Janie is attacked by a rabid dog and saved by Tea Cake. At last they reach the city of Palm Beach, where chaos and destruction await them. Tea Cake is forced to assist in clearing the bodies of the dead. The work is not only vile and difficult but also profoundly racist; white corpses are given coffins while black ones are left in a mass grave covered with quicklime. The racial hierarchy, made obvious during the storm when whites occupied high ground while forcing blacks into the dangerous low-lying land below, is reinforced by these burials.

For today's readers, Hurston's flood evokes the devastation of New Orleans in the aftermath of Hurricane Katrina. In the years since the storm, Hurricane Katrina has become a familiar metaphor—a fashionable tool by which media commentators measure every political catastrophe faced by a presidential administration. Because catastrophes like Katrina focus public attention, reveal institutional shortcomings, and evoke powerful emotional responses, they are easily reduced to casual metaphor. But I want us to try to recapture the initial horror of the tremendous human loss and emotional trauma caused by the storm. Before Hurricane Katrina, New Orleans was a place where, like Janie in the Everglades, many black people lived with poverty and struggle, but also with community and with deep historical and familial connections, and where they made distinctive cultural contributions. This unique black community was severely damaged in August 2005. The order to evacuate came fewer than twenty-four hours before the hurricane made landfall.[7] On the day of the evacuation order, more than one in four individuals in New Orleans lived below the federally defined poverty line, and more than a quarter of New Orleans residents did not own private vehicles. As the storm approached, more than thirty thousand people fled to shelters in the city's Superdome and Convention Center. Those who lacked the resources to get themselves or their families out were forced, like Janie, Tea Cake, and Motor Boat, to endure the storm in their homes.

New Orleans was spared a direct hit, and the city might have swiftly recovered from the extensive, but manageable, damage caused by wind and rain. Yet in the hours after the storm passed, several critical levees failed. As in Hurston's novel, the broken levees unleashed lake waters with frightening force and speed. In vulnerable neighborhoods there was little warning and no means of escape. Stranded, the people waited for relief and rescue that, for days, did not come. The power went out and the floodwaters rose. Food and water became scarce. The city's shelters became centers of disease, hunger, and death. For three days the victims of the storm were left to manage on their own. As they waited, President George W. Bush shared a birthday cake with Senator John McCain, visited a senior citizens' home, gave a speech on the war in Iraq, and played the guitar with a popular country singer. Secretary of State Condoleezza Rice shopped for shoes in New York City and took in a Broadway show. FEMA director Michael Brown sent lighthearted interoffice emails about which shirt and tie he should wear during his live television appearances about the disaster. Despite aggressive and continuing coverage of the destruction on cable news, it seemed that federal government officials refused to recognize what was happening in New Orleans. The contrast between the urgency of the disaster and the paucity of the initial response led many observers to question what caused this inability to see what was happening.

As in Hurston's novel, the storm was a dispassionate and impersonal force, but its destruction was not shared equally. Before the storm, New Orleans was a predominately African American city, and those left in the wake of the hurricane were disproportionately black.[8] Almost exclusively, it was the suffering of black people that was broadcast to a national viewing audience. Poor and black citizens found themselves both more vulnerable to the disaster and less able to recover in its aftermath.[9] Even in the earliest days of the disaster, observers began to note the obvious racial inequality. During a live broadcast on CNN, Representative John Lewis, a senior member of the Congressional Black Caucus, asserted that race was a critical factor influencing both media representations of the disaster and the responses of government officials. Lewis first gained national recognition decades earlier when he was brutally beaten while participating in a voting rights march in Selma, Alabama.[10] The "Bloody Sunday" demonstration was the catalyst leading to passage of the 1965 Voting Rights Act. Throughout his distinguished career, Lewis has enjoyed a certain moral authority on issues of race. His fierce advocacy of domestic civil rights issues and his stance on international human rights concerns have earned him numerous awards, including the NAACP Spingarn Medal and the John F. Kennedy "Profile in Courage" award for lifetime achievement. Even Republican opponents, like John McCain, have written of Lewis as an American of great integrity.[11] In the immediate aftermath of Katrina, Lewis suggested that government officials were reacting inadequately because they considered the lives of black people unworthy of resources and action.[12]

The same argument was made more memorably on September 2, 2005, during a benefit concert. During a live broadcast on NBC, hip-hop artist Kanye West went off script, turned to the cameras, and said: "I hate the way they portray us in the media. You see a black family, it says, 'They're looting.' You see a white family, it says, 'They're looking for food.' And, you know, it's been five days [waiting for federal help] because most of the people are black. And even for me to complain about it, I would be a hypocrite because I've tried to turn away from the TV because it's too hard to watch. . . . We already realize a lot of people that could help are at war right now, fighting another way—and they've given them permission to go down and shoot us! . . . George Bush doesn't care about black people."

These comments churned up a second storm as members of the media, government, and military all sought to deny that race had played any part in the response. The racial aspects of the disaster became a flashpoint for disagreement between black and white Americans.[13] More than five years later, George W. Bush recalled that the moment West accused his administration of racist neglect of Katrina survivors was the low point of his presidency.[14] Yet even as government officials made their denials, black Americans grew increasingly convinced that their government had abandoned them.[15] In the days immediately following the flooding, a Pew Research Center public opinion survey revealed an enormous racial divide. While most Americans (58 percent) felt depressed about the suffering caused by the storm, there were significant differences in how blacks and whites understood the failure to rescue survivors. Seventy percent of African American respondents reported being angry, but only 46 percent of whites were angry. Further, over two-thirds of black respondents (71 percent), versus only 32 percent of whites, believed that responses to the disaster showed that racial inequality is still a major problem. A full 66 percent of blacks believed that the government would have responded faster if the victims were white, while only 17 percent of whites agreed.[16]

The entire nation grieved over the losses in New Orleans, but for black America, the aftermath of Hurricane Katrina forced the question of whether black people were truly American citizens worthy of fair treatment, swift response, and unchallenged rescue. For black Americans the disastrous consequences of wind and water were deepened by the initially slow and then surprisingly militaristic response to black suffering.[17] Black Americans bristled as tens of thousands of African American men, women, and children were labeled "refugees" by the US media, as if the disaster had occurred not on American soil but in a distant country.[18] The refugee label had the effect of rhetorically removing black victims from national responsibility, as though the consequences of the levee failure were to be endured by foreigners rather than by Americans at the bottom of the same hierarchies of race and wealth that had contributed significantly to the disaster itself. As in Hurston's novel, it was these embedded racial wealth inequalities that allowed more white New Orleanians to evacuate before the storm, to return swiftly to the city, and to rebuild in the months following the storm.[19] As it was for Janie and Tea Cake in their hurricane, white residents in New Orleans occupied high ground while blacks sought refuge in the more dangerous territory below. And just as in Hurston's novel, racial hierarchies had life-and-death consequences.

In *Their Eyes Were Watching God,* Tea Cake and Janie finally find their way back home after the storm has subsided. Even then they are not safe. Tea Cake was bitten by a rabid dog while saving Janie, and he ultimately succumbs to madness and delusions. Janie must shoot him to save her own life. Stories from New Orleans in the first days of the flood echoed this plot element as well. Despite the baffling silence of the federal government and the unanswered cries for help, initial media coverage focused on criminal activity rather than on massive human suffering. Left without adequate medical supplies, food, or water, New Orleanians tried to fend for themselves by taking necessary items from stores and businesses. These attempts at survival in a disaster were labeled criminal and were denounced by the very government agencies that failed to provide the urgently needed relief. The governor of Louisiana, Kathleen Blanco, initially voiced her outrage at looters while remaining silent on the lack of coordinated federal response. On August 31, CNN reported that Governor Blanco was "just furious" about lawlessness. "We'll do what it takes to bring law and order to our region," she pledged. On the same day, the Associated Press reported that New Orleans Mayor Ray Nagin had ordered most of the city's dramatically limited police force to halt rescue efforts and to concentrate on stopping looters, who had "grown more aggressive."[20]

Television news reported roving, armed gangs of young black males opportunistically profiting from the tragedy. Reports suggested these men were stealing from electronics stores, raping women trapped in the evacuation centers, and trying to assassinate relief workers.[21] Later evidence showed that most of these young black men were organizing to assist other survivors who were unable to find supplies: the elderly, the sick, and women with children. These men were portrayed as rabid criminals, but their "madness" resulted from trying to save and care for their companions and fellow survivors.[22] In this, they were like Hurston's Tea Cake.

That desperate survivors were portrayed as dangerous criminals was largely a result of the racialized nature of the Katrina disaster. Americans have long connected urban African American communities with crime. Decades of research in sociology, political science, and psychology demonstrate the facile link between blackness and criminality that exists for many Americans.[23] In early reports many US media sources followed a traditional formula of representing black people as dangerous and criminal.[24] Black residents were accused of looting, drug abuse, homicide, and rape during the disaster-evoked chaos. Most of these media-reported crimes were never substantiated, and later research showed that extensive prosocial behavior, not crime, was the primary response of survivors in the days following

Katrina.[25] Still, the alchemy of race and disaster produced a powerful image of chaos and crime that dominated the first news reports.

In this way, Hurricane Katrina became more than an object lesson for preparing for natural disaster, overcoming massive destruction, coping with bureaucratic incompetence, questioning government responsiveness, appreciating civil society's flexibility, celebrating human resilience, or any of the other storylines that emerged in the months and years following the storm. Through its distinctive racial and political character, the debacle became a site for the contestation of black citizenship. Parnell Herbert, a New Orleanian and Katrina survivor whose story is recorded in *Overcoming Katrina: African American Voices from the Crescent City and Beyond,* explains that even the visual images of Katrina told the story of black Americans laying claim to their rights as citizens: "Something that really surprised me was the number of African Americans in New Orleans who had large American flags in their homes. Were they flags that once draped a loved one's casket? Why did the survivors begging for help from the US military forces feel it necessary to wave the American flag, as opposed to a white sheet or blood stained towels?"[26] Herbert's observation reminds us that when they waved their nation's flag, black New Orleanians were making a specific claim of citizenship and belonging. In many ways Hurricane Katrina can be read as Hurston's novel playing out in a contemporary moment: race and class hierarchies structuring the consequences of a natural disaster, powerful white institutions ignoring black suffering, and black men driven mad as they try to rescue others in the aftermath of the storm. But the connections go deeper than these incidental similarities. In Hurston's novel the Everglades hurricane is a definitive event revealing the inequalities of society, but it is not the entirety of

Janie's life. Similarly, the women who endured Katrina's aftermath are more than storm survivors; they are workers, mothers, daughters, aunts, pastors, doctors, friends, and congregants. Their stories begin long before August 29, 2005, and their experiences in the storm are shaped by the social positions they occupied before the levees failed. A racial analysis of the Katrina disaster has become received wisdom, but the story of this historic moment is a story not only of race but of gender.

As the disaster unfolded, black women became the main characters through whose suffering and resilience the media told the story. Just as Janie Mae Crawford is the focus of Hurston's novel, black women were at the eye of the rhetorical storm of Hurricane Katrina. It is on the bodies, minds, and lives of black women that the story of Katrina was written. Photographs of black mothers carrying their infants as they waded through filthy, chest-high water became enduring images of the disaster. Television news and popular magazines used images of desperate, frightened African American women to dramatize the tragedy facing residents as they battled the aftermath of the hurricane with little official assistance. Their suffering became the conduit through which new conversations on race, class, and vulnerability began. They were the bridge over the deadly waters that allowed the rest of America to cross into the agonizing realization of how unequal the country remained at the dawn of the twenty-first century.

Within five days of the storm, national media reports began to shift away from black men represented as looters, rapists, and snipers and to focus instead on black women and children trapped in the city's evacuation centers. These women became the sympathetic victims of the storm. Post-Katrina New Orleans, as read through the lens of Hurston's novel, is a place to begin taking seriously the idea that black women's experiences act as a democratic litmus test for the nation. Legal scholars Lani Guinier and Gerald Torres offered the useful metaphor of the miner's canary for understanding how the political and economic realities of marginal populations indicate the democratic and economic health of the nation. Miners used canaries with sensitive respiratory systems to alert them to poisonous gasses in the atmosphere of the mine. In a similar manner, vulnerable communities of black and brown Americans foreshadow the underlying problems likely to poison the US system. In August 2005, black women of New Orleans became the nation's miner's canary.

Issues of race, gender, and class inequality that affect black women's lives in America point to problems embedded in the fabric of the nation. Katrina rendered those inequalities highly visible. Inadequate evacuation capacity pointed to America's failure to invest in modern public transportation systems. The levee failure was indicative of America's crumbling infrastructure. The delayed government response was a sign of the limitations of federalism and a harbinger of compromised homeland security. The grinding urban poverty revealed by the storm was prophetic of impending economic crisis. The disproportionate burden of the disaster shouldered by African American women was a symbol of the brutal intersections of race, class, and gender that black women confront daily.

The nineteenth- and twentieth-century educator Anna Julia Cooper wrote, "Only the black woman can say 'when and where I enter, in the quiet, undisputed dignity of my womanhood, without violence and without suing or special patronage, then and there the whole . . . race enters with me.' "[27] It is African American women, surviving at the nexus of racialized, gendered, and classed dis-privilege, who mark the progress of the nation. In the 1970s, the African American women of the Combahee River Collective recognized their continuing position, writing, "If Black women were free, it would mean that everyone else would have to be free since our freedom would necessitate the destruction of all the systems of oppression."[28] At the start of the twenty-first century, as the floodwaters rose in New Orleans, the lives of black women once again stood for America's failures to achieve its dream of democratic equality. Hurston's Janie undertakes a voyage of self-understanding, romance, psychic exploration, and communal struggle that represents something larger than her personal story; so, too, do the images and experiences of black women trapped by the flood in New Orleans represent the broader political reality of race, gender, class, and vulnerability in the American state.

Under the headline "Pray for Us," the September 12, 2005, cover of *Newsweek* featured a distressed black woman carrying an infant and a toddler as she raced for an evacuation bus. The caption read "A Katrina refugee and her two children." The *Economist* the same week displayed a weeping black woman in a New Orleans T-shirt, under the headline "The Shaming of America." These two magazine covers capture important elements of how depictions of black women were used to frame the disaster. Early reports repeatedly referred to storm survivors as "refugees" and asked, "How can an American city look like Mogadishu or Port-au-Prince?"[29] Despite being discussed as though they were distant foreigners, these black women retained the power to shame the nation through their suffering. As women and mothers they could represent victimization in a way that male survivors could not. In a country where patriarchal norms still demand that women and children be saved first, the

Cover of the *Economist,* September 10, 2005. Photo: © The Economist
Newspaper Limited, London, September 10, 2005

abandonment of poor black mothers and their children argued that these chivalrous impulses rarely extend to African American women. They shamed the nation because the American narrative is triumphant and collective. Americans take great pride in understanding themselves as a prosperous, just, and fair nation steeped in relative equality and uncompromised liberty. The televised deaths from dehydration of elderly black women in a major urban center did not fit this triumphant narrative.

It is a dangerous enterprise to introduce this text with a journalistic account and a literary frame, because it risks reducing the massive human suffering caused by Hurricane Katrina to little more than a metaphor or literary device. More than fifteen hundred people died in the aftermath of Katrina. More than half a million were permanently displaced. Billions of dollars of property was damaged. Entire communities were wiped away. Homes, schools, churches, and stores were irreparably damaged. Decades of family memories were lost. Centuries of traditions were altered in moments. Years after the storm, the city of New Orleans continues to struggle with the blight, economic devastation, and personal suffering induced by the levee breach. To try to understand the consequences of Katrina through a Harlem Renaissance novel is to risk a dangerous mediation of experience that makes already vulnerable persons into little more than characters in a story.

Despite these dangers, there is something important to be gained from understanding this experience through the lens of fiction. Literary parallels can reveal truths that might otherwise be obscured. That is why I begin this work of social science with a work of fiction. Literature crafts a specific story to reveal a universal truth.[30] I want to make a claim for Janie, as well as for the individual black women whom Janie represents, as an appropriate subject for the study of broader phenomena. It is important to understand political processes through the vulnerable human lives that are part of the larger story. By Henry Louis Gates's reading, *Their Eyes Were Watching God* does its most important political work by subverting our expectations of what counts as political.[31] Like Hurston, I hope to disrupt our assumptions about the study of politics by beginning my investigation of contemporary American politics in the hearts and minds of ordinary black women.

This book is not a work of history, but it relies on black women's history as a frame for understanding contemporary politics. It is not a work of literary criticism, but it relies on literature written by and about black women. It is not a biography, but it gives some black women an opportunity to tell parts of their personal stories. It is not a traditional social science text, but it makes use of empirical data. This book is concerned with understanding the emotional realities of black women's lives in order to answer a political, not a personal, question: What does it mean to be a black woman and an American citizen? Black women are rarely recognized as archetypal citizens. Just as many of Hurston's critics were unwilling to acknowledge Janie's exploration of her psychic reality as politically important, so have political observers largely failed to consider what we can learn about American politics by exploring the psychology of black women. This book is intended to correct that deficiency. I use the lived experiences of African American women as my point of departure for understanding democratic citizenship in the United States. I will provide empirical evidence that the internal worlds of black women are both constituted by and influential in the political realities in which they live.

African American women face unique expectations as citizens of the United States. The particular histories of slavery, Jim Crow, urban segregation, racism, and patriarchy that are woven into the fabric of American politics have created a specific citizenship imperative for African American women—a role and image to which they are expected to conform. We can call this image the "strong black woman." It defines the mantle that the nation, black communities, and black women themselves expect African American women to assume. The social construction of black women's citizenship and identity around the theme of self-sacrificial strength is a recurrent motif in black women's lives and politics. The strong black woman is easily recognizable. She confronts all trials and tribulations. She is a source of unlimited support for her family. She is a motivated, hard-working breadwinner. She is always prepared to do what needs to be done for her family and her people. She is sacrificial and smart. She suppresses her emotional needs while anticipating those of others. She has an irrepressible spirit that is unbroken by a legacy of oppression, poverty, and rejection.[32]

Over the course of this book I will offer a theory of how the strong black woman came to function as a racial and citizenship imperative for black women. I believe that the construct of the strong black woman does not arise from empirical observation of who black women actually are. Instead it is a racial and political construct emanating from the expectations of African American communities and from the needs of the nation that frame black women in very narrow ways. In the language of political theorists, the strong black woman myth is a misrecognition of African American women. But it creates specific expectations for their behavior within the American polity. I first set out a theory of recognition as it relates to contemporary African American women. Then I explore the history of intentional misrecognition of black women. Next I discuss how these misrecognitions contribute to pervasive experiences of shame for black women and try to understand how shame limits the opportunities for African American women as political and thought leaders. Finally, I claim that the imperative of impervious strength is, in part, a shame management strategy that has both emotional and political consequences for black women. Like Hurston's novel, this book is not only a story of achieving personal fulfillment but a call for the creation of new forms of politics rooted in a deep and textured understanding of black women's lives. Empirical social science can illuminate the human experience of politics by forcing us to think about what it means to black women when they seek to fulfill the responsibilities and access the rights of citizenship. This book uses statistical, experimental, and qualitative data to draw out these meanings. It also relies on black feminist traditions that emphasize individual biographies and fictional narratives as entryways to understanding collective race and gender experiences.

Hurston concludes her novel with Janie alone but self-possessed. She has survived personal attacks, rejection, and violence. She has also survived the impersonal, chaotic destruction of the hurricane. We are left with Janie pulling the world around her shoulders. "She pulled in her horizon like a great fish-net. Pulled it from around the waist of the world and draped it over her shoulder. So much of life in its meshes! She called in her soul to come and see." *Their Eyes Were Watching God* never articulates an explicitly political role for Janie. Instead of leading a community or movement, Janie chooses a solitary and contemplative life. But she is not entirely alone. The novel consists of Janie's retelling of her story to her sympathetic girlfriend,

Phoeby, knowing that Phoeby will share the story with other women in town. Although Hurston does not tell us exactly what Phoeby does with Janie's story; we do learn that by listening to Janie, Phoeby comes to feel "ten feet taller." We know that she plans to return home to her husband and demand to be treated more equally. Phoeby's task is to hear Janie's story, be made taller by it, and use it to demand changes in the systems of racism and patriarchy that circumscribe American life. She challenges us because we, as readers, are in the same position relative to Janie. We have heard the story, and it is our job to make politics out of it. The book in your hands is not so much Janie's story as Phoeby's.[33]

"The Bridge Poem"

KATE RUSHIN

This Bridge Called My Back is a groundbreaking anthology of writing by women of color. Edited by Cherríe Moraga and Gloria Anzaldúa, this sweeping collection of poetry, essays, and analytic pieces gathers the voices of black, Latina, and Native American women whose identities have forced them to the margins of the racial, ethnic, and white women's movements of the previous decades. These works challenge patriarchy, misogyny, homophobia, and racism. This Bridge Called My Back is a foundational text of third wave feminism. In it, poet Kate Rushin's "The Bridge Poem" articulates the burdens many African American women experience as a result of attempting to fulfill multiple, competing roles that serve the needs of others more than themselves.

I've had enough
I'm sick of seeing and touching
Both sides of things
Sick of being the damn bridge for everybody

Nobody
Can talk to anybody
Without me
Right?

I explain my mother to my father
my father to my little sister
My little sister to my brother
my brother to the white feminists
The white feminists to the Black church folks
the Black church folks to the ex-hippies
the ex-hippies to the Black separatists
the Black separatists to the artists
the artists to my friends' parents . . .

Then
I've got to explain myself
To everybody

I do more translating
Than the Gawdamn U.N.

Forget it
I'm sick of it.

I'm sick of filling in your gaps

Sick of being your insurance against
the isolation of your self-imposed limitations

Sick of being the crazy at your holiday dinners

Sick of being the odd one at your Sunday Brunches

Sick of being the sole Black friend to 34 individual white
    people

Find another connection to the rest of the world
Find something else to make you legitimate
Find some other way to be political and hip

I will not be the bridge to your womanhood
Your manhood
Your humanness

I'm sick of reminding you not to
Close off too tight for too long

I'm sick of mediating with your worst self
On behalf of your better selves

I am sick
Of having to remind you
To breathe
Before you suffocate
Your own fool self

Forget it
Stretch or drown
Evolve or die

The bridge I must be
Is the bridge to my own power

I must translate
My own fears
Mediate
My own weaknesses

I must be the bridge to nowhere
But my true self
And then
I will be useful

One

Crooked Room

The master's tools will never dismantle the master's house.

—Audre Lorde

Zora Neale Hurston writes Janie Mae Crawford as an irrepressibly independent woman. Janie leaves the economic security of her emotionally deadening first marriage to pursue adventure and love. After the death of her second husband, she flouts social convention and follows her heart into an affair with a much younger man. When her beloved descends into madness and threatens her life, she kills him rather than allow him to destroy her. When she is ready to return home, she does so despite the whispers and scandal occasioned by her unconventional choices. By following this path Janie does not avoid pain, loss, and disappointment, but by choosing her own burdens rather than allowing the burdens of others to be heaped on her back, Janie refutes her grandmother's prophecy that black women are the mules of the world. Janie's quest is about carving out a life that suits her authentic desires rather than conforming to the limiting, often soul-crushing expectations that others have of her. In this way, her personal journey is a model of the struggle many black women face.

This struggle is interestingly mirrored in the post–World War II cognitive psychology research on field dependence. Field dependence studies show how individuals locate the upright in a space. In one study, subjects were placed in a crooked chair in a crooked room and then asked to align themselves vertically. Some perceived themselves as straight only in relation to their surroundings. To the researchers' surprise, some people could be tilted by as much as 35 degrees and report that they were perfectly straight, simply because they were aligned with images that were equally tilted. But not everyone did this: some managed to get themselves more or less upright regardless of how crooked the surrounding images were.[1]

When they confront race and gender stereotypes, black women are standing in a crooked room, and they have to figure out which way is up. Bombarded with warped images of their humanity, some black women tilt and bend themselves to fit the distortion. It may be surprising that some gyrate half-naked in degrading hip-hop videos that reinforce the image of black women's lewdness. It may be shocking that some black women actors seem willing to embody the historically degrading image of Mammy by accepting movie roles where they are cast as the nurturing caretakers of white women and children. It may seem inexplicable that a respected black woman educator would stamp her foot, jab her finger in a black man's face, and scream while trying to make a point on national television, thereby reconfirming the notion that black women are irrationally angry.[2] To understand why black women's public actions and political strategies sometimes seem tilted in ways that accommodate the degrading stereotypes about them, it is important to appreciate the structural constraints that influence their behavior.[3] It can be hard to stand up straight in a crooked room.

The subtitle of this book is an adaptation of Ntozake Shange's choreopoem, *for colored girls who have considered suicide / when the rainbow is enuf. For colored girls* is a definitive artistic, visual, and poetic representation of the experience of the crooked room. It has sold more than a hundred thousand copies. The play was first produced Off-Broadway in 1975. The next year it became a Broadway production, and in 1977 it earned an Obie Award for distinguished production and a Tony Award for Best Featured Actress. The official publication, production, and awards history does not capture the meaning of this piece for African American women. Since its introduction more than thirty years ago, *for colored girls* has been a mainstay in the personal libraries of African American women, of black feminist curriculum, and of black women's local theater productions. Literary scholar Salamishah Tillet describes it as the "black feminist bible," and author Ntozake Shange observes, "Not a day goes by when some young woman somewhere isn't doing a *for colored girls* monologue, making the voice her own, finding her own infinite beauty once again."[4]

Shange's piece viscerally depicts the crooked room that black women confront.[5] The production portrays the harshest and most bitter experiences of black women's lives. Her characters suffer sexual and romantic betrayal, abuse, rape, illegal abortion, heartbreak, and rejection. *For colored girls* has lasting significance for so many because it presents black women's experiences with unflinching rawness that is not primarily concerned with translating these experiences for a broader audience. Its primary goal is to give voice to black women by acknowledging the challenges they face, not to invoke pity or even empathy either from black men or from white viewers. It speaks to and about black women, and it does so by using language, images, and experiences that resonate for black women.

For many who love it, reading or seeing Shange's *for colored girls* is like noticing not that one is alone in the crooked room but, rather, that there are others standing bent, stooped, or surprisingly straight. It is an experience of having someone make visible the slanted images that too frequently remain invisible. "The poems were addressing situations that bridged our secret (unspoken) longing. *For colored girls* still is a women's trip, and the connection we can make through it, with each other and for each other, is to empower us all."[6]

Shange's work exposes the fragility of black women's emotional lives and insists that the agony of their experiences is collective, structural, and not of their own making, but it is not exclusively an exploration of victimization. Though her characters know pain, they also know love, passion, exploration, joy, music, and dance. Despite the incredible obstacles they face, not all of her women are irreparably broken. Results from the psychological studies of the crooked room showed that many respondents did find a way to discern the true upright position even when everything around them was distorted. Hurston's account of Janie Mae Crawford in *Their Eyes Were Watching God* is a literary example of this ability to find the upright, as is Shange's final poem in *for colored girls,* "A Laying on of Hands." Black women's political history is similarly filled with examples of this independence. Black women of the early twentieth-century club movement resisted the lie of black promiscuity by leading a movement for temperance, modesty, and respectability.[7] African American domestic workers resisted the idea of Mammy-like devotion to whites by living outside their employers' homes, protesting unfair labor conditions, and nurturing their own families and communities.[8] Women of the civil rights movement helped change the country, not through angry violence, but through disciplined endurance of racist counter-attacks against their nonviolent struggle. These women managed to stand straight despite the crooked world in which they lived.

Sometimes black women can conquer negative myths, sometimes they are defeated, and sometimes they choose not to fight. Whatever the outcome, we can better understand sisters as citizens when we appreciate the crooked room in which they struggle to stand upright. In the next several chapters I will pose a number of questions about how black women's politics is affected by the crooked images they encounter. Is it possible that black women's organizing efforts and public reactions to issues of sexual assault are linked to their beliefs about the stereotype of black women's promiscuity? Does the pervasive notion of Mammy help explain why black women are suspicious of coalitions with white women? Do black women often defer to black men's religious, familial, and political leadership because they reject the idea that they are angry and domineering? Having a clear view of the distorted images and painful stereotypes that make America a crooked room for African American women is the first step toward understanding how these stereotypes influence black women as political actors.

To learn more about the titled images of the crooked room that contemporary black women encounter in the United States, I conducted focus groups with forty-three African American women in Chicago, New York, and Oakland.[9] As a warm-up task, I asked participants to think about black women as a group and list the stereotypes or myths about them that other people may hold. I then asked them to write down the "facts" about black women as they saw them. They worked in groups and had very lively discussions about both the myths and the facts. Although these women lived in different cities, were of several generations, and had different economic and family circumstances, their discussions formed a coherent picture. They independently arrived at the same three stereotypes that many researchers of African American women's experience also identify: Mammy, Jezebel, and Sapphire.

Like the women in the focus groups, some readers will find these stereotypes familiar, others may never have heard of these myths, and still others may not know the negative connotations attached to them. In the next chapter I will explore the historical and contemporary outlines of the three stereotypes at length, but for the purposes of understanding the general idea of the crooked room, here I offer the brief explanations given by the women in the focus groups. For those of you less familiar with these ideas, I ask you to trust me for a few more pages that Mammy, Jezebel, and Sapphire are common and painful characterizations of black women and that each has a long history in American social and cultural life.

As they identified the main stereotypes, the focus group participants said that black women are seen either as "oversexed" or as "fat mammies who aren't thinking about sex at all." There was broad agreement that white people generally saw them as either promiscuous or asexual. "Jezebel," "maid," and "Mammy" were the terms they used most often to label these stereotypes. Margaret, a fifty-two-year-old woman from the West Beverly neighborhood of Chicago, said, "Just because we are African we're supposed to be wild and all this. We are supposed to be from the jungle and like to have wild sex. Like that is all we think about. Folks think we're hot to trot. Or they think we're Aunt Jemima. It's never in between."

Many talked about the "welfare queen" as an ever-present characterization. Although nearly all the women rejected the hypersexual and Mammy stereotypes, several agreed with the welfare queen myth. "That is not a myth," one participant said. "That belongs on the 'fact' side of the page. There are a lot of black women out here living on the system." Still, everyone agreed that not all black women conformed to the image of welfare cheat, and most argued that the stereotype was damaging even if it was rooted in real behaviors.

The focus group members believed that black men and other black women also perpetuated myths about black women. "Haters," "gold diggers," "overly demanding," and "argumentative" emerged as the main intraracial characterizations of black women. One professional woman in her fifties said, "Black men always try to say that we are manipulative and too bossy and too demanding. They act like they don't know that black women are the backbone of the family. We keep things together. The man may be the head of the household, but we are the backbone and the backbone has got to be strong."

Throughout this book I will return often to these women's voices. Their insights set my research agenda by giving me clues about where to look to understand black women's emotional and political experiences. Their discussions of myths pointed me toward three particular characterizations: hypersexuality, Mammy, and emasculating anger. These were the recurring stereotypes that participants said influence how others saw them. Most of the women also talked about their personal strategies to counter these negative assumptions. "I respect myself, so I know that nobody can call me a ho." "I let my husband be the man in our house, so he never says that mess to me [about being too bossy]. He knows he is my man and God made him the head of our home." "I have never been on welfare. I worked two jobs, but I have never been on welfare." These narratives reveal the ways that black women attempt to stand upright in a room made crooked by the stereotypes about black women as a group.[10]

In their 2003 book *Shifting: The Double Lives of Black Women in America,* Charisse Jones and Kumea Shorter-Gooden report on the results of their African American Women's Voices Project. After surveying and conducting in-depths interviews with hundreds of black women, they discovered that "97 percent acknowledge that they are aware of negative stereotypes of African American women and 80 percent confirm that they have been personally affected by these persistent racist and sexist assumptions."[11] Their book provides detailed evidence of how black women accommodate other people's expectations by shifting their tone of voice, outward behaviors, and expressed attitudes.[12] The women in my focus groups offer additional evidence that black women believe others think negatively about them. Jones and Shorter-Gooden's research shows that this awareness has real effects on how black women see themselves, how they pursue personal relationships, and how they comport themselves at work. I think it also influences how they understand themselves as citizens, what they believe is possible in their relationship with the state, and what they expect from their political organizing.

The Politics of Recognition

We can characterize African American women's struggle with the slanted images of the crooked room as a problem of recognition—an important theme for political philosophers interested in issues of identity, difference, and citizenship.[13] Recognition scholarship derives from the concept, central to Hegelian philosophy, of *Anerkennung,* or mutually affirming recognition that allows citizens to operate as equals within the confines of the social contract.[14] Hegel proposes recognition as an animating struggle of human society and particularly of public life. Anerkennung is a core feature of the relationship between citizens and the state. Citizens want and need more than a fair distribution of resources: they also desire meaningful recognition of their humanity and uniqueness, and they are willing to make sacrifices to get it.

The social contract is the basis of democratic citizenship. Within this contract, individuals subject themselves to rules, constraints, and collective burdens imposed by the state (such as taxes and military service) in exchange for safety and services provided by the state (such as security and social programs). Implied rather than explicit, the social contract is the key to stable, voluntary democratic institutions. The social contract of democratic governments assumes that governing authority derives from consent of the governed rather than from divine command, hereditary connection, or armed capacity. American founding documents draw heavily and explicitly on Enlightenment traditions steeped in the idea of a social contract in which recognition plays a central role. For example, the Declaration of Independence asserts citizens' collective right and responsibility to draft a social contract that allows not only safety and freedom but also the pursuit of happiness.

Although liberal social contract theory is aggressively individualist, Hegel's theory of recognition is aware of reciprocity and of community and social relationships. Taking recognition seriously means understanding that groups are as important as individuals for specifying the correct relationship between the state and its citizens. Citizenship is more than an individual exchange of freedoms for rights; it is also membership in a body politic, a nation, and a community. To be deemed fair, a system must offer its citizens equal opportunities for public recognition, and groups cannot systematically suffer from misrecognition in the form of stereotype and stigma. In the next chapter I describe how this democratic requirement of equal recognition has been violated for African American women in their relationship with the American society and state. But first, I want to pause to explore why political theorists consider recognition so important to the experience of citizenship.

According to Hannah Arendt, the public sphere makes a unique contribution to human self-actualization by offering opportunities for recognition. "The public realm . . . was reserved for individuality; it was the only place where men could show who they really and inexchangeably were. It was for the sake of this chance, and out of love for a body politic that made it possible to them all, that each was more or less willing to share in the burden of justification, defense, and administration of public affairs."[15] People are willing to do the work of citizenship, Arendt suggests, because the public sphere offers them a chance to be seen and recognized as unique individuals. Her reasoning hints that recognition is part of the solution to the collective action problem represented by the democratic social contract, the problem of ensuring contributions to the collective (such as taxes or military service) even when an individual's personal interest might best be served by refusing to contribute. To the extent that people crave recognition opportunities made possible only by participation in the public sphere, recognition acts as a selective incentive, encouraging prosocial behavior and freeing the state from enforcing all contributions through threat of punishment.

Thomas Hobbes, asking why individuals would give up their perfect natural freedom to enter into a social contract that is less free, finds the explanation in the need for safety. Without a state, men may be free, but their lives are "solitary, poor, nasty, brutish, and short."[16] Arendt offers a provocative alternate explanation. People are willing to shoulder the burden of self-government because the public sphere offers a particular, indivisible, nontransferrable good that is otherwise unavailable to them: recognition. Craving recognition of one's special, inexchangeable uniqueness is part of the human condition, and it is soothed only by the opportunity to contribute freely to the public realm.

The problem for marginal and stigmatized group members should be obvious. These citizens face fundamental and continuing threats to their opportunity for accurate recognition. Individuals denied access to the public realm or whose group membership limits their social possibilities cannot be accurately recognized. An individual who is seen primarily as a part of a despised group loses the opportunity to experience the public recognition for which the human self strives. Further, if the group itself is misunderstood, then to the extent that one is seen as a part of this group, that "seeing" is inaccurate. Inaccurate recognition is painful not only to the psyche but also to the political self, the citizen self.

Arendt maps a deep connection between the public and private selves. Misrecognition in public has a profound impact on the private self. "Since our feeling for reality depends utterly upon appearance and therefore upon the existence of a public realm into which things can appear out of the darkness of sheltered existence, even the twilight which illuminates our private and intimate lives is ultimately derived from the much harsher light of the public realm." Despite its importance, Arendt refuses to fetishize the public sphere. Recognition in public begins with nurturing solitude in a protected, autonomous private realm. Individuals need sheltered, private space not available to public view. Without this privacy, life "loses the quality of rising into sight from some darker ground which must remain hidden if it is not to lose its depth in a very real, non-subjective sense."[17]

The need for privacy creates another dilemma for black women. In the next chapter I argue that because of their history as chattel slaves, their labor market participation as domestic workers, and their role as dependents in a punitive modern welfare state, black women in America live under heightened scrutiny by the state. As members of a stigmatized group, African American women lack opportunities for accurate, affirming recognition of the self and yet must contend with hypervisibility imposed by their lower social status. As a group, they have neither the hiding place of private property nor a reasonable expectation of being properly recognized in the public sphere. This situation undermines the intersecting needs for privacy and recognition that underlie the democratic social contract.

Recognition is a useful framework because it emphasizes the interconnection between individuals and groups. Individuals from disempowered social groups desire recognition for their group but also want recognition of their distinctiveness from the group.[18] Thus many African Americans bristle at the idea of color blindness because it suggests that race is irrelevant to identity. They want to be understood as black and thus tied to a history and culture associated with blackness. At the same time, they do not want to be reduced to their racial identity alone. Just recognition means being neither blind to nor blinded by identity differences.

Misrecognition has been a central theme in African American intellectual traditions. In *The Souls of Black Folk*, W. E. B. Du Bois describes the experience of living behind a veil and asks, "How does it feel to be a problem?"[19] This formulation of black life in America emphasizes both the physical barriers imposed by segregation, which make it difficult for black people to be seen, and the dispositional racism that views black life as problematic for the nation. Ralph Ellison's stunning novel *Invisible Man* is a masterful treatment of the recognition crisis faced by black Americans. It opens with a declaration of misrecognition: "I am invisible, understand, simply because people refuse to see me."[20] Ellison's protagonist struggles with multiple forms of misrecognition. He finds that he is sometimes hypervisible, exposed to the aggressive and unwanted gaze of tormentors, and at other times transparent, as though those whom he encounters can simply see through him. Always, racism keeps others from seeing him accurately.

African American feminist scholar bell hooks asserts the primacy of recognition as a precondition for citizenship in her book *Black Looks*. She argues that the very act of looking at individuals from marginal groups is infused with power. To be a person of relative power and privilege viewing a person of less power and privilege is a political act. The gaze of the powerful is neither neutral nor benign; misrecognition hinders the ability of black people to act as citizens. Indeed, hooks asserts, challenging white people's assumptions about what they see when they view black people is a critical step toward liberation and equality.[21]

The misrecognition experienced by black women who attempt to engage in the public sphere is what I mean when I speak of the crooked room. By emphasizing recognition in my analysis, I am making a specific and potentially controversial choice. Why should we be concerned with inaccurate recognition when injustices of distribution seem so much more pressing? Shouldn't we focus on the unequal social, economic, and political structures that profoundly and disproportionately affect black women's material circumstances and opportunities?

Political scientist Patchen Markell points to the limits of politics organized around recognition as the preeminent democratic good. This view of democracy, he writes, assumes that subordinated groups are primarily harmed by "a ubiquitous and deep-seated form of injustice, called 'misrecognition,' which consists in the failure, whether out of malice or out of ignorance, to extend to people the respect or esteem that is due to them in virtue of who they are." While this may be true, Markell argues, recognition is an endogenous process. Humans do not simply have a "true self" that is either recognized or not. Individuals become who they are as a result of being seen: "Recognition [is not] a thing of which one has more or less, rather [it is] a social interaction that can go well or poorly in various ways." Citizenship is therefore bound up with recognition in complicated ways, and justice requires more than demanding to be seen, or to be seen accurately. Engaging in the public sphere through politics is "the ongoing, unpredictable, and eminently political activity through which we become who we are."[22]

Recognition is thus a problematic entry point for a work on African American women's political lives. Recognition scholarship, like its political counterpart, identity politics, is routinely maligned as concerned with symbols rather than substance, cultural battles rather than economic ones, the appearance of power rather than the exercise of it. What difference does it make that other people recognize your uniqueness if you don't have equal access to political and economic resources?

The social and political theorist Nancy Fraser has been critical of the ways that a focus on recognition can silence concerns about economic redistribution. She levels a damning criticism against theorists of multiculturalism who seem concerned more with the culture wars than with the material circumstances of marginal people. But rather than discard recognition as a theoretical framework, Fraser encourages us to see the interplay of recognition and redistribution. Recognition of race, gender, and sexual identity is not, she argues, simply a matter of self-actualization for the citizen, nor is recognition solely a matter of personal interactions among individuals. It is intimately bound to distributive justice: misrecognition is a matter of "institutionalized patterns of cultural value in ways that prevent one from participating as a peer in social life."[23] Distribution inequalities of social, political, and economic goods are related to the inability to "see" citizens from low-status, stigmatized groups accurately. Fair distribution alone cannot solve the problem of misrecognition, nor can accurate recognition alone fairly redistribute resources.

My decision to begin with a framework of recognition politics is based in empirical findings that start with the women in my focus groups. As African American women described the barriers and difficulties they experience, many pointed to issues of misrecognition. The recognition framework also brings to the fore the emotional experiences of black women as a location for political understanding. There are clear connections between public misrecognition and black women's experiences. It is painful to labor under negative stereotypes; my goal is to show the political consequences of that personal pain. Political philosopher Charles Taylor describes the crooked room problem when he writes, "A person or group of people can suffer real damage, real distortion, if the people or society around them mirror back to them a confining or demeaning or contemptible picture of themselves."[24] Although I will address material and structural inequality, this book is primarily about recognition. My task is to explain how black women's citizenship is shaped by their attempts to navigate a room made crooked by stereotypes that have psychic consequences.

Black Women's Crooked Room

Eliza Gallie was a free black woman living in Petersburg, Virginia, before the Civil War. She was divorced, owned property, and had financial resources that made her unusual among free blacks in the Confederate South. In 1853 Gallie was arrested and charged with stealing cabbages from a white man's garden. Autonomous and assertive, she could afford to fight back against the scurrilous claim. She employed several aggressive attorneys who argued her case. But a Southern, white, male legal system declared her guilty and sentenced her to be publicly whipped on her bare back. Historian Suzanne Lebsock reminds us, "She was helpless in the end, the victim of the kind of deliberate humiliation that for most of us is past imagining."[25]

In 2002 historian Chana Kai Lee, not yet forty years old, was a tenured professor at the University of Georgia and the author of an award-winning biography of civil rights leader Fannie Lou Hamer.[26] Complications from lupus caused two severe strokes within a week. Though she was left with disabled speech and diminished physical capacities, her department chair insisted that to keep her job, Lee must immediately return to the classroom. Her physician wrote multiple letters explaining the severity of Lee's condition, but she was pressured to resume teaching because "the state is concerned about sick leave abuse." Reflecting on the humiliating and physically impossible task of addressing a large classroom only weeks after a stroke, Lee saw herself as victimized by familiar stereotypes about black women. "Images of a 'welfare cheat' kept playing in my head. Ph.D. or no Ph.D., tenure or no tenure, I was just like the rest of those lazy black folks: I'd do anything for a cheap ride. I'd take advantage of any situation. I'd exaggerate and manipulate good, responsible, white folks who played by the rules, all to avoid my responsibilities."[27]

Lee's stroke and its humiliating aftermath occurred more than 150 years after Eliza Gallie was publicly flogged for supposedly stealing a white man's cabbage. The country was a profoundly different place in 2002 from what it was in 1853. Black women are no longer enslaved, and they enjoy the constitutional assurance of full citizenship. Centuries of struggle, sacrifice, and achievement have altered basic economic, political, and social realities for black women in vast and meaningful ways. Being required to limp and slur in front of dozens of college students is horrifying, but it is not the same as being publicly whipped.[28] Lee was forced by economic necessity to return to work. Gallie lived in fear of racial murder against which there was no reasonable protection in the United States in 1853. Their experiences are not the same.

Yet there is a thin but tenacious thread connecting Gallie to Lee. Each is a woman of relative economic privilege and freedom. Powerful white institutions subjected both to public humiliation and physical suffering. As a historian, Chana Kai Lee interprets her experience of punishment as resulting from the practice of stereotyping black women as welfare cheats. The jurors in antebellum Petersburg, Virginia, were willing to convict Gallie in part because they believed black women to be dishonest and criminal, willing to steal white men's property even if they owned their own. The two women are linked across centuries of change by a powerful web of myth that punishes individual black women based on assumptions about the group. Their stories are painfully familiar to many African American women who feel that they continue to be mistreated and humiliated as a result of lies told, and widely accepted, about black women as a group. They force us to consider how and why American governments, American popular culture, and even black communities have contributed to the humiliation of African American women. Their experiences also lead us to ask what resources black women use for psychic self-defense and how successful they are.

Although historical myths are seldom imported wholesale into the contemporary era, they are meaningfully connected to twenty-first-century portrayals of black women in public discourse. African American women who exercise their citizenship must also try to manage the negative expectations born of this powerful mythology. Like all citizens, they use politics to lay claim to resources and express public preferences; but sister politics is also about challenging negative images, managing degradation, and resisting or accommodating humiliating public representations.

Statistics reveal the inequality that marks black women's lives. In the United States today more than one in four black women lives in poverty, a rate more than double that of white women.[29] Babies born to black women are two and a half times more likely to die before their first birthday than white babies.[30] Compared to white women, black women are significantly more likely to be the sole wage earner in their household, to never marry, to suffer divorce, or to be widowed young and therefore to have to raise their children without a husband's emotional or financial assistance.[31] Black women heads of households are twice as likely to live in inadequate housing, and they earn 33–50 percent of what their male counterparts earn.[32] Fewer than 30 percent of black women have bachelor's degrees, and the unemployment rate for black women is more than double that for white women.[33] Black women have higher rates of hypertension and diabetes. They are more likely to die of breast cancer and more likely to have a hysterectomy. While HIV-AIDS infections have declined throughout the United States, the highest rate of new cases is among young black women, in whom it is also the leading cause of death.[34] Although a much larger number of black men are incarcerated, African American women are the fastest-growing population of new inmates.[35] Nearly a third of black girls and women are sexually assaulted in their lifetimes.[36] Most of these assaults are perpetrated by black men. On the whole, black women have less education and higher rates of underemployment, poverty, disease, and isolation than white women.

These statistical inequalities do not adequately capture black women's lives. Sisters are more than the sum of their relative disadvantages: they are active agents who craft meaning out of their circumstances and do so in complicated and diverse ways. Despite important commonalities, all African American women do not share the same ideas, beliefs, and feelings. Some join churches, where they find community, opportunities to use their skills, and venues to showcase their talents. Some stay home with their kids and seek out friendship in book clubs. Some are professional working moms who drop the kids at Jack and Jill, then go to their African dance class.[37] Some are poor urban teenagers who know all the words of every hip-hop CD released in the past decade. Some are in committed same-sex relationships and actively fighting for the legal right to marry, and others are desperately trying to get out of abusive marriages. Some are healthy, fit, and strong; others are battling injury, disease, or addiction.

Statistics show that race and gender strongly determine life opportunities for black women. On the other hand, the inherent variety among individual black women's lives sometimes reinforces, sometimes defies, and always complicates the simple story of the numbers. Still, I want to think about black women as a meaningful analytic category. Even if there is no single, universal black female experience, there are enough shared identities, beliefs, and experiences to offer insight into African American women as a group.

Understanding the connection between black women's emotional lives and their politics is difficult because emotional experiences are very intimate. Emotions are so closely linked to individual temperament and experience that it is foolish to make sweeping generalizations based on race and gender. If black women as a group are more likely to be poor and unhealthy, this does not mean that all sisters are sad or angry. How African American women feel about their lives and circumstances depends on the meanings they give to them. But those meanings are often socially constructed. Social ideas like race, gender, and class thus have a powerful effect on personal feelings.

A good example is African American attitudes toward doctors, medicine, and health care. In *Medical Apartheid,* journalist Harriet Washington painstakingly links contemporary black reticence about the American medical establishment to a long and grotesque history of racist experimentation, abuse, and deceit. She begins with descriptions of antebellum gynecological experimentation carried out on unwilling female slaves, discusses the pervasive practices of robbing cemeteries to procure black bodies for medical school anatomy classes, recounts the appalling Tuskegee experiment that allowed black men to suffer and die from untreated syphilis, and reveals how contemporary racial assumptions affect the medical care black patients receive.[38]

Washington's book challenges the pervasive belief that African Americans' suspicion of doctors and hospitals, and their notorious noncompliance with prescribed medical treatments, have no rational basis.[39] If we look at these behaviors through the conventional lens of heroic medical history, then African Americans seem unreasonably apprehensive. When we look though the lens offered by Washington, there is a clear and reasonable link between historical abuses by doctors, black oral traditions that bear witness to these horrors, community beliefs that formed as a result, individual emotions of fear, anger, and distrust in response to these beliefs, and behavior patterns of black patients reflecting this distrust. Just as medical abuse affects black attitudes toward health care, political and social events influence emotions, and emotions affect how we engage in politics. To understand black women as political actors we must explore how intersecting disadvantages based on race, gender, class, and sexuality influence how these women feel and think.

By politics I do not mean exclusively or even primarily voting choices. Electoral participation is important, but politics is much broader. I want to know what obstacles black women see as most onerous in their lives and where they place the responsibility for both creating and removing those obstacles. Under what circumstances do they blame themselves when things go wrong, and when do they implicate a larger system of racial and sexual bias? When do they advocate individual, communal, or political strategies for addressing their concerns? Do they feel that black men or women of other races are allies in these struggles? The answers to these questions connect political realities to socially influenced private emotions.

One connection is through political and emotional responses to common negative stereotypes. Scholars of black women's experience in the United States have highlighted the role of images and myth in creating the powerful ideologies that supported economic and social structures like slavery and Jim Crow. Hateful stereotypes are the tools that build the crooked room. They have tangible consequences when policymakers, acting on assumptions informed by these myths, make choices that disproportionately affect black women's lives. For instance, historian Deborah Gray White argues that myths about black women's lusty availability, set against the gendered expectations of the chaste Victorian era, justified the sexual abuse of enslaved women.[40] Legal scholar Dorothy Roberts describes how, in the twentieth century, negative assumptions about black women's sexuality were used to justify their involuntary sterilization.[41]

As the women in my focus groups identified, three pervasive myths account for the most common forms of misrecognition of black women: sexual promiscuity, emasculating brashness, and Mammy-like devotion to white domestic concerns. These three ideas have long histories in the United States and are drawn from a web of racial and gender stereotypes that also ensnare African American men and implicate white women. They create an interlocking mythology with political implications. Previous scholars have labored to unearth the frightening history of public representation of black women and have carefully traced how the assumptions of hypersexuality, irritating assertiveness, and Mammy-like competence infect policymaking.[42] In the next chapter I describe how these myths affect individual black women as political actors. I cannot tell a clear causal story, drawing neat arrows from stereotypes to black women's emotional lives to their political choices. African American women are too varied, history is too subjective, and causal inferences are too tenuous for such a simple narrative. Still, it is worth trying to understand the messy human experience of the political world.

Two

Myth

Portraying African-American women as stereotypical mammies, matriarchs, welfare recipients, and hot mommas helps justify U.S. Black
women's oppression.

—Patricia Hill Collins, *Black Feminist Thought*

L et us return to Janie Mae Crawford, the protagonist of
Their Eyes Were Watching God, and the personal consequences of misrecognition. Her grandmother, perceiving Janie's blossoming young womanhood as dangerous, arranges her marriage to an older man. She
misperceives Janie as helpless and endangered, and offers her security. Janie chooses her second husband, Jody, because he seems to
offer adventure, opportunity, and freedom. But Jody also misperceives Janie. He sees his possession of the beautiful Janie as a symbol
of his own power. He cannot understand that Janie is curious and
defiant, and instead sees her as simply lovely. Instead of companionship, Jody offers her visibility and status. Her marriages are a crooked
room for Janie. She is confronted with distorted images of herself cast
by others, but she is surprisingly capable of discovering the true
upright. She resists limitations and crafts an independent identity and
self-definition. Still, not until she finds love with Tea Cake does Janie
experience the profoundly transformative experience of being recog-

nized. Tea Cake's recognition of Janie gives her space to grow. Rather than trying to fix her based on an inaccurate understanding of who she is, Tea Cake partners with Janie to pursue shared goals.

The women of *for colored girls* also suffer with burdens imposed by misrecognition. These burdens are imposed both by the structural constraints of white racism and by the intimate and often violent restrictions of black sexism. The Lady in Green laments, "somebody almost walked off wid alla my stuff." She goes on to explain that her spirit, thoughts, ideas, and sense of self were stolen by "a man whose ego walked round like Rodan's shadow / was a man faster n my innocence / waz a lover / I made too much room for." Her experience of romantic and personal betrayal is then echoed by other voices in the poem. They, too, have been violated by men who cannot truly see or recognize them. But unlike Janie Mae Crawford, the colored girls of Shange's work do not find redemptive recognition in a male partner. *for colored girls* does not end with companionate marriage to a loving Tea Cake; indeed, the only proposal in the play is issued by the violent Beau Willie, who demands that Crystal marry him while he dangles their children from a fifth-floor window. *for colored girls* explicitly rejects the notion that recognition is achieved through a male gaze. Instead, these women heal the wounds of misrecognition by learning to see themselves reflected through the empathetic eyes of other black women who share their experiences. The play ends with the women asserting, "I found god in myself & I loved her / I loved her fiercely." This chapter tells the stories of some historic Janie Mae Crawfords and some modern colored girls by discussing the most common forms of misrecognition they must overcome.[1]

The Myth of Promiscuity

In June 2008, popular R&B singer R. Kelly went to trial for allegedly videotaping himself having sex with a teenager. The infamous tape that initiated the suit showed a man urinating on a young girl. On the first day of the trial, a popular urban-music radio station played a twelve-hour, no-commercial block of Kelly's music as a sign of solidarity with the singer. Although the case had taken six years to come to trial, Kelly was acquitted in a few weeks. In December 2009, the African American talk show host Tavis Smiley agreed to publish R. Kelly's memoir through his publishing house, SmileyBooks.[2] In a press release from Kelly's publicist, Smiley is quoted as saying, "We are thrilled to be the conduit through which R. Kelly will tell his own story. He has earned the right to tell his own story his own way." The radio station's demonstration of solidarity with Kelly even before he was acquitted and Smiley's offering him an opportunity to tell his story on his terms despite lingering questions about his role in the sex act are decisions that marginalize the young black woman whom Kelly allegedly abused. They can be read as choices to discount her experience of sexual violation as false or trivial. For many, the seeming consent of the teen on the videotape implied that no harm had been done.

There are several other high-profile moments in the late twentieth century when African American men, accused of sexual assault of a black woman, garnered significant public support among African Americans. In 1991, Supreme Court nominee Clarence Thomas was accused of sexual harassment by Anita Hill, a black woman and former coworker. The three-day questioning of Hill and Thomas was arguably the most spectacular modern confirmation hearing of a

Supreme Court justice. During his testimony, Thomas angrily referred to the often explicit questioning as a "high-tech lynching." After he invoked the specter of lynching, Thomas's approval ratings among black Americans jumped to nearly 50 percent. As a conservative justice whose judicial decisions have uniformly run counter to the political agenda articulated by modern civil rights organizations, Thomas has never again enjoyed such high favorability ratings with black Americans.[3] But in the context of his dispute with Hill, it was Thomas, draped in the history of America's racial violence against black men, who received significant black community support.[4] Hill, meanwhile, was regularly maligned as a race-traitor who allowed her story of sexual harassment to be used by powerful white opponents to harm the credibility of an African American man. Many wondered what she had done to provoke or encourage the harassment.

In 1992, former heavyweight champion Mike Tyson was found guilty of the rape of an African American woman, Desiree Washington. Tyson served three years of a six-year sentence. When he was released from prison, he was hailed as a returning hero by many African American political and social leaders, including the Nation of Islam and the Reverend Al Sharpton.[5] Many questioned Tyson's guilt: because Washington had willingly joined him in his hotel room, her actions, they suggested, invited sexual contact.

Together these moments hint at the continuing power of a common stereotype of black women as particularly promiscuous and sexually immoral. They also reveal complicated African American responses to this misrecognition of black women. In each case the state intervened to punish the alleged sexual abuser of a black woman even while some members of the African American community denounced the woman as "fast" and rallied behind the man who allegedly perpetrated the crimes. In other words, while the myth of black women's hypersexuality may have been historically created and perpetuated by white social, political, and economic institutions, its contemporary manifestations are often seen just as clearly in the internal politics of African American communities.

The promiscuity myth has roots in Southern slaveholding society, which operated by a gendered social and moral code. The Victorian ideal of true womanhood required strict adherence to a code of piety, purity, submissiveness, and domesticity—virtues believed to be inherent in feminine nature.[6] Victorian social codes clearly divided public and private realms, made white men the sole authorities in their homes, and stripped married white women of their property and legal personhood. It also advanced beliefs in the essential chastity, innocence, and weakness of women. African American women's lives and labors in the antebellum South contrasted sharply with this iconic womanhood. Black women were subjected to forced nudity during slave auctions. They often labored in fields with skirts hiked up. They were punished on plantations by being whipped in partial or total nudity. They were banned from legal marriage.[7] The myth of black women as lascivious, seductive, and insatiable was a way of reconciling the forced public exposure and commoditization of black women's bodies with the Victorian ideals of women's modesty and fragility. The idea that black women were hypersexual beings created space for white moral superiority by justifying the brutality of Southern white men.

In his 1785 text *Notes on the State of Virginia,* Thomas Jefferson subjected enslaved blacks to the same "scientific" observation he used on the new nation's vegetation, wildlife, and geography. His observations led him to conclude that white women were clearly superior to black ones. The proof, he argued, was that black men preferred white women "as uniformly as is the preference of the Oranootan for the black women over those of his own species."[8] This single observation combined beliefs in the supremacy of whites, the potentially dangerous desire of black men for white women, and the willingness of black women to have sexual intercourse with apes. This sexual mythology was pervasive during the eighteenth and early nineteenth centuries. Not only were black women described as animalistic and aggressive, they were sometimes cast as vile seductresses who lured white men away from their chaste female counterparts. "As soon as the sexual desires are awakening in the young men of the South," wrote the famous biologist Louis Agassiz in 1843, "they find it easy to gratify themselves by the readiness with which they are met by colored house servants."[9]

Hypersexuality was more than a demeaning and false stereotype; this inaccurate portrayal was intentional. Myth advances specific economic, social, and political motives. In this case, sexual lasciviousness was a deliberate characterization that excused both profit-driven and casual sexual exploitation of black women. Emancipation did not end the social and political usefulness of this sexual stereotype. White men's "right" of access to black women's bodies was an assumption supported both by their history as legal property and by the myth of their sexual promiscuity. This myth meant that neither the law nor social convention allowed that black women might be victims in this arrangement. The rape of black women, like the lynching of black men, was both a deep personal violence and a form of community terrorism that reinforced their vulnerability and lack of self-ownership. As historian E. Frances White writes, "Virtually no legal protection was provided for women who were portrayed as loose and licentious. Under such conditions, black women—promiscuous by definition—found it nearly impossible to convince the legal establishment that men of any race should be prosecuted for sexually assaulting them. The rape of black women was simply no crime at all."[10] The mythology of black women as promiscuous was important to maintaining the profitable exploitation of slave society. In freedom, it remained important as a means of racial and gender control.

The idea of black women's sexual wantonness was important to late nineteenth- and early twentieth-century nation-building efforts. Race and gender science informed public ideas of who was capable of citizenship as the country reestablished the basis of political participation following the Civil War. Science and its growing hegemony of knowledge underlay the nineteenth century's racial ideology and iconography.[11] Classification of human communities through hardening constructs of race and gender was central to nineteenth-century scientific and social scientific projects.[12] The science of race and gender served as a basis for denying full and equal participation in the state. Rigid definitions of masculinity and femininity, and of whiteness and otherness, prescribed specific roles for black women at the dawn of the twentieth century.[13]

The treatment of Saartjie Baartman, the so-called Hottentot Venus, is an iconic example of how black women's bodies became central to the process of arraying human beings in ascending order from apelike to human, African to European, black to white, female to male, savage to civilized. Baartman was a Khoikhoi woman from South Africa who became a canonized exhibit of London's Piccadilly Circus as a result of her supposedly abnormal sexual organs. Her large buttocks and elongated labia subjected her to exhibition both in life and in death.[14] The scientific discourse around the Hottentot Venus found its way into American understandings of race and sex.[15] Black women were seen as physiologically and anatomically different. Their rampant sexuality was easily discerned in their misshapen and exaggerated sexual organs.[16]

In this sense, modernity offered no possibility of more accurate recognition of black women. Instead, the modern, the civilized, and the evolved were defined over and against them. Observation of the primitive, subhuman other was central to defining the advanced, civilized citizen, and black women's supposedly hypersexual bodies were central exhibits in that display. Baartman's genitalia and buttocks served as observable, scientific evidence that black women were not fully civilized. Science was used to underscore the ideological biases of racist, misogynist America, and black women's vulnerability was codified in law. The myth of black women's unrestrained sexuality operated in both slavery and freedom as a means of justifying racial and gender exploitation.

According to historian Darlene Clark Hine, black women created a culture of dissemblance to protect their inner selves from this oppressive sexual myth and their resulting vulnerability.[17] To dissemble is to conceal one's true self. Nineteenth-century black poet Paul Laurence Dunbar hinted that much of black life in America was dissemblance when he wrote, "We wear the mask that grins and lies, / It hides our cheeks and shades our eyes,— / This debt we pay to human guile; / With torn and bleeding hearts we smile."[18] Dunbar understood that in the context of segregation, black people often had to conceal their thoughts and emotions to protect themselves from systems that demanded their happy acquiescence to inequality. Hine's theory of black women's culture of dissemblance builds on

Dunbar's insight and explains the specific ways that gender vulnerability led black women to hide their authentic selves. For decades following the end of Southern slavery, more than three-fourths
of African American women worked primarily as domestic workers.
Their labor put them in proximity and subordinate status to white
men, many of whom held deeply ingrained sexual beliefs about black
women. Further, their race and gender denied them full protection of
the law. These realities meant that black women were particularly
vulnerable to sexual assault. Faced with these circumstances, many
black women sought refuge by donning a mask of asexuality. They
learned to adopt a false identity that provided them some semblance
of protection—of the self if not necessarily of their bodies—in their
hostile and sexually predatory environment. Hine's work shows that
by divulging little about their personal lives, revealing next to nothing about their own interests, triumphs, or defeats, and shielding
their authentic personalities behind a performance of racial and gender tropes, black women crafted a kind of psychic safe-space beyond
the surveillance of the white families for whom they worked. As Hine
writes,

> Because of the interplay of racial animosity, class tensions,
> gender role differentiation, and regional economic varia-
> tions, Black women, as a rule, developed and adhered to a
> cult of secrecy, a culture of dissemblance, to protect the
> sanctity of inner aspects of their lives. The dynamics of
> dissemblance involved creating the appearance of disclo-
> sure, or openness about themselves and their feelings, while
> actually remaining an enigma. Only with secrecy, thus
> achieving a self-imposed invisibility, could ordinary Black

women accrue the psychic space and harness the resources
needed to hold their own in the often one-sided and mis-
matched resistance struggle.[19]

The act of dissemblance was a tactic to find the upright in the
crooked room that, as Hine puts it, "enabled the creation of positive
alternative images of their sexual selves and facilitated Black women's
mental and physical survival in a hostile world."[20] In this sense, black
women's secret realities protected them psychically and socially from
a system of labor exploitation and political powerlessness.

The realities of black women's sexual vulnerability in light of the
assumption of their sexual promiscuity prompted the psychic and
tactical need to hide their real selves behind a facade of openness.
Although born from the necessities of domestic labor and embraced
by many, the culture of dissemblance took on a specific, class-defined
form for middle-class African American women during the first half of
the twentieth century. Women's clubs became a popular tool of social
and political organizing for women in the years following the Civil
War. Among white women, these clubs laid the foundation for suffrage activities, progressivism, and temperance movements in the
early twentieth century. Barred from participation in white women's
organizations, African American women developed their own robust
movement of social uplift through a number of loosely affiliated national organizations focused on racial equality, justice, and moral
hygiene. The National Association of Colored Women (NACW),
founded in 1896, became the largest and most enduring organization
of this movement. Operating under the motto "lifting as we climb,"
the twentieth-century black women's club movement was, in part, an
organized political attempt to counter the myths of sexual licentious-

ness with counterexamples of modesty and respectability. Active from the 1880s through the 1930s, women's clubs made up the largest racial movement of the twentieth century, eclipsing even Garveyism and the modern civil rights movement.[21] Club women's work helped black communities survive economically and politically while offering an alternative image of black women as chaste and temperate. It resisted the painful sexual assumptions at the heart of black women's lived experience, combining the work of community uplift with strategies of promoting religious fidelity, personal moderation, and social respectability. "At the core of essentially every activity of NACW's members was a concern with creating positive images of black women's sexuality."[22]

These stereotypes meant that normal expressions of human sensuality such as wearing visible makeup or revealing clothing, dating openly, and engaging publicly in romantic physical affection could be read as confirming evidence of black women's lewdness. In an effort to resist these stereotypes, black women in public leadership positions buried normal, innocuous expressions of sexuality behind an image of either pristine asexuality or narrowly defined respectable married identity. They aggressively advanced a social agenda that encouraged other black women to follow their example.[23] Having been cast as disreputable, these black women leaders sought to establish their respectability and through that act to lay claim to fair and equal treatment in public life. This "politics of respectability," enacted through a specific culture of dissemblance, is a response to the myth of hypersexuality. Black women who served as schoolteachers, nurses, church mothers, civic leaders, and the like hoped that their public displays of strict sexual respectability would counter existing prejudices and help control the terms by which they would be seen.

If a claim to full citizenship rests on the assertion of a narrowly defined, sexually repressive respectability, then black women must adhere to a rigidly controlled public performance of themselves. Such rigidity can leave little room for complicated realities. Black women's real lives include sexual desire, some include children born outside of marriage, some include loving partnerships not sanctioned by social norms. For those women, the politics of respectability required even greater dissemblance. It forced them to wear a mask. It also meant that many middle-class proponents of respectability were willing to criticize publicly, silence actively, or simply ignore those black women who did not fit its narrow definition of acceptable feminine behavior. Respectability politics implied that women's ability to work on behalf of black communities and to demand fair, just treatment from the state rested on their sterling moral character. Therefore, it was important to present an untarnished self to the public at all times regardless of the difficult, messy human realities women experience. Although this form of dissembling created some emotional space for black women, the politics of respectability failed in important ways. Black women tried to live with dignity and modesty, control their fertility, and work to form lasting, loving relationships with men and with other women, but these efforts occurred in a context of profound degradation of black women's characters and real threats to their physical safety.

The culture of dissemblance may have also left black women's politics without the flexibility to respond to complicated contemporary political realities that evoke the ideas of hypersexuality. Thus, as in the case of the alleged Kelly video, when a teenage girl is filmed in sexual intercourse with an adult man, black women are as likely to denounce her for promiscuity as to hold him accountable for criminal misconduct. Despite their own history of sexual vulnerability in the workplace, black women showed little solidarity with Anita Hill's tale of sexual harassment because her testimony violated the code of dissemblance and invited sexualized scrutiny of black women. Many black women believed that when Desiree Washington made the disreputable choice to accompany Mike Tyson to his hotel room, she terminated her right to say no. The pervasive and long-standing culture of sexual dissemblance means that black women have not become adept at addressing these public moments of intraracial sexual anxiety.

This point is made forcefully by Evelynn Hammonds in her piece "Toward a Genealogy of Black Female Sexuality: The Problematic of Silence," in which she traces the historical sexual and labor exploitations of black women's bodies. Far too many black women reformers, authors, and academics, she argues, have faced these degrading images of black womanhood with relative silence about sexuality. This silence has done little to deconstruct degrading images of black womanhood and has had deleterious material consequences for racial political agendas. For example, Hammonds suggests that mainstream black women writers and activists inadequately addressed the explosion of HIV-AIDS among African American women in part because HIV positive status is associated—in the popular imagination—with uncontrolled sexuality.[24]

Through dissemblance, these middle-class activist African American women sought to respond to and defend against the sexualized myths to frame themselves as "good women" and therefore gain access to the privileges of womanhood. But the privileges of white women were not based on an assumption of equality. They resulted instead from an ideology that saw white women as weak, pure, and needing male protection. The politics of respectability too often conformed to similarly dichotomous thinking about what is bad and good in women.[25] Reactions against the myth of promiscuity meant that these same black women often found it difficult to make claims on the state and society as full citizens. Instead they found themselves battling to share the prison of second-class citizenship with white women.

Social norms surrounding gender have changed dramatically since the beginning of the twentieth century. Advances in birth control make it possible for women to control fertility while remaining sexually active. Changes in the nation's labor needs required middle-class women to work and increased their engagement in the public sphere. Second-wave feminism opened educational opportunities, liberalized divorce laws, and equalized pay so that women were capable of greater personal and financial autonomy. Along with these political and social changes came dramatically different sexual possibilities for women.

Black women coming of age in the latter half of the twentieth century were socialized in this new post-Victorian social ethic, and many chose to drop the mask of dissemblance. Like their white counterparts, African American women tested the boundaries of this autonomous expression of human sexuality. They used birth control, shortened their skirts, and produced erotic cultural products. Like the blues singers of an earlier generation, many expressed rebellious sexual ethics through music.[26] One important space for young black women to express new sexual ethics was in the burgeoning urban culture of hip-hop.[27] In the 1980s, androgynous and husky-voiced MC Lyte pioneered women's hip-hop bravado; Queen Latifah's early persona rested on Afrocentric reclamation of black womanhood; and Salt-n-Pepa unabashedly explored heterosexual female sexual pleasure and empowerment.[28] As 1990s hip-hop culture turned toward exaltation of the gangster, black women continued openly to occupy new sexual terrain. For example, Jada Pinkett, Vivica A. Fox, Kimberly Elise, and Queen Latifah teamed up in 1996 for the black female outlaw film, *Set It Off*. Sexuality was boldly central in the film: Elise plays a single parent, Pinkett a sexually empowered single woman, and Latifah a butch lesbian.[29] Hip-hop was never a progressive, biased-free space for black women's sexual liberation, and the examples I have offered here are troubling and limited, but early hip-hop seemed to hold the promise of a modern blues aesthetic—one that would respond to black women speaking about their own complicated realities of sexual desire, action, autonomy, coercion, ecstasy, and abuse.

But as hip-hop aged, the space for black women's voices narrowed. Overtly sexualized but strikingly one-dimensional artists like Lil' Kim and Foxxy Brown captured some attention in the late 1990s. And by 2011 Nicki Minaj was the undisputed queen of sexy, female hip-hop emcees. But even Kim, Brown, and Minaj are exceptions in this male-dominated industry. As hip-hop grew into a multibillion-dollar, corporate-owned entertainment industry, talented b-girls, breakers, and emcees became increasingly scarce. Instead of offering a forum for sisters to voice their own truths, hip-hop made black women into silent, scantily clad figures who writhe willingly behind male artists.[30] These video vixens submit to having beer poured on their heads, engaging with multiple sexual partners, and being called "bitch" and "ho." Literary scholar Nghana Lewis writes, "Particularly in hip-hop, the discursive abuse of black women registers perhaps more pervasively now than at any other point in the history of American culture."[31] The liberating sexual revolution of late twentieth-century America had one set of implications for white women and a very different one for black girls and women, because it occurred within a long history of understanding black women as unethically sexualized. Hip-hop videos put the Venus Hottentot's exaggerated sexual organs back on display for the voyeuristic pleasure of the paying public. Though separated from her by many decades, corporate-controlled hip-hop music and culture created a new set of tilted images portraying black women as lusty, available, and willing partners.

Hip-hop is not the sole or most problematic cultural force promoting hypersexualized images of women. The sexual objectification of girls and women of all races is standard fare in contemporary American popular culture and marketing. It is profitable for both Madison Avenue and Hollywood. For white women, the emergence of sexualized images reads as a cultural backlash against their expanding political, social, and economic opportunities. MTV's *16 and Pregnant* and the *Real Housewives* series are not accurate portrayals of white women's lived experiences, and evidence shows that media-based sexual objectification has measurable deleterious effects on girls and women.[32] But the implications of sexual images for black American women are different. Although sexism affects all women, black women's relative economic and political weakness makes them more vulnerable to state intervention. The sexualized myths of black women have conspired to narrow the political and social world for sisters.

Not only is the overt sexualization of black women through hip-hop troubling for the sisters themselves, it also has meaningful political consequences. Hip-hop has become the dominant form of youth culture in the United States. But according to political scientist Cathy Cohen, its reliance on open and often gratuitous display of black sexuality has also initiated moral panic in public discourse.[33] Hip-hop's overt sexual themes and images have been blamed for such social problems as crime, academic underperformance, teen pregnancy, welfare dependency, and drug abuse. Cohen argues that race leaders, media voices, and policy makers eschew more complicated analysis of the structural inequalities of inadequate housing, poor nutrition, unequal schools, limited employment opportunities, and racially biased policing as causes for these social ills in favor of a public discourse that blames scantily clad young women for initiating the downfall of their own communities. Primed by centuries of assuming that black women are sexually lewd, this moral panic takes hold easily and directs the terms of public conversations about how to address inequality. Instead of changing structures, too many solutions in the public sphere involve enforced limitations on black women's sexuality.

For example, welfare policy is intimately linked in the American imagination with black women's sexuality. Political scientist Martin Gilens shows that white American opposition to welfare results from whites' fixed beliefs that the system supports unworthy black people who lack a suitable work ethic. Central to this opposition is a belief that black women do not appropriately control their fertility, that they have sex with multiple partners, producing children who must be cared for through tax-supported social welfare programs.[34] Feminist theorist Ange-Marie Hancock has shown that welfare policy is shrouded in a politics of disgust resulting from racialized and gendered stereotypes of black women.[35] The depiction of black women as sexually insatiable breeders suits a slaveholding society that profits from black women's fertility. But for a shrinking postmodern state, black women's assumed lasciviousness and rampant reproduction are threatening. Therefore throughout the twentieth century the state employed involuntary sterilization, pressure to submit to long-term birth control, and restriction of state benefits for large families as a way to control black women's reproduction.[36] The myth of a plantation Jezebel can be deployed to limit today's welfare-dependent mother. It is not just a matter of distorted perceptions; these misrecognitions can be used to punish African American women through policy.

Which is not to deny that black women debate among themselves about the extent to which unwed motherhood is a serious problem. In a Chicago focus group, several over-forty women discussed whether black teenagers needed the state to step in and control their irresponsible sexuality. They had a heated argument about whether teenagers who have more than one child should be forced to submit to a long-term birth control shot.

FRANCINE: I am very opposed to that. It is bad enough that we are literally standing on the street corner handing out condoms to our teenagers. But this is crazy. A law that requires long-term birth control shots? Come on, what are we saying here?

MARGARET: And who are the teenage girls having the most babies? That is like genocide almost. This isn't China! Even though you wish they wouldn't be mothers until they've lived life. But still, who is going to be giving these shots?

IRIS: I have got to disagree. I strongly support it. I am sick of these babies having babies just because they got nothing better to do. Just give them all a shot.

FRANCINE: What are you talking about? I got little nieces. I don't want them getting that shot!

The conversation was complicated and emotional. Women often talked over one another. I was struck by the passion with which Margaret and Francine argued against stereotyping black teenagers, even those with multiple children, as oversexed. Iris, in contrast, insisted that black youth sexuality is pathological and needs to be controlled by public policy.[37] It may seem a stretch to point to antebellum notions of black women's lasciviousness as a source of contemporary emotional and political meaning for black women. But this early characterization of black women has infiltrated the nation's understanding of black women's character in ways that continue to resonate in America's cultural, social, and political fabric. The myth also resonates in the hearts and minds of black women.

Mammy

In 2008, Stephanie Tubbs Jones, the first black woman elected to Congress from Ohio, was serving her fifth term in the House of Representatives. As the representative from the eleventh district, Tubbs Jones had won four reelection campaigns by large margins. In 2004 she also achieved national notoriety as a fierce advocate of voting rights. Her district encompassed much of Cleveland, the city that was the flashpoint of a voting rights controversy after the 2004 presidential election contest between John Kerry and George W. Bush. Voting irregularities in Columbus and Cleveland, home to most of the state's black citizens, caused many to question the honesty of the election. Tubbs Jones led the congressional objection to certifying election results from Ohio. In 2005 she introduced the "Count Every Vote" Act to address irregularities that occurred in her district and across the state of Ohio in 2004. She was also a powerful figure within the Democratic Party, serving on the House Ways and Means committee and as a Democratic National Committee co-chair.

None of this saved her from being called a "Hanky Head" on a popular black political website during the Democratic primaries in 2008. Tubbs Jones served as the campaign co-chair for Senator Hillary Rodham Clinton during her primary battle against Senator Barack Obama. She was one of Clinton's staunchest supporters and most vocal surrogates. Her loyalty to a white woman candidate campaigning against the first black man to win the Democratic nomination endangered Tubbs Jones's electoral solidity within her own district and hurt her national reputation among many black Americans.

On June 3, 2008, the black political website Jack & Jill Politics posted an entry suggesting that Tubbs Jones should be concerned about reelection. "We have a bunch of CBC [Congressional Black Caucus] Hanky Heads that are scrambling for cover, because they are hearing loudly from their districts; many of them went overwhelmingly for Obama, while they were toting Missy Clinton's Water." The blog author called for primary challenges to a number of Congressional Black Caucus members. Topping this list was "Stephanie Tubbs Jones (Hanky Head)." By describing Tubbs Jones this way, Jack & Jill Politics was invoking a common and painful image of black women: the black mammy.

It is important to understand the context of this charge. Tubbs Jones was not called mammy simply because she supported Senator Clinton. In fact, in early polls Clinton led Obama among black voters, but African American women became solid Obama supporters after the New Hampshire and South Carolina primaries. They threw their support behind Obama after a number of troubling events in the campaign. Hillary Clinton choked up during a press interview the day before the New Hampshire primary, which she won even though Obama had led by double digits in late polling. Postelection results showed that white women voters provided Clinton's margin of victory. Many commentators suggested that Hillary's open display of emotion was the key to her win. Then in South Carolina, former president Bill Clinton compared Obama's primary bid to that of Jesse Jackson two decades earlier. Many analysts interpreted his comments as racially biased. This combination of events led many to believe that Hillary was using displays of emotional weakness to solicit white women's votes and that her surrogates were using racial tactics to discourage white support of Obama. In this context, Tubbs Jones's support of Hillary Clinton was seen not as just a personal political strategy but as a deep racial betrayal deserving of the slur "Mammy."

After slavery ended, the myth of lascivious, wanton, and sexually available black women could not alone support a system of domestic labor that required proximity between black women and the white families that employed them. An insatiable breeder was profitable in agricultural slavery because children born to bondswomen became the property of the enslavers regardless of their racial composition. But after slavery's demise, the specter of racial intermixing in a context of (nominal) legal equality became a national anxiety. Black women who labored in white homes had to be reimagined. A seductive, exotic wench would threaten the stability of white families, but an asexual, omnicompetent, devoted servant was ideal.

With the Compromise of 1877, which ended Reconstruction and withdrew federal troops from the South, white secessionists were given the power to craft segregation codes, disfranchise black voters, and revise the Confederate narrative as triumphant rather than traitorous. America's newest citizens, meanwhile, were relegated to forced agricultural peonage through rural sharecropping, grinding urban poverty in the South's new cities, new forms of segregation through the imposition of Jim Crow, and racial terror meted out by the Ku Klux Klan. The white Southern imagination generated myths of black manhood and womanhood that supported these segregationist policies. Mammy was a central figure in this mythmaking.[38] "African American women as mammies served to challenge critics who argued that slavery was harsh and demeaning. After all, [mammies] were depicted as being happy and content with their duties as servants."[39]

Enslaved women working as domestic servants in Southern plantations were taken from their families and forced to nurse white babies while their own infants subsisted on sugar water. They were not voluntary members of the enslaver's family; they were women laboring under coercion and the constant threat of physical and sexual violence. They had no enforceable authority over their white charges and could not even resist the sale and exploitation of their own children. Domestic servants often were not grandmotherly types but teenagers or very young women. It was white supremacist imaginations that remembered these powerless, coerced slave girls as soothing, comfortable, consenting women.

Unlike the bad black woman who was aggressively sexual, Mammy had no personal needs or desires. She was a trusted adviser and confidante whose skills were used exclusively in service of the white families to which she was attached. Mammy was not a protector or defender of black children or communities. She represented a maternal ideal, but not in caring for her own children. Her love, doting, advice, correction, and supervision were reserved exclusively for white women and children. Her loyal affection to white men, women, and children was entirely devoid of sexual desire.

This asexuality is apparent in Mammy's androgynous embodiment. Early twentieth-century artwork that imagined black women as lascivious and uncontrolled represented their physical bodies as gross exaggerations of loosely connected sexual parts.[40] These renderings highlight black women's sexuality by amplifying their breasts, hips, and buttocks. Because Mammy is docile and maternal, she is remembered as big, fat, soft, dark-skinned, and unfeminine. Nothing about the mythical mammy elicits sexual desire from men or hints at sexual desire in Mammy herself.[41]

Mammy was key in the creation of the nation's identity as well. Although she evokes the period of slavery, Mammy becomes important as an idea in the context of freedom and the emergence of black women's citizenship. The Nineteenth Amendment to the Constitution, giving women the right to vote, was ratified in 1920. The culmination of decades of struggle, the amendment opened the way toward full and equal political citizenship for women. Just three years later, in 1923, Mississippi senator John Williams proposed a bill seeking a site for a national Mammy monument. The Richmond, Virginia, chapter of the United Daughters of the Confederacy was prepared to fund the statue "as a gift to the people of the United States . . . a monument in memory of the faithful colored mammies of the South." It would be placed on federal land, in the shadow of the Lincoln Memorial, which had been dedicated a few months earlier, in 1922.[42] The bill passed the Senate just weeks after the same body defeated the Dyer antilynching bill. While refusing to protect African American citizens from domestic terrorism, the Senate referred the Mammy monument bill to the House of Representatives, where fierce and prolonged resistance from the black press, black women's organizations, and ordinary citizens helped to kill it.[43] Just when white women achieved the franchise and the promise of equal citizenship, a group of them sought to memorialize black women's subjugation and inequality.[44]

In supporting a federal monument to Mammy, the Daughters of the Confederacy were not seeking to honor the lives of actual black women who, in both slavery and freedom, provided domestic labor for white families. These women were vulnerable to the sexual and labor exploitation of slaveholders and household employers. They dissembled to mask their true thoughts and personalities in order to gain a modicum of security for themselves and their families. During the Civil War, they helped hide the white family's valuables on Monday only to lead Union troops to the spoils on Tuesday. After emancipation, these women used work stoppages, strikes, carrying home extra food from employers, known as pan-toting, and various forms of indirect resistance to renegotiate their unfair, unwritten labor contracts.[45]

America was not interested in these deeply human and complicated stories of the lives of black female domestics. Instead, it seriously considered a monument that would display black women as the faithful servants of white domesticity. Whenever I am in Washington, DC, I try to imagine the psychic assault I would suffer if I had to walk past a granite Mammy statue while on the National Mall.

Although Mammy was never carved in granite, she was enshrined in the American imagination throughout the first half of the twentieth century.[46] "American films, pancake boxes, and syrup bottles imprinted Mammy on the American psyches more indelibly than before."[47] As the nineteenth century's first certified marketing icon,

Mammy's Cupboard Restaurant, Natchez, Mississippi.
Photo: Melissa V. Harris-Perry

Mammy became hugely influential in the 1880s and 1890s in promotional materials and advertisements that ushered in America's modern commercial age. To this day, monuments to Mammy both large and small remain visible on the American landscape. For example, Mammy's Cupboard is a restaurant and gift shop built inside a twenty-eight-foot-tall skirt of a black Mammy. Originally opened in 1940, it still stands on the roadside in Natchez, Mississippi, serving "home-cooked" meals to Mississippi travelers.

Mammy was much more than a packaging technique; she was also a political icon who played a central role in reunifying the nation in the aftermath of the Civil War. By representing the notion that black women's domestic labor is a natural extension of their skills and desires, she simultaneously justified past enslavement and continuing oppression. "A closer look at how the mammy stereotype was manipulated reveals that she was both a huckster and messenger. Because she was a survivor from the Old South, her continued service to a white mistress, now her northern employer, was a reunifying gesture toward North-South reconciliation."[48]

The life of Hattie McDaniel is a striking allegory for the mythical Mammy. McDaniel was the first African American woman to win an Academy Award, for best supporting actress in 1939 for her performance as Mammy in *Gone with the Wind*. McDaniel's story is a complex mixture of ambition, compromise, resistance, rejection, and success. Whoever she really was, it was her embodiment of Mammy that won her national acclaim, praise, and validation. But McDaniel's story must be seen alongside her father's. In the Civil War, Henry McDaniel was a solider in the Union Army who was shot in the jaw during an intense battle in which his black regiment suffered severe losses at the hands of the Confederacy. McDaniel's biographer describes her father's lifelong battle to receive a pension, medical treat-ment, and recognition from the government for which he fought. Like many other black Union soldiers, he was consistently denied benefits or services from his country. The contrast between the nation's em-brace of Hattie McDaniel's mythical service as mammy and its rejec-tion of Henry McDaniel's actual service as a soldier is a striking metaphor for the racialized and gendered expectations of citizen-ship.[49]

Mammy is symptomatic of consistent and repeated misrecogni-tion. Rather than seeing black female domestic workers accurately as laborers, the Mammy myth portrays them as unwavering in their commitment to the white domestic sphere. In this role, Mammy serves to stabilize the racial and gender order, and therefore the order of the state.[50] By misogynist white supremacist definitions, Mammy is to be hailed as a patriot. By enjoying her servitude, she acts as a healing salve for a nation ruptured by the sins of racism. "Seeing the former slave woman visually transformed into a con-tented servant absolved everyone of past transgressions and future responsibility toward the freed people."[51]

Mammy is the figure of acceptable black womanhood. "Loyal, docile, but fiercely protective of her white folks, she exalted in her servitude."[52] When flesh-and-blood black women working as domes-tic laborers failed to live up to this devoted stereotype, the state asserted that they needed to be retrained to fit the myth. In the early twentieth century, a land grant from the city of Athens, Georgia, and investments from private interests throughout the South established the Black Mammy Memorial Institute.[53] The institute sought to re-train Southern blacks to be dutiful, loyal domestic servants. The resurgence of Mammy symbolism in the early twentieth century was an attempt to superimpose romantic notions of Southern paternalism on contemporary, contractual labor relations.[54] Twentieth-century laboring women needed contracts to protect them from oppressive working conditions and to ensure fair payment of wages that supported their own black families. Mammy, by contrast, needed no employment contract because she was tied to her white family by duty, gratitude, and love. The Black Mammy Memorial Institute, backed with resources from the state and private investors, represents the dependence of white supremacy on black women's faithful service in white households.

Although no contemporary institutions boldly assert the need to retrain black women as mammies, popular culture has re-created her in a new, more palatable version. In American popular culture, black women often appear among white women as magical figures. These modern mammies, like their nineteenth-century counterparts, are capable of solving white women's personal crises without ever hinting at the depth of their own oppressive circumstances. For example, the modern Mammy made several guest appearances on the wildly popular HBO series *Sex and the City*. Though living in New York City, the lead characters—four white women—rarely encountered black women. The few African American women written into the script appeared briefly, with little character development, and were often capable of magically comforting the white women and solving their problems. A black woman chauffer takes Carrie Bradshaw out for a midnight meal after her book party. Her presence immediately soothes Carrie, who has reported in an earlier scene that her "loneliness is palpable." After Miranda becomes a single mother and has trouble quieting her colicky baby, the Emmy-winning actress Lisa Gay Hamilton shows up as a neighbor, never seen before or after, to assist her. She brings a vibrating chair that immediately quiets the infant, reinforcing the notion that black women instinctively understand child rearing in ways that white women do not. When the first film version of *Sex and the City* hit theaters in the summer of 2008, Academy Award–winning actress Jennifer Hudson was cast as Carrie's feisty young assistant. Although her movie role is much more significant than the sister cameos in the series, Hudson's "Louise" is able to fix her boss's love life, website, and personal files even though she is two decades younger.[55] These updates of the Mammy caricature are hardly limited to *Sex and the City*. Contemporary popular culture is replete with black women characters with an instinctive ability to "help Whites get in touch with their better selves."[56]

Responding to Mammy

While the state and popular culture memorialized Mammy as the ultimate expression of black women's patriotism and loyalty, she was reviled in black communities as betraying her own. Mammy suggests an affectionate and consensual (although asexual) relationship between black women and the Southern whites who perpetrated terrible crimes against African Americans. In 1924, responding to the mammy memorial campaign, W. E. B. Du Bois wrote, "Whatever [the Mammy] had of slovenliness or neatness, of degradation or of education she surrendered it to those who lived to lynch her sons and ravish her daughters."[57] Mammy was not only an embarrassing symbol of slavery but an accomplice and conspirator in white supremacy. To be called a Mammy in the black community is to be called a race traitor.

Just as we can see that black women try to craft images of respectability in an effort to resist the hypersexualized myth, we can read other elements of their lives and politics as responsive to the damaging lies of Mammy mythology. A black woman proves that she is not a Mammy by refusing loyalty and coalition with white women and their domestic concerns. Instead, she demonstrates fierce loyalty to race causes, to black families, and to the black domestic sphere. Racial loyalty inures against the harsh community critique of performing the Mammy.[58] To show that they are not mammies, African American women are often required to demonstrate racial loyalty over and above gender solidarity.

I saw evidence of this in my focus group gathering of New York women, who ranged in age from twenty-two to fifty. The group's first written exercise was to list a few adjectives that described themselves and then to make a second list of adjectives that their friends, family, or coworkers might use to describe them. My goal was to discover whether these women felt that their self-image matched the image that others held of them. After writing their self-descriptions, the women read them aloud to the group.

> Kind, giving, understanding, dependable
> Supportive, giving, understanding, cheerful, and in-charge
> Compassionate, self-sufficient, hard worker, independent
> Funny, intelligent, outgoing, and strong
> Independent, long-suffering, loyal, mild-tempered
> Kind, loving, tender, patient
> Loving, homebody, pushover, giving to others
> Motivated, stressed, generous, and focused
> Friendly, good-hearted, sociable, and sweet
> Mine is not like anyone else's. I said that I am loud, pushy, controlling, stand-offish and I am a loner.

Later, when I reviewed what these women said about themselves, I was surprised by how consistently they understood themselves as servants of other people's interests. In thinking of themselves as loving, giving, and devoted to others, they attributed to themselves the classic characteristics of the Mammy ideal. But these women were devoted, giving and long-suffering in the black domestic sphere, not the white. As they talked further, it became clear that their own children, parents, spouses, and communities were the beneficiaries of their self-sacrifice.

Gloria is a single mother from the Bronx whose eighteen-year-old-daughter just received a full scholarship at a prestigious liberal arts college. Gloria works as a youth coordinator in her church and volunteers for the Girl Scouts. She revealed that in 2001, her daughter was a student at a high school near the World Trade Center. She became emotional as she described how, for hours, she did not know whether her daughter survived the attack. Gloria then went on to explain that in 2001 her mother suffered a stroke and was paralyzed on her left side. Gloria now spends a great deal of time visiting her mother at the nursing home. "I just wish that for the elderly things could be different. Our parents worked so hard. They brought us up. And when things happen to them it seems as if they cannot get what they really need. I wish there were laws to make things easier for them." Gloria's emotions, her stress, her concerns were entirely connected to the health and well-being of her family.

Donella is twenty-six and single; she grew up in Brooklyn, where she lives with and cares for her parents, who are in their seventies. She explained to the group that she works part time but has spent several years caring for her now deceased grandmother before her father fell ill and she began providing care for her parents. "I am really worried about my parents getting the best care. It seems like when they are at the doctor they are waiting all day. They just get patted on the shoulder and told to come back in six months. There is no real care." Despite her youth, Donella spent most of the session talking about her family and her concerns and hopes for them.

Tiffany is a married woman in her forties. She described herself as a "late bloomer" because, after twenty years of marriage, she had recently had her first child, then nine months old. She explained that she had always worked two jobs in order to keep herself and her husband living in a "nice house with a big mortgage." Now that she was balancing work and motherhood, she faced some economic hardship. "I had to quit my second job with JC Penney's," she said, "because I refuse to work on weekends. I have to be there for my son on Saturdays and there is no way that I can give up church on Sundays. They need me at my church." Tiffany sees her primary responsibilities as her family and church.

Angelique is a thirty-five-year-old single mother living in Spanish Harlem. She has a twenty-year-old son and a thirteen-year-old daughter. Recently laid off from a job as a temporary secretary, she was visibly distressed about trying to find a job. She also worried that her teenage daughter is "smelling herself" and may be sexually active. But she explained that her biggest concern was her son. "He has two strikes against him. He is black and he is a man. I don't want him to make that third strike."

Although these women described themselves as Mammy-like in their loyal, giving competence, they subvert the myth through where their devotion is directed. It is important not to celebrate this transfer of loyalties from the white domestic sphere to the black community. Unlike the mythical Mammy, these black women are worried about their own families and neighborhoods, but they continue to share with Mammy a potentially dangerous lack of self-regard. They see themselves as the solution to other people's problems, and their effort and concern are almost entirely other-directed. As they resist the role of magical Mammy for white women, they take on the burden of magical woman for their own race.

There are times when this racial loyalty can override shared gender interests with white women. I do not suggest that coalition by race is more natural or right than coalition by gender or vice versa— only that the legacy of Mammy and the resulting suspicions of white women and their motivations can limit the range of political possibilities available to black women. The pioneering study of black women's political attitudes by Claudine Gay and Katherine Tate offers empirical evidence for this concern. Their analysis shows that African American women identify just as strongly with their gender as with their race. Indeed, black women who had a high sense of racial identification also tended to have a greater sense of linked fate with other women. These researchers also found that racial loyalties are more salient when sisters make political judgments and policy choices. Although their findings "soundly repudiate the popular view that gender is irrelevant for black women," the research suggests that "race remains the dominant screen through which black women view politics."[59]

This brings us back to the 2008 Democratic primaries and the characterization of Stephanie Tubbs Jones as Mammy to Hillary Clinton. Here I have to take some responsibility. In February 2008 I published an online article titled "Hillary's Scarlett O'Hara Act." I was working on the text of this chapter at the time, and in the article I argued that the press misunderstood black women's politics when they asked whether sisters would support Hillary Clinton because she was a woman or Barack Obama because he was black. Instead, I argued, we must engage the history of black and white women's power relationships and recognize that African American women do not necessarily perceive white women's empowerment as a path to their own. I wrote, "Black women will not be relegated to the status of supportive Mammy, easing the way for privileged white women to enter the halls of power." The piece was reproduced in dozens of outlets and received hundreds of comments. Some agreed with me: "I am so tired of white women's ignorance and insensitivity to the ways they oppress us as they exercise their entitlement to the privileges of whiteness." Others were angry at me: "So according to you, black women who support Obama are doing so because they no longer want to 'play mammy' to Hillary!" While I did not actually call black women who supported Senator Clinton "Mammy," my article undoubtedly influenced how some African Americans in the world of Internet blogs and online news sites wrote about the contest.[60]

One such site is Jack & Jill Politics.com, whose writers repeatedly referred to Tubbs Jones as a "hanky head" as a way of protesting what they perceived as her misplaced political loyalties. This characterization asserts that Tubbs Jones should not have supported the white woman; she should have been in solidarity with the black man, whom her black constituents overwhelmingly supported during the primaries. It is more poignant because Tubbs Jones physically conformed to the most common stereotypes of the mammy. She was dark skinned, was somewhat overweight, and had an ever-present smile. I do not believe that in her first decade of public service, most African Americans looked at Tubbs Jones and thought "Mammy." But when she stood next to Hillary Clinton, her physical appearance acquired a new historical resonance. I am convinced it was part of the reason she was so readily characterized as Mammy. African American communities were able to deploy the painful legacy of Mammy against their own representative as a way of indicating their displeasure with her political choices.

I don't want to make too much of the Tubbs Jones characterization. Internet blogs are often mean spirited, and name-calling is common. But Jack & Jill Politics is a thoughtful site with often incisive political analysis. Though full of stinging commentary, it also reflects broad trends in black political thought. I think it is important to take seriously how the site framed Tubbs Jones's allegiance to Senator Clinton. For many black women voters, Hillary Clinton's historic bid for the US presidency was not a symbol of gender liberation. The Mammy symbol evokes for them a history of white women who were complicit in racial oppression. The women who agreed with my original post or contributed to further characterizations of Tubbs Jones as "Mammy" felt it was important to hold white women accountable for accepting the benefits of racial privilege even as they suffered from the severe constraints imposed by sexism.

African American women and white women have a tense political relationship. Some white women activists relied on racial arguments in the nineteenth-century struggle for suffrage. For example, feminist pioneer Elizabeth Cady Stanton abandoned the fight for black male suffrage after the Civil War and relied on powerfully articulated racist and anti-immigrant reasoning to make a case for white women's suffrage.[61] In the 1960s and 1970s, second-wave white feminists failed to understand that their concerns with workplace entry were not shared by black women, who had long been wage earners.[62] Research suggests that most contemporary black women express little solidarity with feminist agendas they perceive as dominated by the interests of white women.[63] Lurking behind this political tension is the powerful and painful mythology that depicts black women as faithful servants of white women's needs. As they resist the lie of Mammy, black women often avoid junior-partner status in white women's movements, choosing instead to focus their efforts on bettering black communities. During the 2008 Democratic nomination battle, Obama and Clinton stood as embodied representations of these tensions. As one black women's website reported, "All I have to say . . . is that the days of Mammy are over. There will be no more of this expectation that black women table their own self-interests to support the needs of white women that will not be returning the favor."[64]

Stephanie Tubbs Jones died unexpectedly of a brain aneurysm just a few days before the 2008 Democratic National Convention. The convention nominated Barack Obama as the party's first African American nominee for the US presidency. It did so with the full support of Senator Hillary Clinton and most of her loyal primary supporters. During the convention Tubbs Jones was remembered with great reverence and fondness by the Ohio delegation and by the Democratic Party. No mention of "Mammy" or "hanky head" was made in any of the tributes to her career.

Angry Black Women

On June 18, 2008, Fox News contributor Cal Thomas discussed Democratic presidential candidate Barack Obama's wife, Michelle. Seeking to place her within a larger tradition of angry black women political figures, he said:

Look at the image of angry black women on television. Politically you have Maxine Waters of California, liberal Democrat. She's always angry every time she gets on television. Cynthia McKinney [former congresswoman from Georgia], another angry black woman. And who are the black women you see on the local news at night in cities all over the country. They're usually angry about something. They've had a son who has been shot in a drive-by shooting. They are angry at Bush. So you don't really have a profile of non-angry black women . . . [except] Oprah Winfrey.[65]

Thomas's observations invoke a third powerful stereotype of black women: one that characterizes them as shrill, loud, argumentative, irrationally angry, and verbally abusive. His statement shows the power of stereotypes to shape public perceptions. In his eyes, black women normally appear in public space "angry about something." His first example, Congresswoman Maxine Waters, has been a member of the House of Representatives for more than two decades. She is a senior member of the Congressional Black Caucus and can claim notable legislative achievements affecting urban areas, education, and economic development. She was an early and sustained critic of the war in Iraq. She led a congressional investigation of covert American government involvement in the urban drug trade. Yet the expectation of black women's angry public posture negates the substance of her anger. She is just angry about "something."

Thomas also seems incapable of distinguishing among different black women. He mentions Waters in the same breath as twice-defeated former representative Cynthia McKinney. Both of these elected representatives are equated with women who are the subjects of evening news stories about urban violence. Thomas seems unaware that the black women viewers most often encounter on their nightly news are, in fact, the local anchors and reporters at network affiliates across the country. These poised professionals are invisible in Thomas's analysis. The angry black woman myth renders sisters both invisible and mute. It is emblematic of the misrecognition of African American women. Observers like Thomas cannot see black women unless they conform to this narrow conception of black womanhood, and they cannot hear the substantive political claims these women make.

The academic literature on stereotyping traces the popular representation of black women as uniquely and irrationally angry, obnoxious, and controlling to the 1930s *Amos 'n' Andy* radio show.[66] The nagging, assertive Sapphire character on Amos 'n' Andy gave rise to an oft-repeated trope in popular culture representations of black women, from Aunt Esther on *Sanford and Son* to Pam on *Martin*. The brash, independent, hostile black woman rarely shows vulnerability or empathy. The myth of black women's emasculating anger has not been studied in as much detail as the Jezebel and Mammy images. But the extant literature does suggest that while Sapphire is one name for the myth, the angry black woman has many different shadings and representations: the bad black woman, the black "bitch," and the emasculating matriarch. The relative scholarly invisibility of the angry black woman myth does not mean that it is inconsequential. Quite the opposite is suggested by black feminist scholars Marcyliena Morgan and Dionne Bennett, who write: "The stereotype of the angry, mean Black woman goes unnamed not because it is insignificant, but because it is considered an essential characteristic of Black femininity *regardless* of the other stereotypical roles a Black woman may be accused of occupying. These stereotypes are more than representations; they are representations that shape realities."[67] In other words, it is not studied because many researchers accept the stereotype.

What is the reality that the angry black woman myth shapes? The respondents in my Chicago focus group of black women under thirty-five discussed how others saw them. Their self-descriptions were like those of the women in New York: kind, giving, and tender; but when they reflected on how their friends and family thought about them, a very different picture emerged.

Sassy, Mouthy, Attitude

Aggressive, Go-getter, and a self-starter

Strong, nice, juicy, smart, spoiled, outgoing, friendly

Crazy, friendly, self-motivated, hard-working

Crazy, reliable, friendly, conceited, loud, strong, spoiled, moody

Fun, smart-ass, picky, humorous, bossy, and always having a million things to do

Stubborn, analytic, outgoing, supportive, brutally honest

These young sisters believe that others see them as considerably harsher, sassier, and more aggressive than they see themselves. Women in the Oakland, California, and New York groups showed the same pattern of assessing themselves as gentle, thoughtful, and kind while believing that others more frequently considered them aggressive and brash. It is emotionally taxing to have to manage this disconnect between self and others' perception. There are also political consequences.

Charisse Jones and Kumea Shorter-Gooden use data from hundreds of survey responses and dozens of interviews to document black women's painful experience of "shifting" in their personal lives in order to reject perceptions that they are too aggressive or overly ambitious. "Our research reveals that many Black women feel pressured to calibrate their directness and assertiveness, and minimize their accomplishments and success, to make the men in their lives comfortable with and confident in their manhood." Although sisters may try to modulate their assertiveness at home, they also reported in my focus groups that their friends and family saw them as harsh and independent. Even as they try to manage their images, they feel haunted by negative expectations.[68]

We saw in the previous section that one member of my New York group described herself quite differently from how the other women described themselves. Deborah proclaimed, "I am loud, pushy, controlling, stand-offish and I am a loner. And that is how other people see me too." It seems Deborah has reconciled herself to the expectation of aggression by embracing it as her central identity. She feels upright in the tilted room because she is tilted at the same angle. Maybe this means that she feels no need to "shift" because her self-perception matches how she believes others see her. In the group, Deborah did have a commanding presence, attempted to dominate the discussion, and constantly talked during quiet writing tasks. She had an easy laugh and plenty of opinions. She played the independent, opinionated, domineering black woman perfectly, but the performance was too seamless to be convincing. Deborah never indicated doubt or vulnerability, attributes regularly expressed by the other participants. She may not have been shifting, but I am convinced that her tilted posture was a distortion of her full self.

The workplace is a particularly fraught terrain for black women who try both to earn professional respect and to guard against the expectation that they are irrationally angry. Ivy Kennelly's study of employers' stereotypes of black women reveals that white employers make a number of labor decisions based on their beliefs about black women as single mothers. These employers tend to see all of their black women workers through a single lens. They characterize them as single mothers, worry that their childcare responsibilities will make them unreliable employees, and express concern about their "aggression" and tendency to "complain about everything."[69] Black female workers appear to be conscious of these negative assumptions. A 1997 study by the Center for Women Policy Studies found that 42 percent of black women think it is important to mask issues of race at work.[70] In another study, 56 percent of managerial black women indicated their awareness of stereotypes about black women in their companies.[71]

Alice, a forty-two-year-old woman in my focus group in Oakland, talked about the difficulty of being a black woman in corporate America. "You have to think about how to use the force of being a black woman. When I am at work, and I work in corporate America, I'm not heard. It is because of my color and also because of my size. But sometimes I have to get heard. Then I go up against some fifty-year-old white male and I am up in his face saying, 'You know what? You are wrong. And this is what we need to do.' It is sad and you shouldn't have to do that."

Alice senses that because she is an overweight black woman, her opinions are unimportant to her employer, but she also believes that she has a certain power to make herself heard in critical situations. This force of black womanhood exists because she can become angry and loud, presumably intimidating the fifty-year-old white men with whom she works. In this sense, Alice's anger is a weapon of the weak.[72] Using this force does not necessarily make her feel empowered; instead, she laments that she "shouldn't have to do that." Alice's experience hints that the anger myth may be a double-edged sword. Sisters can sometimes get their way by confirming the expectation that they are threatening and angry, but doing so may leave them feeling that they have not truly been heard at all.

Black women's personal and working lives are not the only places where they must manage a schism between self-perception as kind and good persons and outsiders' expectation that they are obnoxious and angry. Popular culture regularly propagates this myth.[73] Omarosa, an early contestant on the popular reality television show *The Apprentice,* is the archetypal angry black woman. She shouts, lies, undermines other contestants, and earns everyone's contempt. Though just one of dozens of such representations on television, in movies, and throughout advertising, Omarosa is particularly insidious because *The Apprentice* is billed as reality. Her performance suggests that the Sapphire myth is not just the construction of white fantasy.[74]

In clinical psychiatric settings, black women are diagnosed very differently from white counterparts who present with the same symptoms. For instance, black women have considerably higher rates of anxiety disorders than white women. Blacks are diagnosed with higher lifetime rates of simple phobia, social phobia, and agoraphobia. Therapists tend to view African American women as anxious or phobic while perceiving white women who describe similar emotions and behaviors as sad and depressed. Black women are more likely to be described by therapists as hostile and paranoid, and diagnosis for black women is inclined to be more severe than for white women.[75] In these diagnostic differences we see the operation of the social construction of black womanhood that disallows sadness. Therapists are less likely to perceive a black woman as sad; instead, they see her as angry or anxious.[76]

Daniel Patrick Moynihan's 1965 report *The Negro Family: The Case for National Action* is a reasonable place to investigate the policy implications of framing black women as uniquely aggressive. Moynihan's report designated black matriarchy as the principal cause of a culture of pathology that kept black people from achieving equality. Moynihan's research predated the 1964 Civil Rights Act, but instead of identifying the structural barriers facing African American communities, he reported on the assumed deviance of Negro families. This deviance was clear and obvious, he opined, because black families were led by women who seemed to be their households' primary decision makers. Moynihan's conclusions granted two generations of conservative policy makers permission to imagine poor black women as domineering household managers whose unfeminine insistence on control both emasculated potential male partners and destroyed their children's future opportunities.[77] The Moynihan report encouraged the state not to assist black mothers as women doing their best in tough circumstances but instead to blame them as unrelenting cheats who unfairly demanded assistance from the system.[78] "This practice of widespread cultural projection reveals what is so dangerous about the 'Angry Black Woman' stereotype: it holds Black women responsible for power they do not possess, power that is, in fact, being utilized in very real ways by members of other social groups who can claim emotional innocence as they hide behind, and persecute, the 'Black Bitches' of our cultural imaginations."[79]

The Moynihan Report did not create the angry black woman stereotype. It tapped into an existing framework and gave it a new, politically consequential name: the matriarch. Even as it undergirded the conservative social policy agendas of the Reagan Revolution and the Clinton Moderation, the Moynihan report also prompted decades of research, launching first a broad, social problems approach that assumed the existence of black matriarchy and sought to delineate its negative effects, and then a flurry of oppositional research by progressive social scientists and humanists who sought to discredit the report's findings by rendering alternative perspectives on black family life.[80] Perhaps no response was more controversial than Michele Wallace's *Black Macho and the Myth of the Superwoman,* which provoked substantial backlash because Wallace pointed out that black nationalist political movements propagated an equally vicious view of black women as emasculating and aggressive.[81]

Wallace argued that black male political leaders were also invested in framing black women as unnaturally aggressive and independent. Doing so allowed African American political organizations led by black men to ignore feminist challenges to their political agendas and to suppress black women's ambitions for political leadership. Black nationalist organizations nurtured oppositional racial politics while maintaining gendered inequality. Even as black men railed against the emasculating findings of the Moynihan report, they colluded with its assertion that black families and communities can be healthy and strong only when black women assume a subordinate role and allow black men to lead.[82]

Ella Baker was relegated to the position of secretary by Martin Luther King, Jr.[83] Stokely Carmichael told the women of the Student Nonviolent Coordinating Committee that their position in the movement was "prone."[84] In the Black Panther Party sisters had to struggle to stay at the decision making table rather than the kitchen table.[85] Louis Farrakhan encouraged African American women to make sandwiches and send their men off to the Million Man March so that these men could atone and then return from the march ready to assume leadership of black homes and communities.[86] And as black feminist author and filmmaker Toni Cade wrote in her groundbreaking text *The Black Woman* (1970), "When a few toughminded, no-messin'-around politico Sisters began pushing for the right to participate in policy making, the right to help compose position papers for the emerging organization, the group leader would drop his voice into that mellow register specially reserved for the retarded, the incontinent, the lunatic, and say something about the need to be feminine and supportive and blah, blah, blah."[87] I am concerned that in their efforts to evade the Sapphire stereotype, black women may be discouraged from demanding equal consideration of their specific political needs within black political discourse.[88]

This stereotype does not acknowledge black women's anger as a legitimate reaction to unequal circumstances; it is seen as a pathological, irrational desire to control black men, families, and communities. It can be deployed against African American women who dare to question their circumstances, point out inequities, or ask for help. Both white policy makers and black patriarchs can dismiss gendered claims as the ranting of eye-rolling, neck-popping, "oh-no-you-didn't" angry women. Black women's concerns can be ignored and their voices silenced in the name of maintaining calm and rational conversation. Their anger is not experienced as a psychological reality but is seen through an ideology that distorts black women's lived experiences.[89] The angry black woman stereotype hamstrings

sisters who find that they cannot forcefully and convincingly advocate their own interests in the public sphere—either in black political
movements or in American policy environments—because their passion and commitment are misread as irrational.

Stereotypes and Shame

Geraldine is a fifty-five-year-old-black woman living on the west side
of Chicago. During the exercise in which focus group participants
discussed myths and facts, she put down her pen and sighed. "Other
people misunderstand us. They judge us . . . they don't understand
that we go through so many different issues and trials. They don't get
what makes us up into being a complex creature. We're misunderstood." Jezebel, Mammy, and Sapphire are the angles in the crooked
room where black women live. They do not reflect black women's
lived experience; instead, they limit African American women to
prescribed roles that serve the interests of others.

It is hard being misunderstood. Misrecognition subverts the possibility of equal democratic participation. It is psychically painful to
hold an image of yourself while knowing that others hold a different,
more negative image of you. At the turn of the twentieth century
W. E. B. Du Bois named this painful duality double-consciousness.
"It is a peculiar sensation, this double-consciousness, this sense of
always looking at one's self through the eyes of others, of measuring
one's soul by the tape of a world that looks on in amused contempt
and pity." Du Bois did not anticipate how black women's experiences
would further complicate this duality, but he did capture the political
relevance of this psychic experience.[90]

Lusty availability violates the expectations of the chaste Victorian era, but it serves the interests of slavery. Competent independence challenges the ideal that adult women should rely on their husband's judgment, but it allows policy makers to define black families as deviant. Welfare dependence violates the ideal that Americans should be self-reliant, but it provides an easy scapegoat for national dilemmas. Mammy-like devotion to white domesticity reinforces safe norms, but it elicits pandering pity rather than egalitarian respect. Although none of these stereotypes captures the complexity of black women's lives, they have been powerfully and regularly reproduced in American political discourse and popular culture since the Civil War. These myths influence how black women see themselves and how they understand their struggle. Most important, these myths make black women feel ashamed—and shame has sweeping consequences for black women's lives and politics.

"Resisting the Shaming of Shug Avery"

From *The Color Purple*

ALICE WALKER

Alice Walker's The Color Purple *lays bare the suffering and struggle of Celie, a poor, rural, black teen growing into womanhood under circumstances of extreme emotional deprivation and physical and sexual abuse.* The Color Purple *is also a story of resilience, redemption, and the power of loving female relationships, both sexual and platonic. Shug Avery is the novel's most defiant and independent female character. Celie falls in love with Shug, who is the catalyst for her eventual liberation. Many characters in the novel try to humiliate and discredit Shug because she refuses to conform to traditional expectations of Southern womanhood. Celie loves her for precisely these same reasons.*

Dear God,

Mr. —— daddy show up this evening. He a little short shrunk up man with a bald head and gold spectacles. He clear his throat a lot, like everything he say need announcement. Talk with his head leant to the side.

He come right to the point.

Just couldn't rest till you got her in your house, could you? he say, coming up the step.

Mr. —— don't say nothing. Look out cross the railing at the trees, over the top of the well. Eyes rest on the top of Harpo and Sofia house.

Won't you have a seat? I ast, pushing him up a chair. How bout a cool drink of water?

Through the window I hear Shug humming and humming, practicing her little song. I sneak back to her room and shet the window.

Old Mr. —— say to Mr. ——, Just what is it bout this Shug Avery anyway, he say. She is black as tar, she nappy headed. She got legs like baseball bats.

Mr. —— don't say nothing. I drop little spit in Old Mr. —— water.

Why, say Old Mr. ——, she ain't even clean. I hear she got the nasty woman disease.

I twirl the spit round with my finger. I think bout ground glass, wonder how you grind it. But I don't feel mad at all. Just interest.

Mr. —— turn his head slow, watch his daddy drink. Then say, real sad, You ain't got it in you to understand, he say. I love Shug Avery. Always have, always will. I should have married her when I had the chance.

Yeah, say Old Mr. ——. And throwed your life away. (Mr. —— grunt right there.) And a right smart of my money with it. Old Mr. —— clear his throat. Nobody even sure exactly who her daddy is.

I never care who her daddy is, say Mr. ——.

And her mammy take in white people dirty clothes to this day.

Plus all her children got different daddys. It all just to trifling and confuse.

Well, say Mr. —— and turn full face on his daddy, All Shug Avery children got the same daddy. I vouch for that.

Old Mr. —— clear his throat. Well, this my house. This my land. Your boy Harpo in one of my houses, on my land. Weeds come up on my land, I chop 'em up. Trash blow over it I burn it. He rise to go. Hand me his glass. Next time he come I put a little Shug Avery pee in his glass. See how he like that.

Three

Shame

For instance, well-mannered Negroes groan out like that [My people!] when they board a train or a bus and find other Negroes on there with their shoes off, stuffing themselves with fried fish, bananas and peanuts, and throwing the garbage on the floor. Maybe they are not only eating and drinking. The offenders may be "loud talking" the place, and holding back nothing of their private lives, in a voice that embraces the entire coach. The well-dressed Negro shrinks back in his seat at that, shakes his head and sighs, "My people! My people!"

—Zora Neale Hurston, *Dust Tracks on a Road*

One way African American women try to help their daughters stand straight in the crooked room is by telling them inspiring stories. Mothers, grandmas, aunts, and teachers want little black girls to know that they can achieve greatness. So they tell them that Harriet Tubman was a courageous and powerful woman who risked her life by leading more than three hundred slaves to freedom through the Underground Railroad. They explain that Rosa Parks's courageous refusal to give up her seat on a segregated city bus launched the civil rights movement and helped her people earn equal rights. They encourage little girls to watch Venus and Serena Williams play tennis and then remind them that Althea Gibson grew up in Harlem living on welfare, but she eventually won at Wimbledon. They speak of Mae Jemison, who became a doctor and a scientist and was the first black woman astronaut. Or they might talk about how Shirley Chisholm was the first black woman elected to Congress and how she ran for president of the United States. They tell these and other stories to make themselves and their children proud.[1] Families and educators prepare black children to meet racial hostility through a process of socialization meant to negate harmful images of blackness and replace them with role models of courage, resilience, and achievement.[2]

This positive racial identity is important to the psychological well-being of black adolescents and adults.[3] I saw some evidence of the success of this socialization when I conducted a survey at Chicago's 2005 Expo for Today's Black Woman. I asked more than one hundred African American women how they felt about black women today.[4] A substantial majority felt very or extremely proud, hopeful, and inspired. Only a small fraction reported feeling angry, afraid, or discouraged. (For data, see Appendix, table 1.)

Stories of black excellence are particularly powerful for countering derogatory racial images because African Americans have historically relied on "fictive kinship" ties. The term *fictive kinship* refers to connections between members of a group who are unrelated by blood or marriage but who nonetheless share reciprocal social or economic relationships.[5] In this book, I draw on the deep tradition of black fictive kinship when I refer to black women as "sisters." This imagined community of familial ties underscores a voluntary sense of shared identity that maps onto the historical construction of race.

Fictive kinship makes the accomplishments of African Americans relevant to unrelated black individuals. There is a sense in which we are all family.

Fictive kinship is also important to African American political thought and practice. Michael Dawson describes the powerful effect of black linked fate on African American public opinion, showing that individuals identify racial interests with their own self-interest.[6] In my first book, *Barbershops, Bibles, and BET,* I explored how African Americans use ordinary conversation to craft "common sense" racial identities that have consequences for political ideology.[7] Group loyalties and collective commitments influence how black people engage the political world. Within black communities, the actions and ideas of individual members can be censored as traitorous or celebrated as heroic. In order to understand black women's politics, we need to think about the emotional consequences of acting within this family. Fictive kinship, linked fate, and common sense allow black women to draw emotional comfort from other women's courageous and exemplary lives, but there is an insidious corollary to this sisterly pride. If one's sense of self is connected to the positive accomplishments of other African Americans, then it is also linked to negative portrayals and stereotypes of the race. The flip side of pride is shame, and like racial pride, racial shame is an important political emotion.

What Is Shame?

In psychology the study of shame is a relative newcomer. The first book-length treatment of shame as a clinical concern did not appear until 1971, and the emotion remained neglected until the late 1980s.[8]

But in the past two decades shame has become an increasingly important area of inquiry, and psychologists, sociologists, legal scholars, and literary critics have studied the various ways shame influences our lives. Few, however, have asked how it influences our politics.[9]

The emotion of shame has three important elements. The first is social.[10] Individuals feel ashamed in response to a real or imagined audience. We do not feel shame in isolation, only when we transgress a social boundary or break a community expectation. Our internal moral guide may lead us to feel guilt, but shame comes when we fear exposure and evaluation by others. This may be especially true for girls and women, who draw a larger sense of self-identity from their friendly, familial, and romantic relationships.[11] Second, shame is global.[12] It causes us not only to evaluate our actions but to make a judgment about our whole selves. A person may feel guilty about a specific incident but still feel that she is a good person. Shame is more diffuse: it extends beyond a single incident and becomes an evaluation of the self.[13] Psychologists commonly refer to shame as a belief in the malignant self: the idea that your entire person is infected by something inherently bad and potentially contagious. Finally, shame brings a psychological and physical urge to withdraw, submit, or appease others.[14] When we feel ashamed, we tend to drop our heads, avert our eyes, and fold into ourselves. Pride makes us feel taller (think of Phoeby made taller by listening to Janie's story), bolder, and more open; shame makes us want to be smaller, timid, and more closed.[15] "Shame transforms our identity. We experience ourselves as being small and worthless and as being exposed."[16]

Clinical psychologists have traced the corrosive effects of shame in a number of dimensions. It is a common and debilitating effect of childhood sexual abuse.[17] It is implicated in the higher incidence of depression among women and contributes to alcoholism, hostility, social anxiety, personality disorders, and suicide.[18] When individuals feel chronically ashamed, they tend to attribute all negative events to their own failings. Instead of seeing the external world as capable of producing both good and bad outcomes, shamed individuals see themselves as particularly worthy of punishment. Shame eats away at self-esteem and makes every social role more difficult.

Shame is also linked to field dependence. Remember that how we place ourselves in the crooked room is related to the information around us. Some individuals assume that the room must be correct, so they adapt themselves to it, while others can detect that the room itself is askew. When we feel ashamed, we assume the room is straight and that the self is off-kilter. Shame urges us to internalize the crooked room.[19]

It also has physiological effects. Blushing, the most obvious and mundane of these effects, is so closely associated with shame that some people believed African Americans did not experience shame because their blushing was not visible. Thomas Jefferson offered up the ability to blush, along with "flowing hair" and "a more elegant symmetry of form," as evidence of the superior beauty of white women. "Are not the fine mixtures of red and white, the expressions of every passion by greater or less suffusions of colour in the one, preferable to the eternal monotony, which reigns in the countenances, that immoveable veil of black which covers all the emotions of the other race?"[20] Jefferson assumed that because only white women could manifest the outward signs of shame, they alone possessed the virtue of modesty. Such assumptions aside, black people can and do feel the physiological urge to hide and retreat when experiencing shame. Black people are like other individuals: when asked to recall shameful events, they talk about having a strong desire to hide, escape, or disappear, and they display the physical postures of slumping, dropping the head, and avoiding eye contact.[21]

When it is experienced often over many years, shame has far more dramatic consequences.[22] Laboratory experiments have shown that shame causes the body to release the steroid hormone cortisol.[23] The shame-cortisol response is similar to the fear-induced "fight-or-flight" response.[24] When faced with physical danger, our bodies release hormones that prepare us to escape or to fight. When we feel ashamed, our bodies react with hormones that tell us to save our social selves by fleeing. Fight-or-flight is an adaptive response when we need to react quickly to physical danger, but if we face chronic exposure to such danger, the physiological response becomes a key element of post-traumatic stress disorder. The shame-induced cortisol response can be similarly debilitating when cortisol levels are chronically elevated. People who repeatedly suffer social rejection become vulnerable to a variety of health effects.[25] Elevated cortisol can lead to weight gain, heart disease, hardening of the arteries, and decreased immune function.[26]

Because it is a response to social rejection, individuals who do not conform to social norms are more subject to frequent and enduring experiences of shame. Overweight women, for instance, experience significant shame in societies where feminine desirability is defined by thinness.[27] African American women are structurally positioned to experience shame more frequently than others. As a group they posses a number of stigmatized identities and life circumstances: they are more likely to be poor, to be unmarried, to parent children alone, to be overweight, to be physically ill, and to be undereducated and underemployed. Black women who escape many of these circumstances must still contend with damaging racial and gender stereotypes. They are aware that others see them through a distorted lens that renders them socially unacceptable. This sense of social rejection and undesirability may express itself in experiences of chronic shame, with both psychological and physiological effects. Skin color and hair texture, for example, have both been found to evoke a sense of shame that affects black women's feelings of attractiveness, infects familial relationships, shapes expectations for romantic partnership and economic success, and manifests in disordered eating.[28] In this sense, shame is the psychological and physical effect of repeated acts of misrecognition. Black women can expect that the tilted images of the crooked room will be used to judge and sometimes limit them, and through the mechanism of shame, the inability to align themselves with the crooked room can actually make sisters sick.

Although shame can be corrosive to individual psychology, some have argued that it serves important social purposes. Sociologist Erving Goffman shows how shame, disgrace, and embarrassment help craft social order and meaning in everyday life.[29] Because shame is connected to collective rules and shared expectations, it is a basic tool by which societies create moral order.[30] Individuals fear the harsh judgments of their families, friends, and communities, so they present themselves as aligned with external norms.[31] Shame works through real or anticipated social sanctions that punish violations of group rules and thus helps us stay within the lines of acceptable behavior and thought. Shame gives a parent the power to send a withering glance down a long pew on Sunday morning and immediately stop a rowdy child from disrupting a church service. This can be adaptive for the group because it supports the creation and maintenance of tradition, shared identity, and group distinctiveness.[32] Shame that results from expressions of disapproval within the context of loving or respectful relationships is known as reintegrative shaming. It is a social strategy consistent with strong communal norms and can be an important element of a child's development.[33] The girl hushed in church learns what behavior is expected but does not fear that her mother will cease to love her.

Stigmatizing shaming is more insidious. Its purpose is not to keep individuals in a community but to label them as outcasts.[34] Employed in this way, shame can be a destructive force, particularly when it infuses a nation's legal and political practices. The philosopher Martha Nussbaum argues that shame and disgust are unreliable guides for public policy because shame tends to distort. Shaming is not restricted to individuals whose acts transgress the law but is deployed against whole groups based on identity alone: "Societies ubiquitously select certain groups and individuals for shaming, marking them off as 'abnormal' and demanding that they blush at what and who they are."[35] When this form of shaming is codified in law, its effects are pernicious. Shame motivates brutal social practices like honor killing, domestic violence, and foot binding.[36] A state that shames its citizens violates the foundational social contract of liberal democracies: government's commitment to respect individual dignity.[37]

A democratic state can rightfully impose guilt because guilt is focused on bad acts, and this specific focus on behavioral violation can encourage empathy and motivate the guilty to altruistic action. Something different happens when the state seeks to shame its citizens by imposing a lasting stigma on their very identity: it is proclaiming that the person herself or himself is defective. Rather than motivating restitution, shame debilitates and encourages avoidance.[38]

For example, it is reasonable to imprison individuals who break the law, but when former inmates are stripped of the right to vote for the rest of their lives, the state has moved from punishing guilt to imposing shame.[39] Lifetime disfranchisement marks the citizen as defective and unfit for participation in a democracy. The shamed ex-felon is not invited to rejoin the community but instead is forced to the margins.

Though we seldom think of it this way, racism is the act of shaming others based on their identity. Blackness in America is marked by shame. Perhaps more than any other emotion, shame depends on the social context. On an individual level, we feel ashamed because of how we believe people see us or how they would see us if they knew about our hidden transgressions. Shame makes us view our very selves as malignant. But societies also define entire groups as malignant. Historically the United States has done that with African Americans. This collective racial shaming has a disproportionate impact on black women, and black women's attempts to escape or manage shame are part of what motivates their politics.

A Shamed Race

In *The Souls of Black Folk*, W. E. B. Du Bois described the experience of being black in America as a constant awareness that others view one as a problem. "Between me and the other world there is ever an unasked question. . . . How does it feel to be a problem?"[40] This observation captures shame as a defining element of African American life. Being black in America has meant that your very existence is a problem: the object of the slavery question, the miscegenation threat, the Jim Crow solution, the Negro problem, the black family crisis, the welfare dilemma, the crime problem, or the nation's racial scar. The social and political realities of American racial inequality make black people themselves into a constant problem that has to be observed, analyzed, and solved. Blackness has often been framed as a cancer that eats away at the nation.[41] Stigmatizing blackness means that African Americans must constantly contend with social shaming.

Psychologists have found a strong negative correlation between shame and self-esteem.[42] People who feel ashamed, or who are subjected to shaming experiences, tend to form chronically low opinions of themselves. Those with chronically low self-esteem tend to attribute bad outcomes to their own failures. They also tend to focus on negative information that reinforces the idea of their social unacceptability. When researchers exposed people with low self-esteem to words like *unwanted, ignored, rejected, disliked, shunned, rebuffed, neglected, excluded, avoided, isolated, condemned,* and *disapproved,* those individuals showed slower response times on a basic thinking task.[43] The lesson echoes Du Bois. If you are constantly told that you are a problem, you eventually feel that you are a problem; and the more you feel like a problem, the more you notice negative feedback. It is harder to concentrate because you are working to manage the psychological effects of feeling ashamed. In this way, social rejection shapes experiences of the self and the world.

The Jim Crow system forced constant shame on African Americans. In the decades following the end of slavery, white political majorities crafted a social structure to ensure that African Americans would have little opportunity for social, political, or economic equality.[44] "By World War I white Southerners had created an intricate racial system of breathtaking complexity that left no action to chance. In the first place, it disfranchised African Americans and legislated them into segregation. Then it moved from the political to the personal to guarantee white supremacy. The system . . . offered a colored-coded solution for every human deed and thought, from where one might urinate to how far one's ambition might soar."[45]

Jim Crow's tentacles, reaching into all arenas of black life, were a powerful mechanism for the production of shame. The disapproving audience necessary for shame was provided by continuous white surveillance of black public action. African Americans in public spaces labored under the rejecting gaze of white racism, which constantly reinforced the idea that black people were unfit for proximity to whites. Fears of miscegenation underscored the belief that blackness was a contagious disease that had to be quarantined. Separate and unequal public accommodations, from schools to water fountains, gave substance to the infectious undesirability of black people. In 1911, the Southern historian Philip Alexander Bruce defended segregation by pointing to the disgust white Southerners felt at sharing social space with black people. "A feeling of repulsion was reflected in both measures,—a repulsion aroused primarily by the instinct of race preservation; only in the case of intermarriage, it was chiefly physical; in the case of co-education mainly ethical. . . . The primary object of the statute requiring the separation of the race in public vehicles of conveyance was simply to promote the personal comfort and safety of the whites. It was offensive to them to be brought in such close physical contact with the new negro."[46] Thus segregation was breezily justified as necessary for the comfort of whites, who could hardly be blamed for their distaste for contact with African Americans. Blackness was obviously a contagion to which whites should not be forcibly exposed. A black person did not have to commit any bad act. Simply being black in a restricted public space was a criminal act punishable by mob violence. Jim Crow insisted that black people assume a physical posture of shame in all of their dealings with whites. African Americans were expected to slump, hang their heads, avoid eye contact, and avoid bumping or jostling whites in public.[47] For nearly one hundred years this legislated racial shame was enforced with the brutality of the lynch law.

This was not reintegrative shaming; Jim Crow was meant only to stigmatize. It asserted that black people were malignant, that they should be ashamed of who they are, and that whites needed to be protected from unwanted exposure to blackness. The deep and lasting state-sponsored shaming of black people was part of a system of modernity. Jim Crow emerged first and most forcefully in urban spaces where blacks and whites lived, worked, traveled, and played in proximity.[48] Shame in this modern context was a means of social control: it reinforced the idea that "superordinates need not care about shame in the eyes of subordinates."[49] White people in the South were free to act within a broad range of acceptable behaviors, but blacks could operate only within a very narrow space. Shaming is a profoundly modern exercise of power because only the inferior can feel ashamed.[50]

Although Jim Crow drew a bright line of legislated shame around the entire race, women were particular targets. Victorian sensibilities held that women were uniquely endowed with morality and ethics.[51] Because they held authority in domestic matters, women were considered the tender sex whose delicacy required special dispensation in public spaces. The special treatment of fragile women was a signal of civility, and those who treated women rudely or roughly in public were labeled barbarians. But this courtesy was extended only to white women. Black women, regardless of class, education, or status, were potential targets of public abuse, ridicule, and mistreatment in the Jim Crow South. The permissible mistreatment of black women was a vicious form of collective shaming.[52] One site fraught with this tension was public transportation. Historian Blair Kelley's *Right to Ride* vividly illustrates the shame imposed on black women who were shunted from ladies' cars on trains, trapped behind cages on streetcars, and refused passage on buses.[53] By refusing to treat black women as ladies, Jim Crow meted out a gendered form of collective shame.

Systematic, state-sponsored racial shame was central to Jim Crow, but it also continued throughout the twentieth century and in locations beyond the South. The South may have perfected the system of racial surveillance and brutal repercussions for transgressing the racial code, but blacks in the urban North also found themselves the targets of state control. African Americans who came to Philadelphia, Chicago, Detroit, and New York during the Great Migration were easy targets for moral reformers.[54] Scholar Hazel Carby describes America's response to the Great Migration as a moral panic resulting in the strict social and cultural policing of black women's bodies. Carby shows that both dominant white institutions and African American organizations and intellectuals subscribed to the belief that black women, if left unrestrained, were a threat to social order.[55] Ignoring the fact that African Americans were forced to live in substandard housing bounded by restricted racial covenants, the reformers blamed disease and crime on the basic practices of black life.[56] Once again, blackness was defined as a malignancy that had to be cut out and controlled in order to protect the public. Reformers— black and white—held African American women particularly accountable for the "degenerative conditions" of the race. Black women were described as insufficient housekeepers, inattentive mothers, and poor educators of their children.[57] Because women were supposed to maintain society's moral order, any claim about rampant disorder was a burden laid specifically at women's feet. If blackness was a shameful cancer, black women were the main carriers because they reproduced black children. An anonymous "Southern White Woman," reflecting on the race problem in 1904, made this argument forcefully. Black women, she wrote, "are the greatest menace possible to the moral life of any community where they live. And they are evidently the chief instruments of the degradation of the men of their own race. When a man's mother, wife, and daughters are all immoral women, there is no room in his fallen nature for the aspirations of honor and virtue . . . I cannot imagine such a creation as a virtuous black woman."[58]

The Moynihan Report of 1965, entitled *The Negro Family: The Case for National Action*, reasserted that black women's reproduction is shameful. Daniel Patrick Moynihan and his coauthors labeled black women as overbearing matriarchs whose mothering led to greater pathology for their children and widespread failure for their communities.[59] In the 1980s, the Reagan administration publicly shamed black mothers with a false narrative about "welfare queens."[60] Abuse of the social safety net by welfare-dependent black mothers was conveniently blamed for the nation's difficult economic circumstances. Here, too, black mothers were cast as carriers of a malignancy. "These stories [of welfare-dependent black mothers] merged into one giant pathology of a metastasizing welfare system pushed to its limits by irresponsible, oversexed black girls."[61] These black mothers were not regarded as the worthy recipients of government aid but instead were portrayed as lazy, dishonest, and irresponsible. This framing legitimated the bureaucratic supervision of poor mothers by public assistance agencies and created more opportunities for state-sponsored shaming. "Means- and morals-testing allows welfare bureaucrats to place recipients under surveillance to check for cheating or lapses in eligibility. This probing forces recipients to assume a submissive stance lest offended caseworkers throw them off the rolls. . . . Bureaucrats often berate and degrade the mothers who pack the welfare office, adding to the humiliation of begging for public assistance."[62] Further shaming black women for their reproductive choices, the state also perpetrated the involuntary sterilization of poor women throughout the middle of the twentieth century.[63] Black women in their role as mothers and potential mothers are subjected to surveillance, judgment, and physical invasion. It is not hard to imagine how these experiences produce lasting shame.

Shame and its attendant physiological effects may be partly implicated in racially disparate maternal health outcomes.[64] African American women are much more likely to have low-birth-weight babies, to endure infant mortality, and to have worse maternal health during their pregnancies and in the first postpartum year.[65] Recent research on the effects of stress on birth outcomes shows a substantial racial difference in psychosocial stress.[66] Researchers found that infant birth weight suffered in conjunction with a mother's perception of racism—an effect that was independent of medical and social variables.[67] This means that the racism black women feel throughout their lives affects the health of their infants. Black pregnancy is not just a personal life event; it occurs within a sociopolitical context of shame and stress.

These examples are not an exhaustive accounting of how racial shaming is deployed to enforce hierarchy, sustain inequality, and create scapegoats. They only hint at the pervasiveness of socially rejecting experiences that routinely mark black American lives. Expectations of virtue and women's role as mothers make African American women especially vulnerable to this collective shame. Stigmatizing shame such as that deployed against African Americans affects not only those who directly encounter the social rejection but the entire class of citizens who share an identity trait. There is no possibility of accurate, democratic recognition of citizens who are subjected to stigmatizing shame. Racism functions by stereotyping all members of a group based on a set of assumed negative characteristics. This means that the shaming experiences of the welfare office affect not only the poor mother who encounters them directly but all African American women, regardless of social class or marital or parental status.

Racial shaming is made particularly insidious by the element of fictive kinship. African Americans' sense of connection to other black people is generally psychologically and politically positive. Those with a stronger sense of black identity tend to have higher self-esteem and better mental health, and they are more active politically.[68] But fictive kinship also makes African Americans more vulnerable to collective shame. If it is possible for one person's good actions to serve as "a credit to the race," then one person's bad actions may "shame the race." When explaining this concept to African American audiences, I sometimes ask them to recall how they felt when they learned that the DC Sniper was a black man. This is greeted with knowing groans. I then point out that white women rarely feel the same sense of shame when the embarrassing acts of white celebrities or the violent acts of white assailants are reported in the nightly news. Ethnic and racial groups differ in shame proneness: for African Americans, shame is not exclusively focused on personal inadequacies but is equally affected by social and interpersonal concerns.[69]

The epigraph to this chapter is emblematic of collective racial shaming. This brief selection from Zora Neale Hurston's autobiography, *Dust Tracks on a Road*, reveals the friction of interracial class tension within the Jim Crow South. I am less interested in the class politics revealed by Hurston here that have been the subject of considerable academic inquiry; instead, I want to focus on the mechanism of collective shame.[70]

Hurston's passage is both revealing and troubling. The middle-class "well-mannered Negro" shrinks with humiliation caused by the actions of her working-class racial counterparts, finding these "offenders" shameful because of her own class sensibilities. She judges them harshly because they are not dissembling. Rather than hiding behind a mask of respectability and silence, they are talking loudly and "holding back nothing." Their honest self-revelation rejects the imperative of respectability that would make them more palatable to white observers. The well-mannered Negro is both possessive of these black people—*my* people—and harshly judgmental of them. I want to suggest that the well-dressed Negro is experiencing the effects of racial shame. She worries that she will be misrecognized; whites will make no distinction between her (well-mannered and well-dressed) and them (loud and dirty). Because race is such a powerful determinant of public recognition in the Jim Crow South, she knows that she will be judged along with all of her people. Interdependent social networks and a sense of shared identity expose African American women to more sources of shaming.

Black people can be collectively punished for the actions (or imagined actions) of a single person.[71] Southern lynch mobs and

Northern white race riots made no allowance for the innocent people in the path of their murderous hunts for "black criminals." American racial terror was predicated on precisely this unwillingness to distinguish among black people. Terrorism targets its victims not for their actions but for their identity. African Americans developed a keen sense of how individual behavior was linked to collective susceptibility.

Contemporary black life is still marked by this corporate vulnerability. The myths, lies, and stereotypes perpetuated about any part of the race can have far-reaching emotional effects. Just as stories of courage and accomplishment induce pride, the stories of pathology or criminality induce shame. As the psychologist Stephen Dale Jefferson has written, "The difficulty involved in hiding such a readily apparent aspect of the self may leave many African Americans feeling exposed, and feelings of exposure are synonymous with shame."[72] There is reason to believe that black women are particularly susceptible to stigmatizing shame. Laboratory research shows that women report significantly greater shame and guilt tendencies than men.[73] Women were more likely than men to report a need to please others and to be liked, and social rejection therefore tends to result in greater self-denigration. When they are socially rejected, women experience more negative thoughts and feelings about themselves and report greater guilt and shame.[74] Although racism shames all African Americans, women are both particular targets of shame and more vulnerable to its effects.

Let's return for a moment to the stories of Eliza Gallie and Chana Kai Lee from chapter 1. Recall that as punishment for allegedly stealing cabbages from a white man in 1853, Gallie is forced to endure a public flogging in half nakedness.[75] This punishment was meant to both hurt and humiliate her. The sentence denied Gallie even the modicum of respectable treatment that, under nineteenth-century social codes, her gender should have afforded. Thus the state enacts its punishment in part by shaming her. When Chana Kai Lee was forced to return to work mere weeks after suffering a stroke, her overwhelming emotion was a sense of shame. She describes feeling weak, helpless, and embarrassed when the effects of the stroke impaired her speech so significantly that she could not complete a lecture. By Lee's account, she was as distressed by her university's willingness to subject her to this experience of profound shame as she was by the physical effects of the stroke.[76] The stories of both Gallie and Lee allow us to glimpse some of the ways that shame has been integral to black women's experiences of inequality.

African American women are of course not the only stigmatized group vulnerable to shaming by the state. Because stigma is socially constructed, the potential for shaming based on identity depends on historical and social realities. Historians have used national shame to explain the political actions of Germany after World War I and of defeated Confederates after the American Civil War.[77] The most extensive work on the political power of shame in contemporary America has emerged from queer theorists. Scholars of gay and transgender identities and experiences in America have employed shame as a central analytic construct for understanding the political choices and tactics fueling public LGBT (lesbian, gay, bisexual, and transgender) movements for equality.[78] My point is not that shame is uniquely politically relevant for black women; rather, my goal is to show the specific ways that shame is meaningful for black women's politics.

Racial Strategies for Resisting Shame

Shame is among the most psychically painful human emotions because it cuts to the core of one's sense of self-worth; people therefore work hard to minimize their exposure to shaming circumstances. In the case of stigmatizing shame, this may mean trying to escape the source of the stigma. Personal shame brings a physical desire to hide and flee, and collective shame prompts a similar response among African Americans. Some attempt to flee shameful racial stereotypes by trying to distinguish themselves from other African Americans. They try to suppress the racial attributes that are most noticeable to whites.[79]

This shrinking away from the shame-inducing reality of blackness can mean adopting identities or behaviors that are meant to counter negative assumptions. African American women in corporate positions advise younger colleagues not to wear their hair in braids or dreadlocks so that superiors will not think they have "radical" personal or political commitments.[80] Black upperclassmen at predominately white universities say to black freshmen, "Don't be late to class. You will probably be the only black student in there and you don't want to shame the race." Comedian turned racial commentator Bill Cosby has advocated racial distancing as an adaptive strategy for African Americans. He identifies urban youth culture as the source of continuing racial inequality in America. As a remedy, he suggests that black people stop listening to hip-hop, stop naming their children in ways consistent with black cultural norms, and stop using black English.[81] Cosby not only promotes racial distancing as an appropriate strategy for achieving racial equality but has also distanced himself from the racial practices he considers pathological.

I have always felt as if he were shouting, I am not like them! I am different and therefore not shameful! As in Hurston's passage, Cosby seems to be shaking his head and mumbling, "my people!"

For most African Americans, withdrawing from blackness is a poor shame-management strategy. The history of American racial prejudice suggests that outside observers are unlikely to notice fine distinctions when judging members of a stigmatized group. The trouble with stigma is precisely that it allows a signal characteristic to overdetermine life chances for the entire group, regardless of individual variation. Further, fleeing blackness can rupture fictive kinship networks and make individuals vulnerable to shaming from their own community. Racial networks can be effective at shaming group members who try to exit. African Americans may compose a subordinate group that controls fewer resources than whites, but they may control more of the resources that a black individual cares about—such as familial ties, potential romantic partners, and social esteem. Although racial distancing may allow individuals to escape the shaming gaze of whites, it may make them more susceptible to humiliation imposed by other African Americans. In attempting to escape racial shame by trying to appear raceless, one may risk becoming rootless.[82]

Rather than flee blackness, some African Americans retreat into the race and reduce their exposure to potentially shaming public space. An interesting analogy is the way patients with poor reading capacity experience shame in medical settings. Adults with low functional literacy find it very difficult to tell physicians about their medical needs. The difficulty arises because these patients feel deeply ashamed of their low literacy in front of high-status doctors. Shame keeps them from asking for the medical help they need.[83] A similar shame sometimes keeps black women from asking for the political help they deserve as citizens. We shame black women for their dependence on public assistance; therefore, any black woman or group of black women making demands on the government is potentially a target of shame. They may prefer to stay silent and find a way to cope with a difficult circumstance rather than be exposed to the shaming experience of presenting their needs.

Remember that shame also has a physiological component. Researchers have shown that short-term exposures to shaming experiences cause the body to release hormones telling the body to hide, flee, or accommodate. There is reason to believe that sustained exposure to shame can cause chronically elevated cortisol levels in members of stigmatized groups.[84] Not only must African Americans overcome structural and psychological barriers to political action; they must also counter real physiological barriers. It is harder to engage the external world when you feel ashamed. It is particularly difficult to engage politically, because, as I discussed in chapter 1, political action requires demanding recognition. Shaming is a problem of consistent and intentional misrecognition. Making demands on the state means asking the state and society to see you and pay attention to your interests. Asking for recognition is a nearly impossible physical task when you feel ashamed.

Finally, shame is implicated in a response known as humiliated fury.[85] Rage helps to ward off shame by protecting the self from further exposure.[86] Shame is first directed toward the self, but if the experience is too painful, it can be turned outward. The hostility is redirected in retaliation toward the rejecting other. If, however, the person or group who makes you feel ashamed is of higher status, it may not be possible to direct fury toward them. Instead, the rage may be directed at safer targets. Shame-prone individuals appear generally disposed to blame others for negative events, perhaps as a way of defending against the overwhelming global experience of shame.[87]

The "angry black woman" stereotype may have its origins in the shame-rage spiral. If African American women's position at the intersection of race and gender makes them uniquely vulnerable to shaming, it may also make them particularly susceptible to the humiliated fury that shame provokes. In an effort to protect their core sense of worth, black women must shunt some of the demeaning and painful stereotypes away from themselves. Anger is an effective, if sometimes destructive, way to accomplish this self-protection. Not only do black women find themselves in personal shame-rage spirals, but they are victimized by others' anger-based shame management. African American men are also subjected to racial and gender stigma that makes them vulnerable to shame. Strength, independence, and invulnerability are the received social norms of masculinity in the United States, but black men's racial and class status requires them to interact with a world that often makes them feel weak, inadequate, or helpless.[88] Research shows that men are particularly uncomfortable with the humiliation that results from this sense of weakness. In an attempt to mask this shame, men can react with violence and anger.[89] When we consider the impact of shame on black women, we must consider intersecting sources of conflict: black women's own vulnerability to collective shaming and their need to manage the collateral effects of men's shame.

I want to pause here for an important caveat: these processes are not deterministic. Not every African American living under Jim Crow felt constantly ashamed; not every black woman who must apply for public assistance feels ashamed; not all African Americans try to distance themselves from blackness; and not every black man who feels ashamed will fly into a violent rage. Exposure to shame and its negative effects depends on inherent differences of temperament and on structural realities that cause differences in vulnerability. It is tempting, but undoubtedly inaccurate, to explain individual or group behavior with a single, totalizing psychological theory. Still, even though it does not explain everything, the influence of shame on black political life has received too little attention from political scientists.

Pecola

The most comprehensive examination of the psychological and social effects of racial shame on African American women is not a work of social science; it is a novel. Toni Morrison's *The Bluest Eye*, a brief and piercing work of fiction that delineates the corrosive intergenerational impact of shame, was published a full year before Helen Block Lewis's groundbreaking monograph, *Shame and Guilt Neurosis*, defined shame as a fertile field of psychological inquiry. Yet Morrison's text anticipates what three subsequent decades of empirical research have shown about the debilitating psychological effects of shame. In addition, Morrison describes the terrible damage that sustained racial shaming can cause in African American communities. She accomplishes this through the story of a little black girl named Pecola Breedlove. Pecola lives in a shabby storefront with her mother, Pauline, her father, Cholly, and her older brother, Sammy, in Depression era Ohio. She descends into madness while praying fervently for blue eyes, which she believes can save her from her life of grinding poverty, social rejection, domestic violence, and, ultimately, incestuous rape. Although Pecola's sad existence is the motivating force of the narrative, the story exquisitely illustrates the durable, traumatic, sweeping effects of racial shame.[90]

The Bluest Eye is narrated in multiple voices, but it is mostly framed by the voice of a child, Claudia, who is Pecola's classmate.[91] Claudia is not sophisticated or experienced enough to understand the reasons for the awful events she witnesses, but she has unfettered emotional insight into the darkness and brutality of Pecola's circumstances and her own. By telling us this story through the eyes of a child, Morrison encourages us to focus on the emotions and moods that she evokes.[92] We are supposed to read the heart of this story, and at its heart are many incarnations of shame.

Morrison tells us immediately that "Pecola was having her father's baby." The reader knows the awful outcome that is lurking but must struggle, along with Claudia, to understand why. The first emotion Claudia reveals is shame. She has caught a cold, and her mother's constant grumbling as she cares for her makes Claudia feel that her sickness is shameful. "My mother's anger humiliates me; her words chafe my cheeks, and I am crying. . . . I believe she despises my weaknesses for letting the sickness 'take holt.' " Claudia is receiving a lesson about the imperative of strength. She realizes she must learn not to be sick so that she does not burden others; her mother's gruffness is a lesson of shaming her toward strength. But this embarrassment at weakness is temporary. Claudia's is a loving family, and she learns that her mother "is not angry at me, but at my sickness." There is no stigmatizing shame here; with her family she is truly safe. Claudia's shame is balanced by a sense of belonging. "So when I think of autumn, I think of somebody with hands who does not want me to die." This loving context provides the sharp contrast to the painful shame that Pecola experiences.[93]

Unlike Claudia's poor but respectable family, the Breedloves (Pecola's family) are marginal members of the community, marked by their physical ugliness, the depth of their poverty, and the inexplicably violent behavior of the father, Cholly. Morrison tells us that even when the Breedloves tried to make a life for themselves, humiliation intruded and disrupted their best efforts at compassionate love. In 1941, everyone is poor, but the Breedloves are poor in a shabby way. There are no loving memories attached to their home. As they look around their crooked room, the only emotion they feel is shame. "Occasionally an item provoked a physical reaction: an increase of acid irritation in the upper intestinal tract, a light flush of perspiration at the back of the neck as circumstances surrounding the piece of furniture were recalled." With this description, Morrison precisely captures the physiological experience of shame. We then learn that the source of the shame is the humiliating experience of trying to buy a new couch. Two white men deliver the couch, and when they take it off the truck, it has a large slash in the upholstery. The Breedloves try to send the couch back, but the white men refuse to take it. Trying to have something new and beautiful, they receive something broken instead. It is a moment the delivery drivers will rarely think of again, but their impunity is absolute. Because they are poor and black, the Breedloves are required to accept something inferior, and their powerlessness to resist this inferiority stays with them forever. "If you had to pay $4.80 a month for a sofa that started off split, no good, and humiliating—you couldn't take any joy in owning it. And the joylessness stank, pervading everything."[94]

Pecola, in whom the Breedloves' shame is most concentrated, embodies the emotion in her physical posture: "Concealed, veiled, eclipsed—peeping out from behind the shroud very seldom, and then only to yearn for the return of her mask." To cope with the violence in her home, Pecola learns to imagine herself invisible. She can make her entire body disappear, but somehow her eyes always remain, bearing witness to the brutality between her parents. The rest of Pecola's world is marked by rejection. Schoolchildren torment her. Storekeepers do not acknowledge her and shudder at having to take money from her hand. Strangers lure her into acts of violence against innocent animals. In the end, her own father rapes her. All Pecola wants to do is hide. "Pecola tucked her head in—a funny, sad, helpless movement. A kind of hunching of the shoulders, pulling in of the neck, as though she wanted to cover her ears."[95]

But the shame is not really Pecola's. It is hers only as an inheritance from her parents and community. She is hardly alone in hating her blackness. Although her fervent desire for blue eyes is the novel's clearest example of self-hatred borne of racial shame, other black characters also find whiteness beautiful and blackness ugly. Older black women chastise Claudia for dissecting and destroying her white baby doll, lovingly given as a Christmas gift. Soaphead Church comes from a family of mixed-race ancestry who consistently and consciously marry "up" in order to move their children farther from blackness. Geraldine is a brown-skinned woman who holds on tightly to an attitude of respectability meant to distinguish her colored family from the "niggers" around her.

Pecola's mother, Pauline Breedlove, has embraced the role of mammy for a wealthy white family. In a pivotal moment, Pauline abuses and rejects Pecola after Pecola accidentally spills a blueberry pie in the white folks' kitchen where Pauline works. "Polly," as Mrs. Breedlove is called by her white charge, soothes and reassures "the little pink and yellow girl" with an affection she never shows her own children. These actions are inexplicable at first, but Morrison allows us to see how they emerge from Pauline's great need for love, beauty, and order. When the ugliness of her life makes beauty and order impossible in her own home, she escapes the shame by clinging to the trappings of whiteness. Pauline is not a frivolous woman. She was once a lonely young bride living in Ohio, deeply ashamed of her country manners and dress when confronted with the black women she met in her new town. Lonely and rejected, she took refuge in the movies. There, Morrison tells us, Pauline learned to adore the world of physical beauty and romantic love embodied by the screen stars. It is a vicious lesson because "in equating physical beauty with virtue, she stripped her mind, bound it, and collected self-contempt by the heap." Absorbing white standards of beauty and virtue made her ashamed and unable to love herself, her children, or her life. "More and more she neglected her house, her children, her man—they were like the afterthoughts one has just before sleep, the early-morning and late-evening edges of her day, the dark edges that made the daily life with the Fishers lighter, more delicate, more lovely. Here she could arrange things, clean things, line things up in neat rows. Here her foot flopped around on deep pile carpets, and there was no uneven sound. Here she found beauty, order, cleanliness and praise." Pauline hides from her shameful blackness and poverty by embracing her role as mammy.[96]

The most destructive shame of all comes from Cholly Breedlove. The reader knows from the beginning that he will rape his young daughter. Morrison does not romanticize or ask the reader to feel sympathy for him; but she does require us to understand that Cholly's violence is part of a long spiral of shame. She takes us back to Cholly's adolescent flirtation with a girl named Darlene, leading to his first sexual encounter. It begins sweetly, if a bit diffidently. There is giggling, tickling, and exploring one another's bodies. He does not know the girl well, nor does he love her, but their encounter is affectionate, gentle, and mutual. Everything changes when two white hunters discover the young couple in the woods. They shine a flashlight on Cholly and Darlene and demand that he "get on wid it. An' make it good, nigger." Darlene's shame is absolute. She shields her face with her hands and dissociates from the experience. Cholly's shame is also extreme and his reaction is "violence born of total helplessness." Through their abusive observation, the white men make Cholly their instrument of raping the young Darlene. Their gaze turns innocence into violence, consent into force, and loving into shaming. Cholly's anger is directed toward his fellow victim. "Never did he once consider directing his hatred toward the hunters. Such an emotion would have destroyed him. They were big, white, armed men. He was small, black, helpless." Instead he hates Darlene and becomes sick every time he looks at her or thinks of her.[97]

Morrison needs the reader to see this moment. She wants readers to know that more than being left on a trash heap by his mother, more than being raised by an elderly aunt who dies in his youth, more than being rejected by his father in favor of a craps game, it is this moment of shame at the hands of the white hunters that sets off the spiral that eventually ends in Cholly's rape of his own daughter. Morrison wants us to know that Cholly is still reeling with shame on that Saturday in spring years later when he rapes Pecola. Perhaps even when he rapes her a second time soon afterward and she becomes pregnant with his child. Morrison teaches us that the pathologies of this family are not innate to themselves. The seeds of Pecola's destruction are planted by the shaming gaze of white supremacy.

Two decades before clinical psychologists conceived a theory of the collective effects of shame, Morrison's painful tale of the Breedloves explicates the burden of shame that black girls and women carry. Through Claudia's jealous rage about Shirley Temple, Morrison reveals how black girls are forced to live in a world that declares Shirley Temple beautiful and worthy and bestows on her the chance to dance with Bojangles, whose loving, affirming glances are denied to little black girls like Claudia. Along with Claudia we can be outraged by a world that negates and erases black girls. When the community learns that Pecola is pregnant by her father, most hope that the baby will die, but Claudia and her sister don't share this desire. "Our astonishment was short-lived, for it gave way to a curious kind of defensive shame." Despite the others' wishes, Claudia "felt a need for someone to want the black baby to live—just to counteract the universal love of white baby dolls." But the shame is too deep, Morrison tells us; Pecola's baby dies.[98]

After the infant's death, Pecola descends into madness and spends her life walking the streets of her little town. Her utter destruction is an indictment of American racism. It is also a warning to African American communities of the consequences of internalizing "dominant standards of value and beauty with little or no inspection of or reflection on the effects to itself or to its individual members."[99] Pecola's story is not typical or pervasive: most black men do not cope with the internalized shame of racism by sexually abusing their adolescent daughters. Yet her story is instructive because it details the abhorrent possibilities of shame. Morrison writes that her intention with the novel is to focus on "how something as grotesque as the demonization of an entire race could take root inside the most delicate member of society: a child; the most vulnerable member: a female. In trying to dramatize the devastation that even casual racial contempt can cause, I chose a unique situation, not a representative one."[100]

The Politics of Shame

At its core, shame is an emotional response to misrecognition. Research suggests that an infant's first experience of shame occurs when the beloved parent fails for the first time to recognize the child by mirroring its facial expressions and mood. In an infant's earliest interactions it discovers its power by the sustained eye contact and attention of the caregiver. The parent greets the waking baby with the wide eyes of enthusiasm. As the caregiver lifts the crying infant from the crib, he or she grimaces with concern about the baby's tears. When baby wants to play, the parent smiles and coos. Together baby and beloved create a dyad based on the caregiver's open recognition of the infant's needs and emotional states. The infant grows confident in its own worthiness because when it has needs the caregiver recognizes and meets them. Though utterly dependent on the adult for its needs, the infant comes to feel powerful through this attachment. Recognition by the adult conveys safety, worth, and self-esteem. But inevitably, the day arrives when baby's attempts to engage the parent are met with distraction or disapproval. The caregiver looks away, stares blankly, seems uninterested or even angry about baby's attempt to engage. Psychologists believe that these first failures to receive clear facial signals of recognition from the beloved caregiver initiate our first experience of shame; unable to provoke recognition and mirroring, the infant feels its first sense of powerlessness.[101]

Every child, no matter how vigilant and loving the caregiver, will eventually encounter a violation of recognition and the experience of shame. In this sense, individual shame and its physical and psychic consequences are constitutive of our humanity—part of the very fabric of human experience.[102] This does not mean that shame is our sole or definitive emotional experience as humans. Shame is soothed by responsive interactions that, over time, reduce instances of misrecognition to infrequent anomalies, but unique psychic and emotional damage is wrought on those children who face chronic, abusive refusal to recognize their needs and desires. This intense and repeated shaming without reparation can have lasting consequences for individuals.[103]

From this story of individual shame we can derive a theory of how collective shame operates for those who suffer continuing experiences of misrecognition by the social and political world. If personal misrecognition leads to individual shame, we can expect that social and political misrecognition is likely to result in collective shaming. As infants we rely on parents to recognize and mirror us. We develop our sense of worthy self by provoking recognition and experiencing positive reflections of ourselves in the eyes of the adults we depend on. As adults we rely on the social world of our jobs, families, places of worship, schools, media, and government to provide those opportunities for recognition and accurate mirroring. For stigmatized groups, the social world is not a positive mirror but a carnival mirror, with images of the self stretched or shrunken by a distorting surface that cannot produce an accurate image. If individual shame is constitutive of the human experience, so, too, is collective shame constitutive to the experience of stigmatized groups. I have argued in this chapter that black women are particularly—although not uniquely—vulnerable to the physical and psychological effects of chronic shaming because the tilted images of the crooked room in which they find themselves cause continual misrecognition. In the next chapter I illustrate these processes by exploring how two contemporary disasters led to public shaming of black women.

Four

Disaster

I was herded like cattle like everybody else regardless of my ability to pay for services. Nobody cared. I was just as low on that totem pole as that lady who was on welfare with five kids.

—Denise Roubion-Johnson, Hurricane Katrina survivor

To commemorate the first anniversary of Hurricane Katrina in August 2006, HBO premiered a documentary film directed by the African American filmmaker Spike Lee. *When The Levees Broke: A Requiem in Four Acts* uses the enduring images of human suffering in New Orleans and the compelling narratives of hurricane victims to capture the tragedy of the disaster.[1] Although the film is political in its thesis and conclusions, it is fundamentally an emotional tale about the heart of the experience of Katrina for the people of New Orleans.

The most compelling citizen survivor to share her story in Lee's movie is Phyllis Montana-Leblanc. Her personal testimony and stinging analysis are the captivating thread holding the film together. Irrepressible, honest, insightful, and frequently profane, Leblanc is the impassioned voice of New Orleanians who were abandoned in the aftermath of the storm. Without a hint of irony she moves seamlessly between cursing the "fuckers" in local, state, and federal government who left her and her neighbors to die and praising the "Lord God Almighty" who delivered them from the flood. She describes being hungry, hot, exhausted, and frightened. She recounts being herded like an animal, treated like a slave, and shunted from place to place, all in an accent and idiom that belong fully and exclusively to the people of New Orleans. Though it is her personal story, to listen to Leblanc is to hear the city itself speaking. In 2008 she expanded on her role in Lee's documentary by publishing a memoir titled *Not Just the Levees Broke*.[2] The text, one of the most powerful first-person accounts by an African American woman to emerge from the storm, has a raw, urgent immediacy; it reads more like spoken language than written text. Having begun this book with a view of Hurricane Katrina framed by Zora Neale Hurston's fictional account in *Their Eyes Were Watching God*, let us now return to Katrina, this time guided by the true story of Phyllis Montana-Leblanc.

Recognition and Visual Disaster

Like all New Orleans natives, Leblanc is both cautious and confident about storms. She does not evacuate for every bad forecast but instead tries to discern how serious the storm is likely to be. In the days leading up to Katrina she finds the news reports confusing and is unsure about evacuating. "Every time they tell us there's a hurricane, people begin running for their lives and nothing happens." Ultimately Leblanc and her sister choose to stay in the city because their elderly mother "says her legs are hurting . . . and we both know we aren't leaving our mama." So, like many New Orleanians connected by deep social networks, Leblanc stays in the path of the storm because it is impossible to imagine leaving part of her family behind. As a result, she and her husband, along with her mother, sister, and nephew, are trapped when her apartment complex is first battered by Katrina's winds then flooded by the levee breach. As days pass without electricity, gas, or running water, Leblanc desperately tries to call for help. Finally she gets through to an operator but is frustrated to learn that the operator cannot connect her to 911 or help her in any substantive way. Through her fear and agony she questions the operator, saying, "I am a person, a living breathing person with a heart beating inside of a body, and you can't help me?"[3]

Leblanc's demand that the operator acknowledge her as a "living breathing person" is a request for recognition. She is asking to be seen and to be recognized as a human who was in need and deserving of help. Throughout her memoir, Leblanc repeats this craving for recognition. She and her family have dire material needs—for safety, food, water, shelter, clothing, medicine, and rest—but they also need to feel that someone acknowledges their humanity. Repeatedly she recounts instances of misrecognition and the shame it brings. Over and over she resists these shaming moments by reasserting her humanity. Her story makes recognition a critical part of the struggle for survival.

Phyllis Montana-Leblanc reminds us that in addition to being a physical disaster, Hurricane Katrina was a catastrophe of misrecognition. When the levees failed in New Orleans—trapping thousands of Americans and destroying a major city—it became one of the few televised American tragedies.[4] Until the events in New Orleans, only the destruction of the World Trade Center in 2001 had allowed Americans to share their fellow citizens' trauma in real time. Unlike September 11, a single, terrible moment replayed by the media, the horror of New Orleans increased daily, produced new images of agony and death, and generated increasingly awful narratives of suffering. Americans throughout the nation witnessed hours of grisly footage and the destruction of one of America's most distinctive cities. The nation was able to watch the faces of their fellow citizens as they were unable to feed their children, comfort their parents, or find their partners.

And we did watch. A Pew Foundation survey conducted within days of the disaster showed that Americans were glued to their televisions.[5] Seventy percent of Americans reported that they paid very close attention to news of the hurricane—nearly twice as many as said they paid close attention to the war in Iraq. In addition, nearly 90 percent of Americans received most of their information about the disaster from television. About half of these viewers reported that the cable news channels CNN, MSNBC, and CNBC were their primary source of information. These sources offered blanket coverage of the disaster, beaming thousands of images of destruction and suffering into American homes. Because it was so highly visible, Hurricane Katrina offered many opportunities for recognition and misrecognition. Issues of race, gender, and politics were literally framed by what Americans saw.

If most Americans were watching the same unfolding tragedy from the same news sources, it is reasonable to expect that they formed a general consensus about the disaster and its meaning. No such consensus existed. Data collected in the weeks and months following the levee breach show that black and white Americans had vastly different opinions about the storm despite having seen very similar images. This reinforces the lesson that recognition is always a matter of interpreting and giving meaning to the images we encounter. For example, one academic study offered evidence that the coverage of Katrina differed markedly between the black press and mainstream newspapers. Black papers were far more likely to refer to race and poverty and far less likely to attribute the situation of those left in New Orleans to their individual responsibility.[6] Another study showed that media coverage actually made the residents of local communities that hosted Katrina evacuees less supportive of the poor and of African Americans.[7]

Hurricane Katrina was not color-blind in its effects, and Americans were not color-blind in their interpretations of the disaster. There was a vast racial disparity between how black and white Americans understood the lessons of the storm. Nearly all respondents to this early Pew survey were discontent with the government's response to the emergency, but white and black Americans viewed the disaster across a wide perceptual gulf. While 71 percent of blacks believed that the Katrina disaster showed that racial inequality remains a major problem in the country, a majority of whites (56 percent) felt that racial inequality was not a particularly important lesson of the disaster. Seventy-seven percent of African Americans believed the federal government response was fair or poor, and although a majority of whites agreed, the percent was much smaller (55 percent). In a stunning racial disjuncture, 66 percent of African American respondents believed that if most of the victims had been white, the response would have been faster. Seventy-seven percent of whites believed that race made no difference.

In short, while most white Americans saw the hurricane's aftermath as tragic, they understood it primarily as a natural disaster followed by technical and bureaucratic failures. Most black Americans saw it as a racial disaster. For black Americans, the catastrophe was not just a matter of slow government response; the lack of coordinated response was itself an indication that black people did not matter to the government. This racial gap suggests that many African Americans believed that their white counterparts misperceived the realities of the storm. By this interpretation, white Americans were not recognizing the role played by racial inequality and bias, and because they could not or would not recognize it, they would surely fail to address it.

The connection between recognition and potential political action was important. Survey data make clear that the vicarious experience of the disaster had immediate and dramatic political consequences. The Pew study reported that 67 percent of Americans believed that President George W. Bush could have done more in his handling of the relief effort, and nearly 60 percent rated the federal government's response as fair or poor.[8] The disaster also caused many Americans to reconsider the nation's security, with 42 percent reporting that the events surrounding Hurricane Katrina made them feel less confident that the government could handle a major terrorist attack. In the aftermath of the hurricane, President Bush's job approval ratings plummeted and never fully rebounded.[9] The Democratic Party won a majority in the House of Representatives and the Senate and won the White House in 2008. Many observers point to the Katrina disaster as both a national tragedy and a political turning point.[10] The failure of the Bush administration to respond to the crisis in New Orleans mattered politically.

Although the partisan effects of recognition became obvious in the years following Katrina, the racial terms of recognition mattered as well. Throughout her nightmare Leblanc is convinced that the refusal to acknowledge her humanity is related to her race. After a five-day ordeal, she and her husband finally reach Louis Armstrong

Airport, where they await evacuation. The airport has become a place of squalor, filth, and death. Feeling trapped and frightened, she becomes increasingly distraught and worries they may never escape to a safe location. A core feature of her anguish is her sense that the officials in charge of the rescue are cruel and unwilling to acknowledge her. This uncaring attitude is embodied in the expressionless, armed guards in the airport. Leblanc becomes irate watching their robotic responses to such enormous distress. "My emotions are starting to crumble. My mind is falling apart and I don't care anymore. This is wrong and it is driving me crazy. I can't hold it together anymore. . . . 'This is inhuman! We are human beings! Look at us, look at us!' They never budge. They never even look at me and I know they can hear me because I am standing right under them at the bottom of the escalators." For Leblanc this refusal to recognize her is not incidental but racial. Her experience of surviving Katrina repeatedly draws forth an analogy to slavery. When she finally makes it to an evacuation center in Houston and takes her first shower in nearly a week, she begins to weep as she reflects on her experience.

> I burst into tears, but soft tears so nobody can hear me. My heart is so broken. My government, in my country, does not care about me, us: the Chocolate People. The tears fall down my face soft and quick, but fall hard on the wooden plank underneath my feet. And then I feel like a slave again. I mean, I know that I could never insult the history of my ancestors by comparing what I am going through with what they endured. But this has the "air of enslavement." That is how I feel. So I decide to try to wash that feeling away with that little tiny piece of soap.

Leblanc's tears are not just personal; they are political. Her suffering is not solely about the loss of home, the agony of hunger, or the separation from family; Leblanc weeps the tears of an abandoned citizen. She recognizes herself as linked to a tradition of black suffering. For her, Katrina is a form of temporary enslavement. She is haunted by nightmares for months afterward. One recurring dream combines her sense of racial and political betrayal. "Sometimes in my dreams I see the mayor of New Orleans, the governor of Louisiana, and the president of the United States watching me die and they are laughing and they are all saying that I'm just one less nigger in the world."[11]

In chapter 3 I argued that shame is an emotional response to misrecognition. This is true at both the individual and the collective level. Phyllis Montana-Leblanc uses the word *shame* throughout her memoir. She repeatedly experiences shame during the evacuation when she is ignored or misrecognized by others, especially those in positions of authority. While waiting to board a flight at Louis Armstrong Airport, she waits in a very long line to retrieve a bagged meal. As she stands in line, she notices that black people in the line are being treated differently from their white counterparts. White storm victims are encouraged or allowed to request specific items in their bag, but African Americans are told that they must accept whatever is given.

> The people who are giving out the food bags are mostly white and the people making requests for a particular type of cookie or chips are being satisfied and when the black people ask for the same they are told that they can only get what is left over, but then another white person requests their

choice and gets it. I saw this with my own two weary eyes. I
just take what is given to me and walk away, feeling somewhat shameful and honestly like a nigger, an animal.

Her sister experiences shame for needing to rely on charity. She says,
"I feel so ashamed of myself. I mean people are feeding us! And
cheaply, I might add. It might seem like I don't appreciate what
they're doing, but I do. I'm rather taking a shot at how our government has left us in a position to have to make people feed us like a
pack of animals."[12]

When Leblanc first sees images of the flooded city, at the Houston evacuation center, her anger returns as she thinks of how many
people have died in the flood. But as she watches the devastation
wrought on her home and remembers the long delay in government
response, she again wants to hang her head. "I can't believe my eyes.
The water from the levees has practically covered our entire city!
They don't show bodies but they are saying that tens of thousands
are 'feared dead, drowned.' 'Feared'? What in the fuck do they mean,
'feared?' Had they come when we got hit, there would be no 'feared.'
I just put my head down in shame and walk back to where Ron is
sitting."[13]

Leblanc's memoir encourages us to consider the political effects
of the misrecognition that accompanied Hurricane Katrina. Leblanc
is not the only African American survivor to speak of shaming and
humiliation as core aspects of the experience. D'Ann Penner and
Keith Ferdinand collected dozens of oral histories from displaced
black New Orleanians in their book *Overcoming Katrina: African
American Voices from the Crescent City and Beyond.* Many of their
narrators tell of being shamed by military and government personnel

who misperceive them as dangerous, poor, and criminal.[14] One of the narrators, Denise Rubion-Johnson, is a middle-class black nurse who was trapped in New Orleans because her husband, a stroke survivor, was too ill to evacuate. During the storm she finds a room at University Hospital for her husband and son and offers her nursing assistance in exchange. She is trapped along with patients and other medical staff for more than five days without necessary equipment or supplies. The first rescuers who appear are local people in small boats. When military personnel finally arrive, on the sixth day after the levee breach, they treat the survivors roughly rather than with compassion. Roubion-Johnson attributes this behavior to racial discrimination.

> We were labeled as "poor black people," and we looked the part. We were smelly, so it didn't matter that I live in this Eastover house that I built, and I drive a Lexus RX 350, and I make a substantial income. None of that was relevant. Katrina was the great equalizer. I got frisked just like the woman next to me from the housing project. I had to stand in line in the hot sun, just like everybody else. I had to go to the bathroom, just like everybody else. I got yelled at to shut up, just like everybody else.[15]

Rubion-Johnson's description shows how collective humiliation arises from the stereotypes of the crooked room. She is adamant that no person, black or white, rich or poor, deserved to be treated badly in these difficult circumstances. She is also clear that the rough treatment she gets is related to the negative race and class stereotypes that influence how black Americans are perceived.

Emotional Effects

We are hardly surprised when victims of a disaster have profound emotional reactions. It is more remarkable when those who are not directly victimized experience negative emotional consequences simply as a result of their vicarious exposure to the vulnerability of others. Because Americans consumed many hours of visual Katrina coverage, the emotional effects of the disaster were not limited to immediate survivors. Just as race was directly implicated in how Leblanc understood her experience, so, too, did black and white Americans viewing the disaster from a distance have very different emotional responses to what they saw.

The responses of African Americans were more pronounced than those of their white counterparts. The Pew Foundation survey conducted immediately after Katrina asked respondents, "Have you yourself felt angry because of what's happened in areas affected by the hurricane?" Although a significant proportion of whites (46 percent) responded that they were angry, the feeling was much more prevalent among African Americans. Seventy percent of black respondents reported that the events surrounding Katrina made them angry. African Americans were also much more likely (71 percent) than white respondents (55 percent) to report that they "felt depressed because of what's happened in areas affected by the hurricane."[16]

The Katrina Disaster Study, on which I was a lead researcher, offers further insight into the racial and emotional reactions measured by Pew. Our survey was conducted approximately one month after the initial levee breaches. We asked respondents, "In the past five weeks since the Hurricane Katrina disaster how often have you

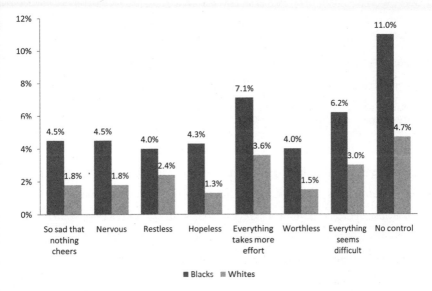

Percentages of blacks and whites who felt certain emotions "very often" in the weeks after Hurricane Katrina. Source: University of Chicago Center for the Study of Race, Politics and Culture Katrina Disaster Study

felt: so sad that nothing could cheer you up; nervous; restless or fidgety; hopeless; that everything was an effort; worthless; that difficulties were piling up so high you could not overcome them; and that you are unable to control the important things in your life." For each emotion, respondents could report that they felt this very often, fairly often, not too often, hardly ever, or never.[17]

The results show consistent differences between African American and white respondents. Approximately twice the proportion of African Americans reported the highest level of each negative emotion. They were twice as likely to report being sad, nervous, restless, and hopeless, as well as to feel overwhelmed, worthless, and as though everything takes more effort. The most dramatic response is that more than one in ten African Americans reported very often feeling that they are unable to control the important things in their lives.[18]

These data suggest that the aftermath of Hurricane Katrina provoked different patterns of emotional response in black and white Americans. Although all Americans reacted strongly, the impact seems to have been more deeply felt among African Americans. They also seem to have been somewhat more debilitated. When asked if their emotions in response to Katrina had interfered with life activities, 67 percent of whites reported that they had felt no impairment versus only 58 percent of blacks. A full 42 percent of black Americans reported that their negative emotions had interfered with their life activities. (For additional survey data, see Appendix, table 2.)

Most African Americans throughout the country had little reason to fear that their homes, neighborhoods, and city would be destroyed by a hurricane. So why were black people more distressed than whites? It could be that black people are generally more sad and anxious. There is some research suggesting that African Americans report chronically higher levels of emotional distress than whites do, but the evidence is mixed.[19] In some studies black Americans report fewer symptoms of sadness. In other studies, the racial disparity in negative emotions disappears when you control for class.[20] There is no clear, compelling evidence that black people express chronically higher levels of negative emotion. But my analysis of data from the Katrina Disaster Study shows that when income, education, gender, and age are accounted for, race still has a strong and significant correlation with reported mental distress following this event.

Is it possible that the post-Katrina emotional disparity is the result of African Americans' always responding to national crises with more negative emotions than their white counterparts? The racial responses to September 11 suggest not. There is no meaningful gap in the emotional responses of black and white Americans to September 11, 2001.[21] The only meaningful short-term difference in emotional responses is geographic. Residents of New York experienced more negative emotions, and follow-up studies revealed that New Yorkers were still experiencing emotional suffering six months after the attacks, when much of the country had begun to return to more normal psychological functioning. Proximity to the disaster left New Yorkers more shaken at the outset and more distressed in the long term. To the extent that there are differences in average emotional responses between blacks and whites immediately following the attacks, it appears that whites, not blacks, were more distressed. It is unlikely that we can explain the racial gap in the response to Katrina as part of a persistent racial pattern of response to disaster.

I believe the reason for the racial disparity in emotional response to Katrina lies not in the essential psychology of black Americans but in the racial dynamics voiced by Phyllis Montana-Leblanc. The explanation of why whites and blacks feel so differently about Katrina lies in racialized beliefs about the failure of government to respond to the needs of African Americans. I saw this connection when I visited New Orleans in November 2005, just seven weeks after the levee breach and long before I read Leblanc's memoir. There I conducted dozens of interviews with survivors of the storm. I also attended several community meetings led by Mayor Ray Nagin and his Bring Back New Orleans Commission. The emotional devastation of those who had lived through the storm was palpable. Everyone I spoke with had been displaced following the city's mandatory evacuation; most had sustained unimaginable loss of personal property; many had survived the nightmarish conditions of the Superdome or Convention Center; some were still searching for missing family members and friends; and a few had confirmed that family members had died during the storm. As survivors of the storm, they showed classic symptoms of post-traumatic shock disorder.[22] I was not surprised to find people enduring painful and raw emotions, but I was stunned by the nearly universal agreement among African American survivors that their suffering was related to their status as second-class citizens. Most of Katrina's black survivors echoed Leblanc's belief that race explained their poor treatment in the storm's aftermath.

The November 14, 2005, meeting of Mayor Nagin's Bring Back New Orleans Commission was held in a large ballroom at the Sheraton Hotel in downtown New Orleans, which had become a kind of headquarters for municipal action. Mayor Nagin presided over the meeting, and the official panel included representatives from several federal agencies and local utility companies, as well as elected officials and community leaders. After an update on the state of the city and the pace of recovery, members of the audience were allowed to come to a central microphone and address the panel.

The first four persons who spoke were white residents from Uptown and Garden District areas with a variety of concerns about power outages, mold, and health issues. The fifth speaker was an African American man who owned his own trucking business. As a local contractor, he expressed outrage at the "storm followers" who were making "$18 per hour while I can only manage to get $15 per hour." In an impassioned plea to the mayor he shouted, "Listen. I got four hundred black men ready to work and we are being talked to like dogs. This is our city and we are being treated like second-class citizens." The audience broke into unrestrained applause. When the next African American man spoke, he pleaded for a moment "to pause and recognize the loss of thousands of people. The nation paused on 9–11, but not now. No one cares about our losses. I am a homeowner who is homeless. I am a taxpayer and a voter. I placed my trust in the elected officials to do what is right but instead we got nothing. We are not refugees, we are Americans."

A black woman who had stood holding her sleeping toddler in her arms while listening to the first seven speakers continued the theme of government accountability. She said:

> I was one of the people left behind. I was stuck on a roof in New Orleans East. I am a taxpayer and a registered voter. I am happy but I am not rich. I have been shifted to five hotels all around the country. I am tired. I have never asked Louisiana for anything. I just want a place to call my own. I didn't need help before this. I was doing for myself and for my children. Mr. Mayor, all I want is a home for my children for Christmas.

Then a black man who lost his home in the Ninth Ward and was displaced first to Denver and then to Dallas confronted the mayor, saying:

> What is really going on? You are asking us to come back to work. I served this city for 35 years and we are watching foreigners get paid to rebuild it while we are sitting on the curb. There is something going on, Mr. Mayor. I understand about the dollar bill situation, but I want to come back and function for my people, for New Orleans. It is wrong for us

to be turned down. I was willing to stay an extra year to help my city. This is my home. These are my roots. We are not in Texas. We are here.

Like Phyllis Montana-Leblanc, who yelled at the armed guards at Louis Armstrong Airport "look at me," these African American survivors were demanding recognition from their government. It is clear that Katrina survivors, as Leblanc wrote, understood their experience in terms of citizenship. I wanted to know if other black Americans, those not directly affected by the storm, were also experiencing negative emotions as a result of a sense of racial betrayal.[23]

Using data from the Katrina Disaster Study, I created a statistical model to determine if African Americans' negative emotions in the weeks following Katrina were related to their racial and political beliefs, and in particular whether these emotions were linked to their feelings about slavery and Jim Crow. In the Katrina Disaster Study survey, we asked a series of questions about support for federal reparations for African Americans as compensation for historic injustices. People in our study were asked: (1) Do you think the federal government should or should not pay money to African Americans whose ancestors were slaves as compensation for that slavery? (2) Do you think the federal government should or should not pay money to African Americans as compensation for the system of antiblack violence and legal segregation known as Jim Crow? and (3) Do you think that reparations should or should not be paid to survivors and their descendants of large, violent, twentieth-century antiblack riots such as those that occurred in Tulsa, Oklahoma, and Rosewood, Florida?

These beliefs about reparations had a meaningful correlation with black Americans' responses to Katrina, even after we took into account such personal characteristics as age, income, and education, as well as other political views such as partisanship and strength of racial identification. Those who support federal reparations for slavery, Jim Crow, and twentieth-century race riots felt worse in the weeks following Katrina. Remember, we did not ask people to predict the *likelihood* of reparations. Readers should not assume that the clear majority of black respondents who believe the federal government *should* provide reparations are optimistic that it *will* provide them. Support for such remuneration is better understood as recognition of the lingering effect of racial injustice and the government's failure to acknowledge or make amends for it. African Americans reported feeling greater levels of sadness and distress in the weeks following Katrina if they also believed that the federal government still owed black Americans for centuries of previous injustices.[24]

Leblanc thought of her enslaved ancestors as she endured the aftermath of Katrina, and her memory of their suffering provided a context for understanding her own. These data suggest that she was not alone in that comparison. The disparity between black and white emotional responses to Katrina grows out of differing racial meanings given to the events. Those who believed the government owed reparation to black Americans for prior racial injustices were especially distraught. The emotional disparity emerges because only a tiny fraction of whites (less than 10 percent) share African Americans' overwhelming belief (greater than 75 percent) that such reparations are justified. September 11 proved to be a rallying point of American identity. Americans largely shared a sense of vulnerability and loss in the days, weeks, and months following 9/11. Katrina did not provoke such a uniform emotional response. Black people found themselves relatively more isolated in their grief and fury. At the core of this differing response are the racial and political meanings that black people assigned to the Katrina disaster. Leblanc sums it up best: "When Hurricane Katrina blew on me, I folded. I still, to this day, can't believe that I crumbled that badly. It wasn't so much Katrina, but how nobody came to help us, and when they did, so many people had already drowned, and most in their own homes."[25]

Policy Consequences

Phyllis Montana-Leblanc is not the only African American who experienced emotional trauma following Katrina. The data I have just discussed is evidence that this emotional trauma stretched far beyond direct survivors of the disaster and extended to black Americans throughout the country. Given that Leblanc's emotional story represents the experience of many other black Americans, what are the political consequences of this disaster of misrecognition?

In the introduction to this book, I argued that black women were Katrina's most visible victims. During the earliest days of disaster coverage, the suffering of women and children shifted media narratives away from law and order and toward outrage over the slow government response. Despite the role that black women played in this shift, we have significant historical evidence (see chapter 2) that American black women are characterized by a number of negative stereotypes. Building on these findings, it is reasonable to ask if the visual representation of Katrina victims as black women had meaningful social and political consequences. In short, does it matter differently to black and white Americans if they think of Katrina as a storm primarily victimizing black women? To answer this question I

Newsweek photo of black mother and two children
used to dramatize the Katrina disaster. Photo: Richard Alan
Hannon/*The Advocate*/September 11, 2005, Capital
City Press, Baton Rouge, LA

turn to more data from the Katrina Disaster Study. This study included a randomized experiment to explore whether framing Katrina
as a black woman's disaster affected the ways that Americans responded to it.[26]

The design was straightforward. Each person who answered the
survey was randomly assigned to one of two images of storm victims:

Newsweek photo of white storm victims used to dramatize the Katrina disaster. Photo: *Times-Picayune*/Landov

they saw either a "black mother" picture or a "white family" picture. The black mother image was taken from the cover of the September 12, 2001, issue of *Newsweek,* and the other appeared inside the same issue. Altogether 251 black Americans were assigned to the black mother condition while 236 were shown the white family image. Among white respondents, 345 viewed the black mother image and 358 saw the white family.[27]

In addition to varying the picture, we varied the accompanying description. Half of our survey respondents received a description that included the word *refugee,* and half received a statement that included the word *American.* Thus, a survey respondent received a caption stating either "More than 100,000 Americans were displaced from their homes as a result of the Katrina disaster" or "More than

100,000 refugees were displaced from their homes as a result of the Katrina disaster." The "refugee" and "American" labels were meant to reinforce misrecognition of survivors as foreigners or to encourage recognition of these survivors as fellow citizens. As we saw from the statements of New Orleanians at the Bring Back New Orleans meeting, "refugee" was a humiliating and irritating label for many black people, who wanted media discussions of the storm to emphasize their American identity. This manipulation allows us to assess whether the word *refugee* encourages misrecognition.

After giving our respondents one of the two images and captions, we asked them to choose between two statements: (1) The federal government should spend whatever is necessary to rebuild the city and to restore refugees [Americans] to their homes, and (2) Although this is a great tragedy, the federal government must not commit too many funds to rebuilding until we know how we will pay for it.

Regardless of the picture or caption study participants received, the results reveal a significant gap between blacks and whites. Overall, 79 percent of African American respondents but only 33 percent of white respondents believed that the government should spend whatever was necessary to rebuild New Orleans and restore victims to their homes. This difference existed regardless of the frame they were given. For African Americans, the desire to rebuild and restore was increased significantly—by 8 to 14 percentage points—when they saw the black mother picture.

The effect of the black mother image was very different for white respondents. Not only did they display much weaker support for government spending overall, but the black mother image made white respondents even less likely, by 2 to 6 percentage points, to respond that the federal government should spend whatever is necessary. This effect was particularly strong for white respondents who were shown the black mother picture along with the word *refugee:* the likelihood of their supporting government spending fell by up to 8 percentage points. Although the total magnitude of the effect is small, there is a statistically significant impact on white attitudes.

Together these findings reveal that African American women were critical to the post-Katrina disaster experience. As they attempted to survive the storm and its aftermath, black women were often treated in ways that made them feel ashamed and dehumanized. They felt that because of their race, their government refused to acknowledge or respond to their needs as human beings and citizens. This survey shows through experimental manipulation that black women survivors elicited a less enthusiastic response from white Americans than white survivors did. When black women storm victims were framed as refugees, few white Americans felt a compelling need to spend collective resources to help them. Recall that even as infants we feel shame when the powerful caregiver refuses to respond to us. It evokes a physical and emotional response rooted in humiliation and self-loathing. As a group, black Americans experience Hurricane Katrina as a collective refusal by the powerful caregiver (the state) to see and recognize their needs.

These racial misrecognitions had real effects. Tens of thousands of disaster victims were looking for shelter in the months following the storm. A study conducted by the National Fair Housing Alliance (NFHA) demonstrates that black survivors encountered significant, demonstrable discrimination in their search for shelter. From mid-September until mid-December, the NFHA conducted testing in Alabama, Florida, Georgia, Tennessee, and Texas. They found that while white victims were given accurate information and were offered a break on rent because they had survived the storm, black potential renters did not have phone messages returned, were not told about apartment availability, and were quoted higher prices for rent and security deposits.[28] The NFHA findings are only one example of a broad pattern of racial bias that black survivors encountered, but they are instructive because they reveal the prejudices these citizens encountered in the basic attempt to secure shelter. Misrecognition is not only about the emotional experience of rejection and humiliation; it also has material consequences.

These lessons of Hurricane Katrina are applicable beyond incidents of natural calamity. To expand our understanding of race, gender, and shame as part of the experience of disaster, I turn to a very different event: the public discourse surrounding the accusation that members of the Duke lacrosse team committed rape. In this case, black women began as powerfully mobilized public actors prepared to take action on behalf of another black woman. By the time the case ended, they had become the objects of a public campaign to shame and silence them.

Social Disaster: The Duke Lacrosse Case

In March 2006, players from the Duke University lacrosse team hired Crystal Mangum, an African American woman and a stripper, to perform at a party. Afterward, Mangum alleged that several players had forcibly raped her. Mangum was a black single mother who attended North Carolina Central University (NCCU), a historically black college also located in Durham. She alleged that members of the team victimized her verbally and physically, shouting racial epithets before forcing her into a room where she was sexually assaulted by several young men. Shortly after she made her statement to Durham police, Ryan McFadyen, a member of the lacrosse team, sent an email to fellow party attendees claiming he wanted "to have some strippers over. . . . I plan on killing the bitches as soon as the [sic] walk in and proceding [sic] to cut their skin off while cumming in my duke issue spandex."[29] McFadyen's email was cited in a probable cause affidavit issued by the Durham County courts. After this email was released to the public, the Duke lacrosse coach resigned, the university cancelled the team's remaining games, and many in Durham's community took the content of the email as an admission of guilt and an indication of a pattern of violent imaginings about black women. Within days, Durham's district attorney, Michael Nifong, filed charges and made press statements assuring the public that he had strong evidence of the players' guilt. Durham's African American community organized in support of the alleged victim. The story became national news and stayed on the front pages of local papers for more than a year.

By 2007, however, everything had changed. The alleged victim was thoroughly discredited. Physical and DNA evidence cleared the young men of any sexual misconduct. The accuser's history of drug use, sexual promiscuity, and mental health problems was made public. Michael Nifong lost his job as district attorney and was ultimately disbarred for his aggressive handling of the case. The city of Durham was named in a lawsuit brought by the team members and their parents, alleging that the young men had been deeply scarred, professionally hampered, and financially strained by the false charges against them.[30] The case and its handling by the media have multiple layers of race, gender, and class meaning: town-gown relations between majority-white Duke University and predominantly black Durham; anxieties about moral debauchery among elite college athletes;

questions of institutional inequity between predominantly white and historically black colleges; concerns about trial-by-media for high-profile criminal investigations; issues of prosecutorial misconduct brought on by political ambition. All of these subjects and more were fodder for journalists, bloggers, scholars, and workplace conversations.[31] The case is also emblematic of the multiple ways in which shame operates in race and gender politics.

As the story of alleged sexual assault was unfolding, a group of eighty-eight Duke University faculty members took out a full-page advertisement in a campus publication, the *Chronicle*. The ad, titled "What does a social disaster sound like?" included quotations from several Duke University students who indicated that as women or as racial minorities they regularly experienced alienation and harassment on campus. After presenting these students' views, the advertisement asserted, "The students know that the disaster didn't begin on March 13 and won't end with what the police say or the court decides. Like all disasters, this one has a history. And what lies beneath what we're hearing from our students are questions about the future."[32]

The ad clearly expressed these faculty members' sense that issues of race and sexual violence were ongoing concerns on campus. Although they never stated that the lacrosse players were guilty of rape, the piece demonstrated that these faculty members did not view their primary allegiance as resting with the accused students. Instead it implicated the known actions of the players (the party, hiring a stripper, sending the email) as participatory actions in a larger social disaster. Part of the text read:

> We are listening to our students. We're also listening to the
> Durham community, to Duke staff, and to each other. Re-

gardless of the results of the police investigation, what is apparent everyday now is the anger and fear of many students who know themselves to be objects of racism and sexism; who see illuminated in this moment's extraordinary spotlight what they live with everyday. They know that it isn't just Duke, it isn't everybody, and it isn't just individuals making this disaster.

But it is a disaster nonetheless.[33]

Less than a year after Hurricane Katrina revealed patterns of festering racial inequality and prompted national conversations about black citizenship, these eighty-eight members of the Duke faculty chose to frame the lacrosse scandal as a disaster. In the long shadow of Hurricane Katrina, this choice is an important clue to the multiple meanings associated with the rape accusation. In this context, *disaster* evokes a sense of unequal vulnerability to supposedly neutral processes. The faculty members were drawing a link between the abandonment of black citizens in the aftermath of Katrina and the sense of vulnerability that many black men, white women, and especially black women felt on Duke's campus. The levee breach drew national attention to inequality in New Orleans; the faculty hoped that the rape accusation could be the impetus to discuss racial and gender inequality on elite college campuses.

The case did draw national attention. In January 2007, CBS conducted a national survey as part of its ongoing political polling. The survey asked about George W. Bush's performance as president and about the war in Iraq; it gauged support for Democratic primary candidates Hillary Clinton and Barack Obama; and it asked about a number of current political issues. Among these were questions about the ongoing Duke lacrosse sexual assault case. A full 58 percent of those questioned were following the case very or somewhat closely. This does not approach the level of attention that Americans gave Katrina, but it shows that the case had drawn a broad audience of interested Americans. By the time of the survey, in January 2007, only 26 percent of respondents believed that the three accused players had probably committed a serious crime. But when asked if race has played an important role in the case, 17 percent said that it was the most important factor, and another 27 percent said it was a contributing factor. Americans were paying attention to the Duke case, and a substantial minority saw it as a case with racial implications.[34]

The poll also showed significant racial differences in how closely individuals were following the case, their presumption of the players' likely guilt, and their beliefs about the role of race in the case. A slightly higher percentage of African American respondents were paying moderate or close attention to the case (61 percent of blacks versus 57 percent of whites). Nearly half of black respondents (46 percent) believed that the Duke players were likely guilty of a crime, while fewer than one quarter of whites (19 percent) agreed with them. Also, nearly 30 percent of African Americans responded that race was the single most important factor in the case—more than double the number of whites who felt this way (14 percent). These gaps in racial perception of the case resemble the patterns of racial difference in perceptions of Hurricane Katrina.

That race was central to the national conversation about the case suggests that the faculty were in a sense correct in trying to frame the issue as a race and gender disaster. Their characterization took center stage in the months following the initial rape accusation and the eventual determination of the lacrosse players' innocence. Eighty-eight faculty and several departments signed the document, but the most visible and vocal organizers were Wahneema Lubiano and Karla Holloway. Both are tenured black women in Duke's Department of African and African-American Studies. Both have spent their academic careers studying and writing about black women's history, literature, and contemporary lives. They understood themselves as uniquely positioned to offer insight about the case by framing it for the campus, the community, and the nation. After all, this is part of what liberal arts professors do; they help their students to contextualize contemporary experiences within larger intellectual frameworks. But as Crystal Mangum's story unraveled, these professors, along with others of "the Duke 88," became the objects of public harassment and ridicule.

It is impossible to understand why Hurricane Katrina evoked racial shame for so many black Americans without understanding the historical context of slavery and Jim Crow. Similarly, to understand the Duke faculty's decision to describe the events of March 2006 as social disaster, it is important to place the Duke case within a broader history. Historian Danielle McGuire's award-winning essay in the *Journal of American History* recounts the horrific story of four black college students returning from their college formal at Florida A&M University on the night of May 2, 1959. The students were pulled over on a lonely road by a group of armed white men, who threatened all of them and, after a struggle, abducted and repeatedly raped Betty Jean Owens. McGuire calls the Tallahassee trial, where an all-white jury convicted Owens's attackers, a watershed moment in US history. It became a flashpoint for black community organizing in the town; it revealed how rape, like lynching, was a form of social terrorism; and it was one of the first times the power of the state was used to protect black women from white male assailants. "We all felt violated, male and female. It was like all of us had been raped," reported one FAMU student involved in the massive protests that accompanied the trial. Thousands of students marched to city hall, considered violent action, and made clear their determination to protect other black women from violation.[35]

For many, the accusations in the Duke lacrosse case evoked the long history of white male violence against black women. Historians remind us that white male slaveholders forced enslaved black women to have sex partners they did not choose and to bear children for profit; some even raped their bondswomen or allowed others to sexually assault them.[36] Historians have also documented how, in the Jim Crow era, when many black women were relegated to domestic labor, they were routinely assaulted, harassed, and violated by white male employers.[37] And historians suggest that just as black men were motivated to flee the lynch mob violence of the South, so did black women during the Great Migration seek relief from the sexual assaults that were an accepted practice.[38] This historically documented sexual exploitation and abuse was the initial framework many black Americans used for contextualizing the charges against the Duke players. Like the students of FAMU and the community of Tallahassee, the NCCU and Durham communities mobilized immediately with community vigils, campus protests, letters of solidarity, fundraising efforts, and statements to the media about their determination to hold the assailants responsible. The community not only focused on the accused but engaged in conversations about race, privilege, inequality, and vulnerability. The African American professors and their white faculty allies at Duke who signed the advertisement were hoping to map the broader social and racial context for the alleged crime. Their sentiments echoed the FAMU student who said "it was like all of us had been raped."

In chapter 2, I pointed out several instances when African American public opinion sided with black men accused of sexual assault rather than with the black women who were their victims—Mike Tyson, Clarence Thomas, R. Kelly. The Duke lacrosse case was dramatically different. The alleged abusers were not African American men but white males from a privileged, predominantly white institution. Whereas Anita Hill and Desiree Washington had no access to an easily available trope to counter the lynching metaphor deployed by their black male abusers, Crystal Mangum's accusations evoked a history of black women as the sexual victims of Southern white men. Mangum thus benefited from a swift response by local and national black communities, who instantly recognized the historical trajectory of her story. The Sunday after the allegations, a local group called black women together to stage a "potbanging," a noise-making protest of banging pots and pans in front of the home where the lacrosse party took place. "We are having a 'Cacerolazo,' or a pots & pans protest, because it is a tool women all over the world use to call out sexual assaulters. Ya'll, a sister—an NCCU student and a mom of two—has been brutally assaulted, and we need to get together and make a big noise!"[39]

But with the release of the DNA evidence and mounting concerns about Mangum's inconsistent story, it became clear that the Duke case was not a repeat of the FAMU event or another example of white men's abusive exploitation of African American women. This young black woman had lied about being raped. The legal and community institutions that had leaped to her defense ended up baffled, hurt, and angry. Her lies reinforced centuries-old assumptions about African American women by evoking the painful Jezebel myth; they silenced and shamed many black women around the country who had defended her. Most critically, because the Duke 88 had used her alleged victimization as a way of talking about continuing realities of race, violence, and vulnerability, her lies undermined the credibility of those broader arguments.

Not only did this case evoke these shameful, centuries-old misrepresentations of black women's lasciviousness, it also prompted painful memories of the more recent case of Tawana Brawley. In November 1987, fifteen-year-old Brawley accused six white men of rape. Brawley's body was covered with dog feces and scrawled with racist epithets. Her clothes were burned and torn. And she seemed profoundly traumatized. The men she named as her assailants included police officers and a New York state prosecutor. Her story, like that of Crystal Mangum's, provoked immediate outrage and elicited high-profile support among African Americans. The Reverend Al Sharpton became her adviser, championing her cause in the media and using her allegations as a way to discuss racism among police and city officials. Respected comedian and social commentator Bill Cosby donated and raised money for her support and legal fees. Hundreds in her hometown marched to support Brawley and protest racialized sexual violence. But in October 1988, the New York grand jury released an extensive and damning report indicating that Brawley's story was fabricated and that she was personally responsible for the abhorrent condition in which she was found. Black feminist legal scholar Patricia Williams writes poignantly about the power of the Brawley case to shame and silence black women: "wild black girl who loves to lie, who is no innocent (in New York television newscasters inadvertently, but repeatedly, referred to her as the "defendant") and whose wiles are the downfall of innocent, jaded, desperate white men; this whore-lette, the symbolic consort of rapacious, saber-rattling, buffoonish black men asserting their manhood. . . . Tawana's terrible story has every black woman's worst fears and experiences wrapped into it. Few will believe a black woman who has been raped by a white man." As Crystal Mangum's story unraveled with spectacular similarity to the Brawley case, it evoked the same shaming anxieties.[40]

On one level the Duke lacrosse case is straightforward. A woman lies about being sexually assaulted. The young men she accuses are assumed by both the press and the legal system to be guilty. A powerful institution bends to the public assumption of guilt and collaterally punishes an entire group of young men associated with the accused. The legal system eventually exonerates these young men. In the aftermath of the findings of innocence, the false accuser and those who uncritically assumed her honesty are subjected to public ridicule, just as they had earlier subjected the innocent young men to ridicule. This is, in many ways, an accurate way to recount this complicated episode. But I want to suggest that the case also gives us a chance to explore some messier interactions among race, gender, and shame in the context of a social rather than natural disaster.

The first comprehensive treatment of the case appeared in the 2007 text *Until Proven Innocent: Political Correctness and the Shameful Injustices of the Duke Lacrosse Rape Case*, by Stuart Taylor Jr. and KC Johnson. Taylor and Johnson explicate the ways that police, prosecutors, university officials, and press ignored facts, shunned procedure, and manufactured certainty about the Duke players' guilt. The authors argue that the impetus of these actions was racial political correctness that assumed the players were guilty not only of rape but of racism. In denouncing this rush to judgment they repeatedly use the words *shame, shameful,* and *ashamed.* By doing so they signal more than a legal assessment of the case: they encourage us to focus as well on its ethical and emotional implications.

The Duke case is a stark reminder that race and gender shaming as a result of misrecognition is not restricted to African American women. The most obvious public shame was reserved for the young white men of the lacrosse team. George Jennison, the father of a team member, wrote about the painful experience his family endured as a result of mischaracterization of his son as a racist and a rapist. He writes, "This pain has often resulted from the characterizations of the young men on the team. All the members of the team were vilified and found immediately guilty by the press and many in the Duke community as well. This story . . . lends itself to extreme depictions. The story of young rich white men raping a young poor black mother was an easier sell than the complex truth."[41] Here Jennison is pointing to an experience not unlike Phyllis Montana-Leblanc's in the aftermath of Hurricane Katrina. As a Katrina victim, Leblanc was denied fair treatment because many saw her through the crooked lens of racial and gender stereotypes. Here the lacrosse player is denied fair treatment because he is perceived to be part of a historical legacy of white male sexual abusers of black women. Both are denied public recognition of their true selves, and both are shamed as a result.

Yet it is deceptively reductive to stop with a simple equivalency, suggesting that at times black women are shamed by misrecognition and other times white men suffer the same fate. In the months and years following the exoneration of the Duke players, Mangum's dishonesty became the basis for a campaign of personal and intellectual shaming of the black women faculty who led the social disaster narrative. Although this shaming was directed at individual faculty members, its goal was not personal but political. Critics of the eighty-eight Duke faculty members who named the case a social disaster capitalized on Mangum's dishonesty to make a public argument against affirmative action and against the study of race and gender in academic institutions. It is reasonable to argue that the personal or professional damage suffered by tenured faculty members is unimportant when compared to the massive, unwelcome, and undeserved shaming of the young men on the lacrosse team. The faculty members are, at worst, only second-order victims of this social disaster. My point is not to evoke sympathy for these faculty members who suffered public humiliation or personal embarrassment but rather to draw attention to some of their experiences. The content of the public campaign against them is rooted in unspoken assumptions about African American women as inadequate producers of academic knowledge and beliefs about race and gender as illegitimate subjects of serious intellectual inquiry. Some commentators exploited the Duke lacrosse case to mount a public campaign against affirmative action policies in higher education hiring. Faculty members who study race and gender were the targets of an intellectual shame campaign that had meaningful political content.

On August 3, 2007, Joseph Bellacosa, a former dean at the St. John's University Law School and former judge of the New York State Court of Appeals, published an editorial in *New York Newsday* titled "Duke Faculty Should Be Shunned by Students." Bellacosa advocated a strategy of public shaming in response to the social disaster article. He wagged an accusatory finger at these faculty members, writing "Duke and especially its 88 should-have-known-better professors were responsible for aiding and abetting Nifong's 'crimes' against his Duke student targets. The DA has had his day of reckoning for what he perpetrated; the 88 should, too." It is important to pay attention to Bellacosa's use of the legal discourse of "aiding and abetting" and his implication that the professors were guilty of crimes against the student athletes. For Bellacosa, by evoking race and gender discourse, the Duke 88 were thereby poisoning public opinion toward the young men. His piece was widely reproduced on blogs and websites. Readers offered assessments of the faculty as "tenured terrorists" and echoed Bellacosa's assessment that the professors were irresponsible, intemperate, and unqualified.[42]

Criticism of these professors went beyond a reaction to the content of their social disaster ad. Commentators who targeted these faculty also sought to discredit their larger academic projects and to cast doubt on the hiring practices that brought them to the university. On January 29, 2007, the *Weekly Standard* published a scathing piece by Charlotte Allen called "Duke's Tenured Vigilantes." Allen not only criticized faculty members for their involvement in the social disaster advertisement, she mocked their academic work as ridiculous, lacking rigor, and based in political rather than intellectual questions. She asserted that "Duke University Press is the laughingstock of the publishing world, offering such titles as *Appropriating Blackness: Performance and the Politics of Authenticity* and *An Archive of Feelings: Trauma, Sexuality and Lesbian Public Cultures*," and goes on to criticize the work of Professor Karla Holloway, whose indictment of racism, sexism, and class bias at Duke was published in an online feminist journal soon after the incident. Holloway argued that despite the legal outcomes of the case, the Duke incident had raised cultural and social issues that required serious investigation. Allen derided Holloway's assertions using precisely the history to which Holloway was pointing.

> The metanarrative they came up with was three parts Mandingo and one part Josephine Baker: rich white plantation owners and their scions lusting after tawny-skinned beauties and concocting fantasies of their outsize sexual appetites so as to rape, abuse, and prostitute them with impunity. It mattered little that all three accused lacrosse players hailed from the Northeast, or that there have been few, if any, actual incidents of gang rapes of black women by wealthy white men during the last 40 years.[43]

Allen's skillful inversion of the history of sexual assault against black women suggests that discussing this history is nothing more than political ax-grinding rather than scholarly invocation of connections between historical experiences of oppression and contemporary power dynamics. This rhetorical move casts into doubt the entire history of black women's physical and sexual subjugation simply because Crystal Mangum lied about the assault in March 2006. The image of Jezebel is used to shame both contemporary black feminist scholars and the historical women whose lives are their source material. Allen describes these professors as "vigilantes," thereby linking them with the history of racially provoked mob violence that took the lives of hundreds of black men, women, and children during the decades following the Civil War.[44] The metaphor is clear: just as lynch mobs are the illegitimate, uninformed, violent enemies of the rule of law, so, too, are these professors an illegitimate and dangerous threat to orderly academic inquiry and discourse.

Taylor and Johnson's *Until Proven Innocent* joins Allen's assessment of black, feminist critical studies as laughable. They carefully trace the professional résumés and personal conduct of several outspoken faculty members who originally signed the social disaster advertisement. They casually deride these professors as " 'diversity' hires" who "advanced while doing comparatively little" and characterize them as bad citizens: not only unqualified but ungrateful, unpatriotic, and dangerous to the impressionable students they teach. "Professors like Lubiano, Holloway, Chin, Deutsch, Houston, and others trained in the race-class-gender approach generally consider American society deeply flawed, with the majority and the powerful oppressing women, minorities, and the poor. For these faculty members, the lacrosse case was too tempting not to exploit. And they did not hesitate to vent their class hatred against their own students."[45]

Taylor and Johnson never attack these professors based on their race or gender identity. In fact, they are equally virulent in their critique of white male professors like Peter Wood and William Chafe. Neither they nor most other public critics of the Duke 88 specifically claim that Lubiano, Holloway, or other black women are undeserving of their academic positions because they are black women. Instead, these critics attack race and gender as objects of study, and they deride the intellectual and political assumptions underlying such studies. For example, although Peter Wood is a white man, his academic career is defined by his commitment to research on race and American racism.[46] William Chafe's distinguished career as an American historian is based on his research about and commitment to racial and gender equality.[47] Thus it is not the hiring of a black woman that wastes university resources; it is taking race and gender seriously as objects of academic inquiry. Taylor and Johnson decry as shameful an entire institutional structure at Duke—and by extension at other universities—that provides the resources, public space, authority, and academic freedom for these "farcical" "activist professors" to "babble" about racism and sexism as they defend a dishonest, sexually unethical black woman. "In the era of political correctness and craven university administrations, the charge of racism, unsubstantiated but accompanied by a few demonstrations and angry rhetorical perorations, suffices to paralyze a campus, to destroy a reputation, and to compel an administration into submission."[48]

Race is important even to the authors' denunciation of Michael Nifong, whose overzealous prosecutorial impulses they link to his political ambition. Nifong was facing reelection in the predominantly black city of Durham, North Carolina. Taylor and Johnson, along with many other observers, point to this looming political campaign as the primary reason Nifong behaved so irresponsibly. Through the arrest and indictment of the Duke lacrosse players, he hoped to position himself as champion of Durham's black community and thereby handily win reelection as district attorney and possibly develop political capital for future campaigns. Even as they reserve their most virulent attacks for Nifong, a white man, Taylor and Johnson implicate the corrupting influence of black political power. Many of the seemingly neutral ethical critiques leveled by Taylor, Johnson, and others thus contain powerful racial implications.

I am not a neutral observer of the Duke case. I earned my PhD at Duke in 1999. Faculty members who were part of the group of eighty-eight taught several of the courses I took in graduate school. Professors Wahneema Lubiano and William Chafe were members of my dissertation committee. Because Duke is my alma mater, I followed the events of the case and its aftermath very closely. Having been trained as a black feminist scholar by these academics, I am attached to the intellectual projects that came under attack from critics of the Duke 88. A basic assumption of black feminist scholarship is that researchers need not be personally removed from the issues we investigate. Black feminist scholarship assumes that experiential knowledge has equal weight with empirical evidence drawn from more traditional sources of social scientific and humanist research.[49] This insistence on lived experience as a valid source of knowledge is precisely what is in dispute between the Duke 88 and their critics. The social disaster ad argued that the faculty had gained important insights about the case and its social and cultural meaning by listening to the testimonies of students. This epistemological claim was scorned as ridiculous when the weight of DNA evidence showed that Crystal Mangum was being dishonest about the sexual assault. These black women professors, their students, and their faculty colleagues were told to be ashamed of ever believing that their own experiences, beliefs, and feelings were valid.

There is strong evidence to suggest that black women bore the brunt of this shaming. Laura Smart Richman and Charles Jonassaint are researchers who were conducting a study at Duke University on the physiological effects of race and stress when the lacrosse rape accusation rocked the campus. At the start of their study, these researchers hypothesized that race-related stressors have pernicious and meaningful psychological and physical effects on African Americans. They tested whether students reacted differently to being shown a video that heightened their sense of student identity (a basketball highlights film) or a video meant to heighten their racial identity (video clips of Martin Luther King Jr.). After viewing one of the two videos, students had to deliver a brief videotaped speech about a personal experience of discrimination. By forcing participants to give a speech that would be videotaped, the experiment was designed to create stress. Moreover, it was the sort of stress readily associated with shame, because it implied that the participants were being viewed and judged.[50]

After this procedure, the researchers collected saliva from the participants and tested the samples for cortisol to determine if those who were prompted to think about discrimination felt more stress when identifying as a student or when identifying as African American. This research has clear implications for the general theory of racial recognition and shame I presented in chapter 3. Recall from that chapter that cortisol is one of the physiological responses to shame and is also implicated in a number of negative psychological and health outcomes. Thus, this study was well suited to examine how a sense of identity—we might even say a sense of citizenship within the Duke nation—served either to protect black students or to expose them to racial shame and its attendant physical production of cortisol.

The research, useful even in its original design, became an extraordinary study of race, shame, and cortisol when Crystal Mangum made her rape allegations against members of the Duke lacrosse team approximately halfway through the researchers' data collection process. Suddenly they found themselves observing a natural experiment. If racial stress affects cortisol levels, they were in a perfect position to observe the effects of a real-life, rather than laboratory-created, racial stressor.

The results from this study are striking. The lacrosse case elicited significantly higher stress levels, as measured by cortisol production, among one group of study participants: black women. To a

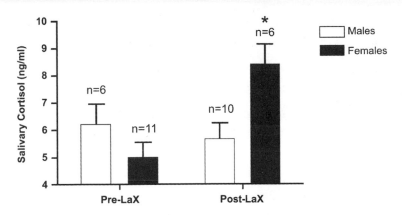

Mean of salivary cortisol levels before and after Duke lacrosse scandal, by sex. Source: Laura Smart Richman and Charles Jonassaint, "The Effects of Race-Related Stress on Cortisol Reactivity in the Laboratory: Implications of the Duke Lacrosse Scandal," *Annals of Behavioral Medicine* 35 (2007). Reproduced with permission.

significantly greater extent than other participants, their bodies were carrying the stress and shame of the event.

In the heady and difficult days of the lacrosse scandal, African American women bore a particular burden on Duke's campus. They experienced particularly high levels of stress and a heightened sense of alienation. "Such alterations in physiological processes and adrenocorticol responses in particular," write Richman and Jonassaint, "can have a negative impact on long-term health outcomes. Cortisol hyperreactivity is related to increased susceptibility to infectious diseases, and chronic cortisol elevations under long-term stress conditions have been associated with depression."[51] In the aftermath of the scandal African American women at Duke University experienced a substantially heightened level of the corrosive, illness-producing, stress hormone cortisol. In the introduction to this book I claimed that the story of Hurricane Katrina was written on the bodies of black women. This study provides evidence that the lacrosse scandal was literally written on the bodies of black women at Duke. This is indeed what a social disaster feels like for African American women.

My goal in presenting the Duke case is not to exonerate the Duke 88—though they committed no crime. Nor am I interested in condemning their critics, who made a number of important contributions to our understanding of a complicated case, or in adjudicating who is right by some standard of my own creation. I want to understand the processes of public discourse that emerged in this case and, in particular, how that discourse affected black women. In the example of Hurricane Katrina, many black women experienced shame as a result of misrecognition caused by their identity as "refugees" from a presumably violent and poor city. In the Duke case, race and gender scholars are publicly shamed because their work is characterized as intellectually insufficient when it leads them to publicly support a black woman who turns out to be dishonest. The class privilege of Duke professors compared to many Katrina survivors is obvious. But in each case, assumptions about race, gender, and black women's identity are important elements framing the ways that they are recognized or misrecognized in the public sphere. Together these two very different kinds of disaster reveal some of the many complicated ways that race and gender shaming occur within American political and social systems.

Responding with Strength

Politics is not just about thinking; it is also about feeling. Emotions are an important part of how we engage our political world. Sometimes we imagine that citizens gather information about candidates, parties, and policies and then use that information to make reasoned decisions about their choices in elections or their options for collective action. But this sterile rationality obscures the truth that our emotions are critical to our politics.[52] Citizens form attachments to political parties long before they can articulate a policy rationale for their loyalties.[53] Paralyzing fear or vengeful anger helps explain many foreign policy choices. Hopeful, inspired happiness can explain why people vote for some candidates. Compassion can encourage efforts toward global justice and social change.[54]

Shame, too, can affect who we are politically, telling us to avoid the public space or provoking us to rage. But African American politics is not entirely, or even primarily, a history of political withdrawal or irrational aggression. African Americans, and black women in particular, have somehow found the emotional resources necessary for sustained resistance against inequality. Black women's activism reminds us that psychological theories are not deterministic and that even shame may motivate political action. Psychologist Janice Lindsay-Hartz reminds us, "Experiences of shame may support our commitment to a destructive social reality; indeed racism is often supported by this mechanism when minorities become ashamed of their racial or ethnic identity. At times, it may be healthier to work to change others' views of reality, rather than to give in to shame and accept the status quo view of reality."[55]

Black women in America have resisted and challenged the shaming ideologies about them in both formal and informal ways. One of the most enduring symbols of this resistance is Sojourner Truth. Her insistence on being recognized as a woman pushed back against a nineteenth-century ideology that portrayed black women as animalistic sexual beasts of burden whose physical and reproductive labor could rightfully be harnessed to enrich slaveholders. Truth's 1851 speech at the Women's Rights Convention in Akron, Ohio, articulated a space for black women in a country that sought to strip them of human dignity.

> Nobody eber helps me into carriages, or ober mud-puddles, or gives me any best place. And ar'n't I a woman? . . . I have plowed and planted and gathered into barns, and no man could head me—and ar'n't I a woman? I could work as much and eat as much as a man, (when I could get it,) and bear de lash as well—and ar'n't I a woman? I have borne thirteen children, and seen 'em mos' all sold off into slavery, and when I cried out with a mother's grief, none but Jesus heard —and ar'n't I a woman?

Truth defines black womanhood as struggle and the overcoming of adversity, unlike white "ladyhood," which is understood as a life of privilege and ease. She locates the source of her feminine identity in labor and survival.[56]

Charlotte, a sixty-two-year-old African American woman in my Chicago focus group, explains the difference between white and black women by saying that black women can make miraculous events occur with little help or resources. "You know how black women are. We know how to make do, honey. We do with what we don't have. A white woman might cry because her family got nothing to eat. But if we got a chicken outside and some rice in the cabinet we are going to make a full meal out of that. White women they don't know how to handle it. They don't know what to do." Like her orator foremother, this contemporary black woman is deeply attached to a self-definition rooted in strength.

Phyllis Montana-Leblanc called on a self-image as strong to help her survive the terror of Hurricane Katrina. "I don't know if anyone who's never experienced this before can imagine sitting and waiting for disaster to strike and not knowing if today is your last day alive. The pressure on my heart is so intense that I want to just crawl inside of a closet with earplugs and a blanket, close my eyes, and make it all just go away. . . . I choose to hang on to who I am: a strong black woman."[57]

To protect against the shaming assault of race and gender stereotypes, many sisters retreat behind a sense of mythic strength, creating a collective self-image of imperviousness. In their struggle to stand upright in the crooked room, African American women have crafted a new frame of reference: the strong black woman. W. E. B. Du Bois wrote that the amused contempt of others not only makes an individual feel bad; it requires the whole race to use "dogged strength [to keep from being] torn asunder." African American women's use of dogged strength to keep from being torn asunder gives rise to the strong black woman. She, too, is part of African American women's repertoire of strategies for resisting shame but the strength myth has emotional and political consequences of its own.

"No Mirrors in My Nana's House"

Sweet Honey in the Rock

LYRICS BY YSAYE MARIA BARNWELL

Sweet Honey in the Rock is a Grammy Award–winning vocal group of black women vocalists founded in 1973 by Bernice Johnson Reagon. The group's members have changed during its long tenure, but it retains a core of five vocalists and a sign-language interpreter. Their performances are deeply embodied celebrations of black women's lived experiences. The group's name is derived from Psalm 81:16: "But you would be fed with the finest of wheat; with honey from the rock I would satisfy you." Sign-language interpreter Dr. Ysaye Barnwell joined Sweet Honey in the Rock in 1979 and appears in more than thirty recordings with the group. She is the author of one of the group's most popular recordings, "No Mirrors in My Nana's House." It is a stirring piece that reveals how the loving protection of black women can shield black girls from a painful world that seeks to negate their beauty and worth. In 1998 the lyrics became a children's book published by Harcourt Brace.

There were no mirrors in my Nana's house,
no mirrors in my Nana's house.
There were no mirrors in my Nana's house,
no mirrors in my Nana's house.
And the beauty that I saw in everything
was in her eyes (like the rising of the sun).

I never knew that my skin was too black.
I never knew that my nose was too flat.
I never knew that my clothes didn't fit.
I never knew there were things that I'd missed,
cause the beauty in everything
was in her eyes (like the rising of the sun);
. . . was in her eyes.

There were no mirrors in my Nana's house,
no mirrors in my Nana's house.
And the beauty that I saw in everything
was in her eyes (like the rising of the sun).

I was intrigued by the cracks in the walls.
I tasted, with joy, the dust that would fall.
The noise in the hallway was music to me.
The trash and the rubbish just cushioned my feet.
And the beauty in everything
was in her eyes (like the rising of the sun).
. . . was in her eyes.

There were no mirrors in my Nana's house,
no mirrors in my Nana's house.
And the beauty that I saw in everything
was in her eyes (like the rising of the sun).

The world outside was a magical place.
I only knew love.
I never knew hate,
and the beauty in everything
was in her eyes (like the rising of the sun).
. . . was in her eyes.

There were no mirrors in my Nana's house,
no mirrors in my Nana's house.
There were no mirrors in my Nana's house,
no mirrors in my Nana's house.
And the beauty that I saw in everything
was in her eyes (like the rising of the sun).

Five

Strength

These suprahuman women have been denied the "luxuries" of failure, nervous breakdowns, leisured existences, or anything else that would suggest that they are complex, multidimensional characters. They must swallow their pain, gird their loins against trouble . . . , and persist in spite of adversity.

—Trudier Harris, *Saints, Sinners, Saviors: Strong Black Women in African American Literature*

The picture I have painted so far is pretty dismal. African American women are standing in a room skewed by stereotypes that deny their humanity and distort them into ugly caricatures of their true selves. As they struggle to find the upright in this crooked room, they are beset by the emotional, physiological, and political consequences of race and gender shaming. This shaming has tangible, even disastrous consequences: it can decrease their opportunities for recognition by the state, reduce the effectiveness of speaking on their own behalf, and set off spirals of fury that lead to further victimization. Under these conditions, one might expect to see black women in public life rarely, if at all. The realities of black women as church organizers, community activists, and elected officials indicate that sisters have developed strategies to push back against both the stereotypes and the shame.

One way black women have demonstrated their agency under difficult circumstances is by crafting alternative images of themselves. The *strong black woman* is the most pervasive and widely accepted of these self-constructions. By its idealized description, black women are motivated, hardworking breadwinners who suppress their emotional needs while anticipating those of others.[1] Their irrepressible spirit is unbroken by the legacy of oppression, poverty, and rejection.[2] Whereas the negative iconography of black women as lewd, angry, or unnaturally devoted to their domestic employers is reproduced by the state and in mainstream popular culture, the image of black women as unassailable, tough, and independent is nurtured within black communities.[3] You can hear this insistence on strength in the music of popular black women artists across generations. Think of Aretha Franklin belting out an anthem of independent self-reliance, "Sisters are doing it for themselves." Or picture Mary J. Blige assuring her listeners, "You can't keep a good woman down." Even young Alicia Keys promises, "I am superwoman, yes I am."

The strong black woman serves as a constructive role model because black women draw encouragement and self-assurance from an icon able to overcome great obstacles. She offers hope to people who often face difficult circumstances. Independence and self-reliance can be crucial to building and maintaining a positive image of blackness in a society that often seeks to negate and vilify it. African American women do not define themselves as Jezebels, Mammies, or Sapphires; instead they call themselves strong and proudly drape the mantle of self-denying independence across their shoulders. This itself is a triumph of emotional and political resistance because black women have consistently demanded a right to name themselves. But there are dangers to allowing this symbol to remain unchallenged at the center of African American understandings of womanhood.[4] When black women are expected to be super-strong, they cannot be simply human.

What begins as empowering self-definition can quickly become a prison. By adopting and reproducing the icon of the strong black woman, African American women help craft an expectation that they should be autonomously responsible and self-denying caregivers in their homes and communities.[5] This means that they are validated, admired, and praised based on how they behave, not on who they are.[6] Loss of social standing is an ever-present threat for individuals whose social acceptance is based on behavioral traits rather than unconditional human value. Any mistake, bad act, or bad outcome can be translated into a global sense of failure.[7] While all individuals are publicly judged by their actions, the strong black woman imperative is unusual in that it requires tremendous personal fortitude from a group with few structural resources. It thus exposes black women to more opportunities for shaming.[8] African American women hold up the strong black woman as a shield against the shame-inducing negative stereotypes of the crooked room. To protect against always being seen as inferior, they declare themselves uniquely capable, but this strength is a shield full of holes; it sets up new possibilities for being misrecognized.

Through the ideal of the strong black woman, African American women are subject not only to historically rooted racist and sexist characterizations of black women as a group but also to a matrix of unrealistic intraracial expectations that construct black women as unshakeable, unassailable, and naturally strong. Many African

American women have internalized self-reliance as central to their identities. They believe that to be a good black woman is to be strong; therefore, strength is foundational to who they are. As long as they can present themselves as self-sacrificial and independent, their identities feel firmly rooted. While this attachment to strength may be adaptive, it also creates dangerous exposure for black women— routine human weakness and fragility are potential sources of shame. "Society," comments the psychologist Regina Romero, "expects the African American woman to handle losses, traumas, failed relationships, and the dual oppressions of racism and sexism. Falling short of this expectation is viewed by many African American women as a personal failure. This may bring about intense feelings of shame that they work hard to contain."[9]

In many ways the strong black woman is like John Henry. Legend holds that John Henry, a black man and former slave, was hired as a steel driver for the Chesapeake and Ohio Railway. The workers building the C&O's new line were moving along quickly until they reached Big Bend Mountain. The mountain was too vast to build around, so the line had to go through it. As the story goes, John Henry was the strongest, fastest, most powerful man working the rails. One day, a salesman came to camp, boasting that his steam-powered machine could outdrill any man. John Henry chose to challenge the machine and won, driving fourteen feet to the drill's nine. At the end, just as he broke through the rock, John Henry collapsed. As the well-known song goes, "He died with the hammer in his hand."[10]

African Americans tell the story of John Henry as an example of black men's strength, but public health scholars have shown that trying to emulate him can actually make black men weak. Epidemiologist Sherman James and his colleagues use the term *John Henryism* to describe an active coping style prevalent among African American men. Like the legendary steel driving man, these men try to use raw strength to tackle life's challenges. If they have few socioeconomic resources, however, these John Henrys have a greater likelihood of developing cardiovascular disease. Trying to meet the challenges of life the way John Henry met the challenge of the steam drill has very real health consequences.[11] The strong black woman image has similar consequences for black women who must fulfill a mandate for self-reliance while having few personal, social, and economic resources available to them. Simultaneously empowering and destructive for individual psyches, the symbol also has complex effects on the way black women understand their political world.

Although psychologists and popular culture have given sustained attention to the health and psychological consequences of the strength myth, no one has yet offered a systematic analysis of its political consequences. The strong black woman shares traits with all three of the stereotypes we examined in chapter 2. She looks suspiciously like Mammy except that her loyalties are firmly with black communities. While not subjected to the racial dynamics of Mammy, her devotion to racial community may leave sisters without the room to organize for themselves. The strong black woman has incorporated elements of the Jezebel myth because she does not require physical or economic protection from men. She cares for herself and her own children whether she has a male partner or not. The strong black woman looks like a way to channel the angry Sapphire in a socially acceptable direction. Black women may believe that their anger must always be in service of others and rarely used in their own defense. Given these connections with negative stereotypes, we should not be surprised to find that this myth has political consequences. One way to understand these consequences may be through the theory of a just world.

Psychologists have found that people's belief in a just world helps explain how they react to innocent victims of negative life circumstances. People become cognitively frustrated when presented with stories of victims who suffer through little fault of their own. They can deal with this frustration in two ways: they can conclude that the world is an unjust place, or they can decide that the victim is somehow to blame. Most people reconcile their psychological distress by blaming the victim. Even when we know that suffering is undeserved, it is psychologically easier to blame the victim rather than give up the idea that the world is basically fair. In some studies, respondents were given a way to compensate the victim, in which case they were happy to make the world seem fair again through their actions. But when they had no chance to make things right and were faced with the knowledge that the innocent victim would continue to suffer, many people tried to find a way to understand this suffering by denigrating the victim.[12]

These effects worked the other direction as well. People want to believe that individuals who receive good outcomes deserve them. One early experiment studied subjects who were told that a fellow student had won a cash prize in a lottery. Even though this lottery was entirely random, respondents tended to believe that the student who won the cash prize was a harder worker than those who lost the lottery. They assumed that the unearned privileges must be related to some inherent, if invisible, qualities in the winner. In other studies, researchers showed subjects a videotape of people learning a task. In one study the learners were punished for incorrect answers with electric shocks (the "learners" were actors and the shocks were faked). In another study they were simply told that their answers were wrong. People expressed much lower opinions of those who were given electric shocks even though they did not get any more answers wrong. When the victim had no possibility of finding relief from the ordeal, or when the victim took on the role of martyr by voluntarily remaining in the painful experiment, viewers decided that the victim deserved the treatment.[13]

These studies show that most people believe in a just world. When the idea of justice and fairness is threatened by the suffering of innocents, people will work hard to maintain a sense of balance even if it means rationalizing that innocent people deserved to suffer.[14] The idea that black women are supposed to be super-strong and invulnerable is a similar psychological distortion, which encourages black women to believe that persistent racial and gender inequality is deserved. As a group, black women have few economic or political resources with which to adjust the structures of government or society to compensate themselves or other victims of inequality. The cognitive need to see the world as a just place requires them to provide some explanation for black women's circumstances. One way to do so is by believing that inequality must be the result of insufficient effort. The standard set by the ideal of the strong black woman is impossible to maintain. Its insistence that black women can always make a way out of no way sets the stage for failure. Sometimes there really is no way, and not even capable, dedicated, smart black women can carve space out of nothing. Of course, this is true for all individuals, but when black women expect themselves to be capable of superhuman tasks, normal humanity is considered failure and that failure can be used to rationalize continuing inequality.

This sort of psychological distortion can encourage support of political agendas focused on individual effort rather than structural change. When citizens are presented with social and political facts, either in their own direct experience or through media presentations, these facts can take on very different meanings depending on the interpretive frame through which they are encountered. The strong black woman myth is a powerful frame for black women—one that discourages attention to the structural sources of inequality.[15] Research shows that certain dispositional frames lead people toward individualist explanations for the causes of inequality.[16] Elected officials can strategically employ moral frames to justify their stances on public policy in order to manipulate voters who would normally oppose their preferred policy.[17] Frames can influence interpretations of controversial public policies.[18] Television news frames can significantly alter how audiences understand the root causes of social problems. For example, political scientist Shanto Iyengar employed an experimental strategy that offered five different media stories about the causes of poverty. Some used structural frames that explained poverty as nationwide in scope and related to unemployment and social programs. Other stories used narratives of particular victims of poverty: a family who cannot afford heat, the homeless, and an unemployed worker. Overall, the narratives of individual cases of poverty elicited more blame for individual circumstances and choices rather than structural explanations of poverty. This work demonstrates that "when poverty is framed as a societal outcome, people point to societal or governmental explanations; when poverty is framed in terms of particular victims of poverty, . . . people point instead to dispositional explanations."[19] Frames are not only available through politicians and the media. Citizens also have individual political predispositions that act as frames. The most obvious is partisan identification—partisan loyalty is a lens through which new political information is filtered and interpreted.[20]

The strong black woman myth is a political frame for African Americans. It assumes that black women are essentially strong, capable, and unassailable, and when information about black women's inequality is encountered, the myth frames that inequality as resulting, at least in part, from the inability to live up to this inborn capacity. The strong black woman thus encourages black women to overemphasize the role of the individual in life outcomes. The psychological need to maintain belief in a just world, combined with the tendency to use dispositional frames to understand inequality, means that powerful psychological forces are at work when black women enter the political world. I have made several empirical tests of these possibilities. First, I wanted to determine if black women actually view strength as a common and important self-definition. Second, I wanted to learn if black women's sense of self-reliance makes them happier with their lives. Last, I wanted to explore whether there is any evidence that this myth of the strong black woman has meaningful political implications. To test these possibilities, I looked at evidence from several surveys, an experimental study, and my focus groups. These empirical sources add a new dimension to our understanding of how African American women negotiate cultural and political standards of self-sacrificial strength.

Black Women's Self-Definition

"Picture number nine is definitely a strong woman," says Gloria, a talkative and opinionated fifty-year-old black woman in my New

York focus group. Picture number nine, one of the two dozen images of women that Gloria considered, shows a young black woman standing on a deserted urban street, holding a girl child. Both the woman and the girl are staring intently into the camera. The women in the other pictures are of various ages, ethnicities, and national origins. Some are photographed alone; others are with partners, with other women, or with children. Some are at work, some are at home, and some are vacationing.

Participants in all of the focus groups were asked to look at each photo and then list the ones that depicted strong women. Some thought a group of Latina waitresses were strong, but others thought they looked simply young and carefree. Some thought an older white couple embracing in an intimate dance depicted strength. Others felt that the couple did not convey anything about strength. Some thought a white woman mechanic was a strong photo, but others disagreed. The one subject nearly every respondent chose as strong was the woman in photo number nine. For the women in the focus groups, this young woman represented struggle, self-reliance, and strength: "You know she is strong because she is struggling to raise her child in a ghetto." "You can tell from that picture what she is thinking: I got my baby and we're going to get through this together." "You can see the strength in her eyes: I can do this even if the daddy isn't around." "She is strong just because she made it. She survived."

The women in my focus groups spoke frequently and admiringly of black women's strength. African American women outside my small groups also seem attached to self-reliance as an ideal. In March 2005, Chicago's major convention center, McCormick Place, hosted the thirteenth annual Expo for Today's Black Woman. The expo, sponsored by a local radio and television station, was widely publicized throughout the city as an opportunity to "showcase the talents and serve the needs of Today's Black Woman." The event provided an opportunity to observe how contemporary black women actively construct their self-concept. Thousands of African American women came together to seek solutions to their life challenges by exploring them with other black women.

That the expo is a commercial endeavor undoubtedly influences how problems are framed and solutions are offered. Even so, the organizers had a sincere goal of addressing issues important to black women. The advisory panel included black women who are college professors, owners of small businesses, print and broadcast journalists, community organizers, church officers, and elected officials. It is fair to see the expo as a space where black women explicitly sought to understand themselves at the intersections of race and gender. The seminars reflected a broad range of social, personal, and political issues. Aspiring authors could learn about publishing, and novice real estate investors could learn how to tap the value of their homes. There were seminars on health, weight control, and living with HIV-AIDS. There was a session for navigating sex and dating as a single woman and another on strengthening one's marriage. Entrepreneurs discussed small business opportunities, and community leaders hosted discussions of black Americans in the criminal justice system. The expo provided a structured space for black women to reflect on themselves and the concerns that dominate their lives.

The opening pages of the printed program contained official letters from then Chicago mayor Richard Daley and Illinois governor Rod Blagojevich. Mayor Daley's letter greeted expo attendees and asserted that the event "brings a sense of pride and community to African American women and men." The governor went further, stating, "We, as a state, work diligently to ensure that women, and particularly minority women, have the same opportunities for success as men. This year's event will help to empower and enlighten you, as African American women, to achieve all of your goals and dreams." Both the mayor and governor were featured prominently in the promotional materials of the event. These letters reflected the state's recognition of the attendees' consumer power as well as their potential political power. Black women attending the expo were seen as worthy of official recognition and their empowerment was explicitly encouraged by the state.

During the expo a team of graduate students from the University of Chicago conducted brief surveys with 125 attendees to learn more about how they described African American women in relation to other groups. The survey began with an open-ended question: "We recognize that everyone is an individual. However, there are some characteristics that individuals in groups share in common. Please write down three words or phrases that describe black women, black men, white women, and white men." Each respondent was asked to provide these descriptions without prompting or interference by the researcher. (For survey data, see Appendix, table 3.)

The results are striking for several reasons. The most frequently used term in any category is the word *strong* as a description of black women, employed by more than one in five respondents. The five most commonly used words account for more than half of total responses about black women. Given free rein to use any words they chose, these respondents showed remarkable agreement: they defined black women as strong, beautiful, smart, independent, and kind. These descriptions fit a classic positive depiction of the strong black woman. The next four most frequent responses also largely reinforced the strong black woman ideal. Black women described sisters as religious, powerful, aggressive, and giving. It seems that they have largely received the message that black women are strong and good people. When asked to reflect on their characteristics, the image of the strong black woman comes immediately to mind.

The expo respondents were not a randomly selected national sample, but they are an interesting and important group. Women at the expo came together with the express purpose of thinking of themselves as black women, spending time with other black women, and finding solutions to their common concerns. When prompted to think about their group identity, they consistently defined themselves as strong. This suggests the power of the self-reliance discourse among black women.

Respondents at the expo offered similar descriptions of black men. Again, *strong* was the most frequently used descriptor. African American men were also defined as handsome, smart, powerful, kind, and determined. But these descriptions varied much more widely. The top five categories accounted for just over a third of all responses. There was a less unified sense of black men as a group. Beyond the top five categories, the descriptions turned negative. The next five most frequently used descriptors were angry, irresponsible, selfish, independent, and aggressive. While strong, handsome, kind black men are the clear corollaries of strong, beautiful, kind black women, there is a lurking sense that these sisters see black men as very different from themselves.

When consciously thinking of themselves at the intersection of race and gender, as at the expo, black women are generally, but not universally, positive about black men. They describe black men as much like themselves, but with many more negative characteristics.

There is evidence here of an intraracial tension around gender. I do not want to exaggerate the significance of this finding, but it does hint at potentially important political possibilities. It may indicate that black women feel solidarity with but also responsibility for their less competent or less trustworthy brothers. Maybe as strong women they expect to carry the load for the race. Alternately, perhaps there is a seed of feminism here if black women believe themselves to be more capable leaders than their male counterparts.

Whatever similarities they expressed with black men, the women at the expo defined white men and women as very different from themselves and black men. White men, in an inversion of the characteristics that American society values, were seen as rich, dishonest, arrogant, mean, and powerful.[21] Although the respondents believed that white men are wealthy, this access to greater resources was not paired with desirable personal characteristics. Instead, white men's economic success was not thought to mitigate their arrogance and meanness. There is a vast and striking difference in how respondents described white women compared to black women. White women were passive, stupid, dishonest, arrogant, and privileged—the opposite of the portrait painted of black women. Not one person used "strong" or "independent" in connection with white women. This is evidence that black women perceive white women's lives and characters as distant from their own. They see themselves as having far less in common with white women than with black men.

It is important to remember that these respondents were thinking of white women in the abstract, not responding to any specific person. To say that black women as a group think of white women as weak, passive, and stupid does not mean that they think of every white woman this way. Had they been asked about, say, Hillary

Clinton or been prompted to reflect on particular white women in their lives, the results might have been quite different. Still, there are important political implications. If these results hold in a general population, such an enormous gulf in the perceived characters of black and white women makes it hard to imagine African American women having much faith in cross-racial, gender-based political coalitions. Political solidarity must have some basis in a sense of shared identities and interests. African American women do not appear to see white women as natural political coalition partners. By valuing their own strength and denigrating that of their white counterparts, they reject any notion of similarity with white women.

These results may be jarring. We are accustomed to hearing about white Americans' opinions of African Americans. Historical accounts of race in America revolve around the changing feelings and attitudes of whites. News media focus on stories of white prejudice or tolerance. Entire subfields of public opinion research in political science, psychology, and sociology focus on the sources and effects of stereotypes that whites hold of blacks. It is much less common to reverse the gaze and ask black Americans what they think about whites. When African American women were allowed to openly express their dominant understandings of themselves and of other groups, they revealed a pervasive self-understanding rooted in the idea of strength. They also made clear their sense that white men and women do not share these essential characteristics. In a country where rugged individualism, the Protestant work ethic, and personal sacrifice are key aspects of the national identity, black women have a heightened sense that their personhood is defined by their strength and independence. In their own perception, their strength binds them to black men, whom they also understand as strong, but distinguishes them from white men and women, whose wealth and privilege are associated with negative character traits.

The women in the focus groups provide a more detailed understanding of the idea of strength. As they discussed what strength means to them, they suggested that it is "just a given when we are talking about black women." They explained that strong women are able to handle everything they are given, endure difficult circumstances, act as a backbone for their families, and show both mental and physical toughness. They also described strength as a kind of resilience: "It's like the rubber band effect. You stretch a rubber band as far as you can but it always comes hurling back. The ability to bounce back off whatever."

Mothers were regularly invoked as representatives of strength. Exposed to mothers, grandmothers, aunties, and teachers who were crucial to their own survival and development, these women looked to maternal figures as icons.[22] They saw the photo of a young single mother as an image of strength, as was a photo of an older black woman comforting a girl and boy child.[23] "You can see the strength in her face and it's not from too much sun. That's from worry, that's from encouraging and caring, decision-making." "That is the wisdom of the older black woman."

Both photographs prompted respondents to talk about their own mothers and the lessons of strength they drew from being their daughters. They spoke of their mothers as "remarkable," "independent," and "dependable." Many women described their mothers as the ultimate role models of strength: they were committed to family, available as advisers, stern but loving, and able to cope with difficult circumstances. As they talked about the women in these photographs and reflected on those in their own lives, their descriptions underscored that African American women are deeply attached to an ideal of self-sacrificial strength evidenced by overcoming adversity. Unlike the stereotypes of Jezebel, Mammy, and Sapphire, the strong black woman is widely embraced by these women as a truthful depiction of themselves and the women in their lives. Although they are affected by how others see them, African Americans have developed a communal self-understanding at odds with negative stereotypes. As black women move through their personal lives, work at their jobs, and engage in politics they not only react against external myths but actively create new ones.

The women in my Oakland focus group talked about why they wanted to be thought of as strong. Jackie commented, "I want to be known as a strong woman because strong implies holding things together and being very disciplined and being in charge. It's like glue when I think of strong." Bonita talked about wanting the ability to handle difficult times and circumstances and to help others: "I want to be a strong woman because it means you get up and go when you don't feel like getting up and going. You do things for your family, you do special things for your friends, maybe even strangers."

Although many celebrate strength as an essential and positive characteristic of black women, others are concerned about the psychological implications of attachment to an ideal of self-reliant independence.[24] Social scientists, journalists, essayists, poets, and clinical psychologists have worried that strength has become a race and gender imperative. If African American women are led to believe that strength is an essential, inborn characteristic—a racial rule—then showing weakness or asking for help becomes traitorous. As popular author and psychologist Julia Boyd writes, "Being strong all the time is a burden and doesn't leave us much room to be human."[25] The strength mandate forces black women into painful silences about their own needs even as they push relentlessly to serve others. Even as they celebrated strength, the women in the focus groups expressed concern about its limitations. They worried that their toughness would intimidate men. They complained of never being able to be soft because everyone assumes black women are rocks. They worried that being strong means never having someone be concerned enough to care for you. "They know that you can take care of yourself so they let you do it." And they were particularly worried that self-sacrifice would encourage others to take advantage. "My mom gives too much. If my brother needed extra money she would give it to him. I say he's fifty years old, let him go out there and get two jobs. But she would say 'no, that's my child and so I'm going to be there and help whenever I can.' He takes advantage of her." Black women celebrate their powerful independence yet worry that their self-image leaves little room for personal fragility or reasonable limits.

The Consequences of Self-Reliance

Although the strong black woman is a pervasive symbol among African Americans, it has been subject to severe criticism for several decades. At the Expo for Today's Black Woman, where attendees were so willing to characterize black women as strong, one of the best-attended sessions was "Escape the Cape: The Superwoman Complex." As African American women have increasingly organized on their own behalf in the past half-century, they have also interrogated the limiting effects of the myth of strength.[26] Yet there is little empirical evidence on how self-reliance influences black women's overall quality of life. To address this concern empirically, I turn to the 1995 Detroit Area Study, a detailed survey of several hundred men and women, both black and white, that examined the social influences affecting physical and mental health. Admittedly, this survey is dated and limited in regional scope, but it contains questions that are rarely asked of a large and diverse sample of Americans and therefore is still useful for illuminating the concepts I am interested in here.[27]

The first important finding from the Detroit survey is that black women differ from other groups on a number of social and emotional factors. They lag behind black men and whites in both emotional and physical well-being. More than 50 percent of white men, white women, and black men reported that their physical health was very good or excellent. Among black women, only 41 percent ranked their health in these categories, and more than a quarter rated their health as fair or poor. The same was true of general life satisfaction. In every other race and gender category, at least 50 percent of respondents were completely or very satisfied with their lives, but only 42 percent of black women responded this way. African American women were neither significantly less nor more sad, but they were less satisfied with their lives and physical health. (For survey data, see Appendix, table 4.)

The Detroit study also suggests that black women experience their intimate relationships with friends and family differently from other individuals. While black women reported feeling loved by their friends and families as much as other groups, they also experienced families as a site of demands and burdens and sensed that their families demand too much of them. Black women reported lower quality of health, less satisfaction with their lives, and a greater sense of being burdened. No other group shares this unique constellation of concerns. Despite this, black women felt that they must be strong, independent, and self-reliant. They overwhelmingly believed that they could do anything they set their mind to, that their future depended on themselves alone, that having things done right required doing them yourself, and that signs of defeat were just signals to work harder. Together, these results speak to the particular legacy of the strong black woman as a cultural ideal. Black women feel less well, less satisfied, and more burdened than everyone else and yet they believe it is their responsibility to overcome life obstacles alone and to achieve despite having fewer physical, emotional, and social resources. They are John Henry's sisters.

These differences between black women and other groups can help us test how an insistence on self-reliance and a sense of being burdened by others' demands affects black women's emotional well-being.[28] Is there a relationship between life satisfaction and sense of self-reliance? Perhaps those who depend mostly on themselves are more satisfied with their lives, or perhaps an insistence on independence makes black women feel worse about their lives. I am also interested in the personal stressor measures. We have seen that black women feel more burdened by their families than do individuals from other race and gender categories; now we can test whether those burdens influence life satisfaction.[29] Because the Detroit survey asked the same questions of a relatively large number of people, we can use a statistical technique called regression analysis to compare how these various ideas and beliefs affect each group.[30]

Several key results emerge from this analysis. In summary, the results show that life satisfaction is positively correlated with good health for both black and white women; sense of self-reliance has no statistically significant effects; feeling loved by friends is positively correlated with life satisfaction for all groups except black women; and religiosity is insignificant to black women's life satisfaction. Feeling loved by family contributes to black women's sense of well-being, but the negative effect of burdens associated with family life is larger. (For survey data, see Appendix, table 5.)

Decades of previous research have shown that perceived health has a consistent positive correlation with overall life satisfaction even in populations that are quite healthy on average.[31] The data from the Detroit survey largely confirm this finding. Both black and white women are generally more satisfied with their lives when they feel physically healthy.[32] The coefficient for white women is larger than for African American women, indicating that believing oneself to be in good physical health has greater explanatory power for white women's life satisfaction. It is also important to remember the difference in average health rating. Recall that only 41 percent of black women rated themselves in the highest categories of physical health, whereas 56 percent of white women did. Thus, compared to their white counterparts, black women reap fewer life satisfaction benefits from the good health they experience and they also have significantly lower health self-evaluations.

Importantly, these data do not reveal a role for assumed self-reliance in predicting life satisfaction for any group. People who believe that they are individually responsible for the outcomes in their lives are not systematically more or less satisfied than those with less self-reliant attitudes. For African American women, we might interpret this as a failure of the empowering aspects of the strong black woman myth. According to these data, black women are far more likely than other groups to believe that they are solely responsible for their life outcomes, but that belief does not make them happier or lead to a greater sense of mastery and satisfaction. Nor does it make them less satisfied. It appears that although they cling to a self-definition rooted in strength, black women's life satisfaction is located somewhere else. Two results in the analysis suggest that black women's service to others is negatively related to their life satisfaction. For black and white men and for white women, feeling loved by friends has a substantial and statistically significant relationship to life satisfaction. In fact, for each of these groups, the love and support of friends contributes to life satisfaction more than any other variable in the equation. Although black women report feeling equally loved and cared for by their friends, this feeling has no influence on their life satisfaction.

This does not mean that black women are inadequate friends to one another. On average, they feel that their friends are much less demanding than their families. Already overburdened by the demands of life, black girlfriends may choose not to impose additional demands on one another and instead work to carry their own weight. This may be why these friendships are not as emotionally protective for black women in this sample as for other groups. Importantly, this finding complicates the assumption, common in the self-help literature, that black women can survive the demands of the strong black woman syndrome by leaning on one another. While friendships undoubtedly play a role in supporting and sustaining emotionally wounded black women, they have only limited capacity to undo the difficulties imposed by structural inequality.

It is also important to note that religiosity has no relationship to life satisfaction among the black women in the Detroit study.[33] African American women are profoundly religious: even those who do not frequently attend church tend to profess a belief in God and claim that their religious beliefs guide their daily decision-making.[34] Black women seek professional mental health care less frequently than white women; and when they do seek it, they do so later in life and in later stages of their illness.[35] Communal and religious networks are often the only marginally competent sources of support and counseling available for black women. Given the reliance of black women on church-based counseling, these results are notable. They suggest that although religion may help black women to survive, it does not necessarily make them any more satisfied with their lives. But these data are only suggestive of this dynamic, not definitive. I will discuss black women's religiosity in greater depth in the next chapter.

Black women in the Detroit survey do respond positively to feeling loved and cared for by their families. For them there is a significant positive relationship between life satisfaction and familial love; but this effect must be balanced against the negative influence of black women's family lives on their satisfaction. Feeling that one's family expects too much has a significant negative effect. While black women are happy that their families love them, they are heavily burdened by their family members, and this burden substantially reduces their overall life satisfaction. Together these results underscore the popular critiques of the strong black woman that point to the deep personal costs black women bear as they try to meet the needs of others. Familial pressure can have many sources. Black women are far more likely than white women to be single parents and to face single parenting with fewer resources. Black women's life expectancy outstrips that of black men, meaning that elderly black communities are largely female. Black women thus face being alone in both childrearing years and old age. The data here suggest the possibility that this loneliness is a significant burden.

Class structures in black communities also contribute to these familial burdens. Among black Americans, poverty creates anxiety, stress, and hardship, not only for the poor but also for the middle class. The black middle class, unlike their white counterparts, is not divorced from the black poor. In urban areas, black middle-income neighborhoods tend to be adjacent to poorer and higher-crime communities.[36] Black families rarely enjoy intergenerational wealth. Sisters who have finished college often have less-educated siblings. Daughters who own homes often have parents who do not. Cousins with disposable incomes frequently have loved ones without. This familial proximity to disadvantage means that the financially vulnerable black middle class must often contribute to the incomes of poorer family members. Such leveling amounts to an informal tax on middle-class black families. Women are usually the mediators in this process. It is most often the daughters, wives, sisters, aunties, and grandmothers who negotiate the terms for transfer of goods and services from wealthier family members to poorer ones.[37] These costs are real, both economically and psychologically. These limited, but interesting, results from the Detroit Area Study may hold hints to the psychological effects of these familial processes.

Those who are interested in seeing the statistical results from which I have just drawn these conclusions can consult table 6 in the Appendix. That table will look pretty standard to the social scientists who regularly encounter these sorts of findings. But for readers who are unfamiliar with statistical estimation, it could be confusing. My decision to include tables in this book is to give evidence of the relationships I have just discussed. If you do not want to read the statistics, you can skip the tables without losing the overall argument. However, you can use the tables to gain more insight about my conclusions.

Taken together, the results of the 2005 Survey of the Expo for Today's Black Woman and the 1995 Detroit Area Study provide insight into the prevalence of the strength myth among black women and its influence on their emotional lives. *Strong* is the default category for describing black women, but the myth leaves them sicker, less satisfied, and more burdened than any other group. Even in the face of these disparities, black women maintain a staunch belief in the power of self-reliance. Rugged individualism does not make black women any more satisfied with their lives, but the significant demands placed on them by their families substantially reduce their satisfaction. These data suggest that the myth of strength exacts a real and measurable emotional cost.

The Political Consequences of Self-Reliance

Does the strong black woman imperative influence black women's politics? Remember that this book does not define politics narrowly as vote choice, partisan preference, or engagement with government entities. When I ask here about black women's politics I am asking about the constellation of ideas, beliefs, and attitudes that contribute to how black women see their relationship to society and the state. It is possible that attachment to self-reliance pushes black women in a politically conservative direction by encouraging a politics of self-help rather than one of structural change. The intuition is simple: to the extent that black women believe they are naturally endowed with a superhuman capacity to overcome life's obstacles, they may be less likely to support political agendas and public policies that seek to dismantle the structural barriers facing black women and more likely to support those aimed at individual empowerment.

To test this hypothesis, I returned to the 1995 Detroit Area Study.[38] This time, instead of investigating life satisfaction, I want to know how the same beliefs and attitudes affect racial political ideas. I developed a scale titled "get-over-it." It is a three-item scale that measures the belief that racial inequality stems more from individual effort than from structural barriers. The items used to generate the "get-over-it" scale are the respondent's level of agreement with three items: (1) discrimination against blacks is no longer a problem; (2) blacks have a tendency to blame whites too much for problems that are their own doing; and (3) many groups have worked their way up without special favors, and black people should do the same.[39] Un-surprisingly, African Americans score lower overall on this scale than whites. But black women and men have an average score on this scale that is just above the midpoint, which means they are slightly more likely to be in agreement with these ideas than opposed to them. And there is as much variation among African Americans as among whites. The idea that racial inequality is more a matter of personal behavior than structural barriers has purchase among both blacks and whites. (For survey data, see Appendix, table 7.)

My analysis produced several findings I want to highlight: for African Americans, agreement with the "get-over-it" measure is neg-atively related to liberal political ideology; for all groups, agreement with this measure is positively associated with American patriotism; for black women, agreement with this measure is strongly, positively correlated with assumptions of self-reliance. This last relationship is present only among African American women. Unsurprisingly, black men and women who call themselves politically liberal are much less likely to agree that race discrimination is no longer much of a problem and that black people should simply work harder without pressing for government assistance. This effect is particularly powerful among black men. Yet white political liberalism was unrelated to this measure. Conservative and liberal whites are equally likely to feel that African Americans should get over issues of racial discrimination.

Although political ideology is insignificant for white respondents in this model, patriotism is significantly and positively associated with the get-over-it variable for all groups. This provides some evidence of just-world processing (the cognitive process of conforming one's views to the theory that the world is just) on the part of patriotic respondents. Meritocracy is an important element of the American political and cultural landscape.[40] It is likely that an attachment to the idea of a functioning meritocracy is an important aspect of American patriotism. The need to believe in a just world parallels the need to believe in meritocracy, a need that should be heightened among more patriotic respondents. If I am proud to live in America, I am more likely to discount information that America might be unjust: if African-Americans do not benefit from the current structures, they, not the structures, must be to blame. Importantly, this patriotism effect works across race and gender categories, lending further support to the notion that it is a variation of pervasive just-world effects. Research by social psychologists Zick Rubin and Anne Perplau shows that respondents who have a strong tendency to believe in a just world also tend to be more religious, more authoritarian, more conservative, more supportive of traditional social institutions, more likely to have negative attitudes toward underprivileged groups, and less compelled to engage in political or social action. This finding in the Detroit study data is only suggestive, but it points to real political consequences.[41]

The final important result from this model offers empirical support for the hypothesis that the strong black woman myth makes black women particularly susceptible to dispositional explanations for inequality. For them, the assumption of self-reliance is strongly and positively correlated with the get-over-it scale—more strongly than any other variable in the model. It has this effect only among black women. Agreement with the get-over-it scale both for whites and for black men is independent of their belief in self-reliance; but black women who assume that self-reliance is critical to personal success are significantly more likely to discount a continuing role of discrimination in explaining unequal life circumstances for African Americans. This result offers compelling evidence that, in addition to its emotional costs, the strong black woman myth has political consequences. Among this sample, it contributes to a worldview that not only asks a woman to demonstrate superhuman strength for family, friends, and community but also discourages her from empathizing with the structural difficulties present in her own life and those of other black women.

Following this logic further, I tried to see whether these political implications also influence black women's policy choices. For this exploration, I used the 1999 Chicago African American Attitudes Study, a questionnaire with an embedded experimental manipulation designed to test the policy effects of the strong black woman myth.[42] The first page of the survey included measures of self-esteem, egalitarianism, and individualism. The experimental manipulation was introduced on the second page, in a scenario presented as a human-interest news article about an African American single mother of two named Nikki. At random, subjects were shown one of five different versions of Nikki's story:

CONTROL GROUP, UNRELATED STORY: In the control questionnaire, respondents read a news story entitled "A River Runs Through It," excerpted from the July 12, 1999, *Newsweek* article by the same name. The story concerns the Federal Energy Regulatory Commission's decision to destroy a number of dams throughout the country and was thought to be unrelated to any of the variables of interest.

SCENARIO 1. NO HELP/GOOD OUTCOMES: In the first experimental questionnaire, a created scenario was presented as a human-interest news story entitled "One Woman's Story." The subject, Nikki, is a single mother of two who is working full time, going to school, and trying to raise her two children. She shuns child support, government assistance, and offers of family help, and behaves in stereotypical "strong black woman" fashion. She faces some negative consequences, but overall her self-reliance leads to good outcomes.

SCENARIO 2. NO HELP/BAD OUTCOMES: In the second experimental questionnaire, the scenario is almost identical, except that Nikki's insistence on total self-reliance here brings more negative outcomes, and her strong black woman veneer is subjected to criticism.

SCENARIO 3. SEEKS HELP/GOOD OUTCOMES: In the third experimental questionnaire, Nikki actively seeks child support, accepts government job training, allows her family to help her financially, and reaches out to a community of friends for support. She is still admirable, but she is less the stereotypical "superwoman." These efforts to seek help lead to positive outcomes.

SCENARIO 4. SEEKS HELP/BAD OUTCOMES: In the fourth experimental questionnaire, the otherwise identical Nikki finds that asking for help creates negative consequences.

Each respondent read one of the five possible stories. The survey questions then measured emotional reactions to the story, perceptions of Nikki and perceived closeness to her, and offered participants an opportunity to comment. The remainder of the survey asked for levels of support or opposition to public policies whose implementation would disproportionately affect black women and children. The proposals were in the areas of welfare, child support, child care, juvenile crime, and health care. In my analysis I often collapse the four categories into two: No Help/Good Outcomes and Seeks Help/Bad Outcomes become Traditional Strong Black Woman; and No Help/ Bad Outcomes and Seeks Help/Good Outcomes become Challenge to Strong Black Woman. The imperative of strength suggests that black women should be able to handle life crises without help. The No Help/Good Outcome scenario reinforces this view by validating the choice to be independent. The Seeks Help/Bad Outcome scenario also reinforces the traditional strength imperative by associating requests for assistance with negative consequences. The other two scenarios challenge the traditional strong black woman perspective by suggesting that independence can be negative and help can be positive. The survey thus allows me to explore how images of strong black women affect African American understandings of the social and political world.[43]

To determine if exposure to the Nikki scenarios makes black women less willing to support government interventions that assist black women and children, respondents were asked about their sup-

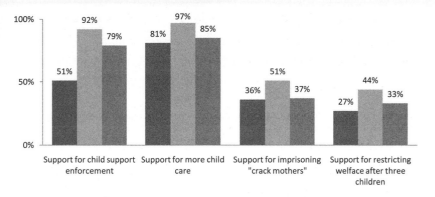

Black women's policy attitudes after exposure to Nikki scenarios

port for ten different policy areas, including stricter welfare laws, government-provided health care, juvenile crime laws, and affirmative action. Their positions on several of these policies were significantly affected by exposure to the experimental manipulations.[44]

The traditional strong black woman scenarios elicited a higher level of support for stricter child support enforcement. Black women had a 92 percent probability of supporting this policy when they were exposed to traditional stories, compared to a 79 percent probability in the control group. Women exposed to traditional stories were more likely to support government-provided child care for poor parents. Among those who read a scenario with traditional ideas of black women's strength, the probability of supporting child care climbed from 81 percent to 97 percent.

When exposed to scenarios that reinforce a traditional image of the strong black woman, respondents were significantly harsher about punishing drug-addicted mothers. While the control group had only about a one in three probability of supporting this policy, more than half of those in the traditional groups supported the proposal that "crack mothers" should be imprisoned. Respondents who read traditional strength scenarios were also significantly more likely to support restricting welfare benefits for women who have more than three children. Although they were not more likely to support a time restriction on welfare benefits, black women were more punitive on the issue of welfare and family size when they were exposed to traditional notions of black women's strength. Only a quarter of those in the control group supported this restriction, versus 44 percent of those in the traditional groups.

These results suggest a few conclusions. In this sample, black women's positions on these drug and welfare policies suggest that those who are primed to think about the positive symbol of strength are severely judgmental of other black women whose behavior reinforces negative racial stereotypes. Women who have just been reminded of the "strong black woman" become harshly critical of the "crack mother" and the "welfare queen." The strong black woman, a symbol embraced in opposition to the pejorative symbols of black womanhood perpetuated by a hostile dominant culture, seems to intensify black women's negative reactions to those symbols. While she operates as a point of pride and inspiration, she also seems to impel black women toward more conservative policy positions and harsher political judgments against sisters who fail to meet the standards the myth imposes. A black woman may need help from government and her children's father, but if she *chooses* to take crack or have additional children, she should be punished. Again, because these data are drawn from a small sample in a single city, they are only suggestive. But they point to the real and consequential ways that the strong black woman narrative intervenes in black political thought. Narratives that reinforce the idea that black women can and should make it on their own strength have potentially conservative effects on African American policy positions. The image of mythic strength can focus black attitudes on individual faults, shortcomings, and accountabilities and may direct attention away from the communal responsibilities and strategies available to African Americans.

The strong black woman is a complicated cultural myth. On one hand, she is a deeply empowering symbol of endurance and hope. Her unassailable spirit is uplifting. Her courage in the face of seemingly insurmountable adversity emboldens black men and women when facing their own life challenges. But in her perfection, the strong black woman is also harmful. Her titanic strength does violence to the spirits of black women when it becomes an imperative for their daily lives. When seeking help means showing unacceptable weakness, actual black women, unlike their mythical counterpart, face depression, anxiety, and loneliness. The strong black woman is not meant to be Pollyanna. Rather, she is expected to show negative emotion, but that emotion is anger, not sadness. The neck-rolling, finger-snapping, tooth-sucking demands of an angry black woman are entirely consistent with the myth of strength. But this no-nonsense, take-no-prisoners woman offers no expectation that the black woman is supposed to be happy, content, or fulfilled. Her sometimes explosive anger is part of what distinguishes her from the ideal of white femininity. This right to own and express anger is among the more potentially powerful psychological and political elements of the construction of black women's strength. That the black woman is not denied an angry voice within an authentic definition of her femininity makes her a powerful ally for both black men and white women in their political struggles.

The emotional consequences for black women are not solely

individual. The mental health of marginalized people has important political implications. Feminist theorist bell hooks contends, "The mental-health dilemmas of black people . . . are very real. They persist in our daily life and they undermine our capacity to live fully and joyously. They even prevent us from participating in organized collective struggle aimed at ending domination and transforming society."[45] The icon of the strong black woman is a bridge between black women's emotional lives and their politics. African American women perceive and describe themselves as strong, beautiful, independent, and kind—self-definitions that are both positive and powerful. The strong black woman does battle against the vicious stereotypes of black women perpetuated by racism and patriarchy. But while she creates a standard for self-improvement and racial empowerment, she also encourages silence in the face of structural barriers. As an orientation toward the world built on a set of beliefs about the intrinsic qualities of African American women and about how those qualities may be appropriately manifested in the way black women think, speak, and act, the strong black woman has both emotional and political consequences.

Strong in the Lord

The icon of the strong black woman encourages African American women to confront the considerable challenges of their lives independently. Recall that a desire for recognition is a motivating force for participation in public life. Human beings need material goods, but they also need to feel valued and recognized. This is particularly important in a democracy where citizens expect to have an opportunity to voice their interests and have the government respond to those interests. African American women face specific, damaging, and deeply embedded race and gender stereotypes that make it difficult for them to enjoy accurate recognition in the public sphere. The crooked room created by these stereotypes has psychological consequences for individuals and social and political consequences for black women as a group. The strong black woman ideal is an attempt to straighten these crooked images. But even though the strong black woman is a more positive image than Jezebel, Mammy, or Sapphire, she is still inadequate to allow black women to enjoy the benefits of recognition and therefore to opt into an experience of full citizenship. Still masked behind a facade of impervious strength, black women remain unable to reveal their fragile humanity.

Frances, a thirty-six-year-old woman in my New York focus group, expressed her frustration with the strength imperative:

> Yeah, I am very, very much jaded. You're angry because you arc still going. It's so repetitious. Your life has become so (claps hands three times) you know, every day I have to do this. I have to work. I'm working from check to check. It's like things never get better for me. I never experience a progression. I feel like you never get to make that transition over into the real woman. And I think the real woman's life is a whole lot better than being this extra strong soldier woman. I want to be that real woman, I don't want to be a soldier all my life!

Frances's yearning to give up the role of soldier was echoed by another group member who responded, "As a black woman I just think people expect so much. Everyone expects a lot from you, especially if you characterize yourself as strong. People believe you never need help when actually you do. People think you never cry." Although the strong black woman allows sisters to craft a new role for themselves unconstrained by the most vicious images of the crooked room, they still seek a place where they can be authentic— or "real women," as Frances describes it.

Religious faith, most often expressed through traditions associated with black Christian churches, is one way that African American women have felt free to admit their vulnerability and seek authenticity. Although they may be reluctant to lean on friends, family, or the state, black women have wholeheartedly embraced God as a partner in their struggles. Zora Neale Hurston's *Their Eyes Were Watching God* rarely discusses organized religion. The lead character, Janie Mae Crawford, navigates the difficult world of racial and gender misrecognition without explicitly calling on Jesus to help her. But both God and the church are embedded in her story. When the hurricane bears down on her and her companions, they turn their eyes to God. When she expresses her love to Tea Cake, she tells him that God opened a door for her to find happiness. Janie relies on the divine, but she also understands the limitations of the church. Early in the novel we learn that Janie's grandmother, the one who consigns Janie to a loveless arranged marriage, is herself a woman of God shut out of official religious leadership because of her gender. "Ah wanted to preach a great sermon about colored women sittin' on high, but they wasn't no pulpit for me." Without a sanctioned space from which to share her religious vision, Janie's grandmother can barely imagine a life of freedom for a black woman, and her lack of vision leads her to limit her beloved granddaughter's choices. Perhaps this lack of official opportunity for religious leadership is why Janie does not participate in an organized church. Still, God is present throughout her journey. She consistently finds a purpose greater than herself by engaging the natural and spiritual world around her. One reason Janie is able to stand straight in a crooked room is because she has the mirror of divinity to offer her a clear reflection of who she is. She sums up her story to her friend Phoeby by explaining that every person must "go tuh God and they got tuh find out about livin' fuh theyselves." The insight that everyone must go to God is not only about shared mortality, it is also a call to find the divine presence within that gives meaning to life.[46]

Faith in God plays a similar role for many African American women. Nadine, an older woman in a Chicago focus group, explained that she perceives God as the source of her strength. After describing some of the difficulties she has lived through, she said, "I think strength is measured by what you endure, what you have to take on. The things that have happened to me in my life, the next person may not be able to handle them. And it wasn't because I was so especially strong. I was just me and I dealt with the things as they came. With God's grace I made it." Nadine is testifying to the supportive role of the divine in her life in a way that is very common among African American women. Consider the black spiritual assertion that there is Balm in Gilead.

Some times I feel discouraged,
And think my work's in vain,
But then the Holy Spirit
Revives my soul again

There is a balm in Gilead
To make the wounded whole;
There is a balm in Gilead
To heal the sin sick soul.

In the next chapter I ask whether there truly is a balm in Gilead for African American women.

Six

God

Womanist 1. From *womanish*. (Opp. Of "girlish," i.e., frivolous, irresponsible, not serious.) A black feminist or feminist of color. . . . Traditionally capable, as in: "Mama, I'm walking to Canada and I'm taking you and a bunch of other slaves with me." Reply: "It wouldn't be the first time."

—Alice Walker, *In Search of Our Mothers' Gardens*

Nadine is married and raising two children while studying full time to be a nurse. Joy is an insurance salesperson who is caring for her elderly mother-in-law. Kim is raising three children while working at FedEx, and Michelle is a single woman doing data entry at the county hospital. Ressie is unmarried, has no children, and just enlisted in the US Army Reserves. These women, part of a focus group of African American women who met in Chicago in 2005, face different landscapes of family obligations, employment stress, and personal goals, but as they talked about their struggles and successes, one consistent theme emerged: God is necessary for survival. Reflecting on the anxieties of trying to raise children, her loneliness as she sought romantic partnership, and her exasperation with her job, Kim said:

I think being strong comes from showing forgiveness, having faith in God, learning from other women. In my case it was my grandmother and my great-grandmother. How my great-great-grandmother was a slave. Learning from them and sitting as a child at their knee and hearing them tell stories about how you should want more out of life. Even if life kicks you to the curb just keep fighting. So for me, being strong and strength, they come from faith, being forgiving and trying to keep on.

Most in the group expressed the sense that, as African American women, they have to keep going even when facing enormous challenges and that their faith in God allows them to persevere. Listening to them speak, I had little doubt that they believed their God-centered survival strategy was adaptive, necessary, true, and good. In Kim's narrative, the same God that protected black women under slavery and gave them fortitude to endure bondage is at work in the lives of contemporary black women. This God's forgiveness and strength make black women's continuing struggle possible. Faith in a benevolent and loving God is a common tool black women employ to straighten out the crooked room of race and gender stereotypes. God provides an alternate measuring stick for judging their human worth. When judged against social values rooted in white beauty standards, economic success, political power, or normative domestic arrangements, African American women consistently fall short. By focusing on a divine valuation based on their character, kindness, service, and strength, black women shift the angles of the crooked room and produce a new image for themselves. Faith is a resistance strategy. And faith for many black women derives from the experiences and teaching of African American Protestant churches. The historical and contemporary practices of many of these churches are based in patriarchy. In many ways these black churches create new forms of subjugation for black women through their promotion of inequitable gender leadership and their teachings about male domination in the home. Thus, although God is understood as a companion in the struggle for recognition, the place where many black women come to know God can be just as unequal as the broader political world.

The experiences of faith, celebration, worship, and resistance form the institutional basis of black church life. Black church scholars C. Eric Lincoln and Lawrence Mamiya assert: "The Black Church has no challenger as the cultural womb of the black community."[1] They also remind us that black churches are sustained by membership that is nearly two-thirds female. To assert the centrality of the black church to African American social, cultural, and political practice is therefore to place black women at the center of these processes. The work of women in the black church sustained enslaved communities, undergirded the modern civil rights movement, and mobilized voters throughout the twentieth century.[2]

But even though black women's lives and labors are the very basis of African American church life, they still experience widespread institutionalized gender inequity. One way to think about how black women experience the black church is as a metaphor with the American state: they are citizens of it, but because of their identity, they are still struggling for full recognition within it. It is also important to remember that African American women's sacred lives are about much more than their institutional contributions to church life. Their relationship with the divine is mediated by, but not entirely determined by, their relationship with churches. In this chapter I want to explore how black women's religious beliefs are an important source for understanding the ways that they sometimes resist and sometimes accommodate the crooked images they encounter. Specifically, I want to investigate how black communities' insistence on women's strength means that black women's faith experiences often reflect the same struggle for recognition that marks their political lives. To do this, I begin with a short history about the scholarly study of theology among African Americans, because this academic story has some important parallels to black women's lived experiences of church and faith.

Womanism

In 1964, Joseph Washington Jr., an African American professor of theology, leveled a harsh and controversial critique against African American churches. He claimed that black churches lack the guidance of an overarching theological approach. Asserting a derisive view of black religious traditions, Washington wrote: "There is little theology in Negro Protestantism. Past alienation from the theological roots of Protestantism, social separation from white Protestants and their historical and cultural extensions of the European tradition, addiction to religion as personal salvation by means of moral purity, worship as the primary means of release and the occasion for class identification—these are the bases for the religion of the Negro."[3] While acknowledging the existence of unique patterns of worship among blacks, Washington placed these practices outside of a Christian tradition because they are not guided by an articulated theology. It was a harsh criticism, but one that ultimately launched a robust scholarly response from African American theologians.[4]

By the late 1960s, a group of African American academics sought to fill this void by crafting a distinct African American contribution to systematic theology. This black liberation theology—or just black theology—was born in the context of the waning civil rights movement and the emerging black power movement. Black liberation theologians felt they were responding to the challenge of making Christianity relevant for African Americans who were engaged in political and cultural struggle against white racism. Black theology addressed the need "not only to vindicate the young civil rights workers laboring in the rural South, . . . but also to galvanize the left wing of the Southern-based civil rights movement and reassemble it within the province of the Black Christians who lived in the urban North."[5] Albert Cleage's *The Black Messiah* (1968), James Cone's *Black Theology and Black Power* (1969), and J. Deotis Roberts's *Liberation and Reconciliation: A Black Theology* (1971) are foundational texts of this tradition. At its core, black theology is predicated on the assertion that God has a unique relationship with African Americans. God is not a passive bystander in human history but rather an active participant in the struggles of oppressed and dispossessed people. In the American context this means that God is on the side of blacks as they struggle against the social, political, and economic marginalization caused by the legacy and persistence of white American racism. Liberation is the theological center of this approach, and movements for liberation define the ministry of the historical Jesus and the experiences of his contemporary followers, blacks in America. Because black liberation theology asserts a special relationship between God and black people, it asserts that black people will receive from God what they fail to receive from American social and political structures: recognition. American society and government may be unable or unwilling to recognize and respond to black people, but black liberation theology assures that the divine does recognize the suffering caused by racial inequality. J. Deotis Roberts writes, "God is aware of centuries of undeserved Black suffering. He is aware of our experience of oppression. . . . Black hope stems from the assurance that God seeks the liberation of the oppressed."[6] Black theology articulates both the political and spiritual yearning for a black-centered and Christian-inspired understanding of suffering and resistance, and these theologians trace their ancestry to liberation elements of slave religion.[7]

Black liberation theology was a powerful contribution to the religious academy. It altered the trajectory of systematic theological studies by forcing American theologians to address issues of race, and it produced dozens of books that fundamentally reinterpreted biblical, theological, and sociological meanings of black religious life. But even as black liberation theologians offered stinging commentary on their white counterparts, many of the men in this first generation of scholars failed utterly to grapple with the complicating questions of gender. They theorized a black male Christ to challenge the existing assumptions of a white male Christ. They did not seriously consider that African American women's life experiences and religious beliefs required separate attention. They used the sermons and writings of black male preachers as source material while largely ignoring the writings, preaching, and church life experiences of black women, who actually constituted the majority of black church participants. Black liberation theology's silence on gender is a stunning omission, made possible by the long history of gender inequality in Christian churches of all racial compositions. Women were expected to sit in the pews, receiving messages from men in the pulpit. Their role was to recognize God in their pastor, not to expect or demand that he recognize God in them. Black women were expected to convey their righteousness by being the strong, capable pillars of the church, not by being its vocal leaders. This assumption about women's religious passivity was reflected in the early liberation theology writings that ignored a meaningful analysis or incorporation of black women. But within one generation, African American women theologians, ethicists, and biblical scholars began actively to resist this shortcoming in black liberation theology with insightful research and writing about African American women as Christian actors.

Womanism was the term these black women scholars gave to the work of crafting a fully articulated racialized and gendered theology. *Womanism* was coined as a description of black feminist sensibilities by Alice Walker in her book *In Search of Our Mothers' Gardens.* Walker describes womanism as an intense form of female-centered identification and action most often exhibited among women of color. Womanism lays claim to the intersectional experience of race and gender for women of color. Walker's definition also conveys a sense of the strong black woman. In the epigraph to this chapter, Walker writes that a womanist is "traditionally capable, as in: 'Mama, I'm walking to Canada and I'm taking you and a bunch of other slaves with me.' Reply: 'It wouldn't be the first time.' " This phrasing reveals a great deal: the understated "traditionally capable" is matched by the extraordinary task of freeing oneself and others from slavery. The reply is equally understated: "wouldn't be the first time." Walker conveys the utterly mundane regularity of courageous acts of leadership and communal liberation among black women. Of course, black women would expect themselves and their daughters to perform extraordinary feats. Thus as many black feminist theologians adopted the self-description "womanist," they accepted the imperative of black women's strength.

Delores Williams's *Sisters in the Wilderness* is the foundational text in this tradition. Williams builds a systematic theology that begins with the Genesis story of Hagar. Hagar is the enslaved servant of Sarah. When Sarah fails to produce an heir for her husband, Abraham, she gives Hagar to him as a sexual concubine. Sarah willingly subjected this enslaved woman to sexual violation by her husband. But when Sarah, at nearly one hundred years old, becomes pregnant herself, she becomes jealous about the potential of Hagar's son having a claim to Abraham's legacy. So she casts Hagar and her infant son into the wilderness. Williams reads Hagar's story of enslavement, sexual violation, surrogacy, exile, and vulnerability as a prototype for black women in the United States where their history is replete with these same conditions, and draws a series of lessons about God's relationship to black women. Hagar is expected to bear up under unthinkably difficult conditions, but God does not abandon her even when she has been exiled. Instead, God appears to this woman, comforts her, provides for her, and creates a strategy of survival for her and her child. "God's response to Hagar's (and her child's) situation was survival and involvement."[8]

Growing out of Williams's text, womanist theological research is based on the writings and experiences of African American women. It focuses on the intersections of race, gender, class, and sexual orientation within black religious experiences and represents arguably the most important contribution of contemporary black theology.[9] Its goal is to affirm black women as members of God's beloved community and to assert that God is present in their struggles to be fully participating members of churches, of racial communities, and ultimately of the American state. In short, womanism is the religious academy's attempt to straighten the crooked room by offering black women positive visions of themselves as full citizens. Womanist scholarship has evolved over the past two decades to address issues ranging from homophobia to war to popular culture, but it remains centered on challenging the crooked images of black women in traditional Christian scholarship and practice. Like its secular counterpart, however, it often claims black women's right to equal participation by relying on arguments about their inherent strength. Sisters' capacity, with God's help, to survive in the wilderness is the basis for claiming that their stories should be told and their voices heard. We saw in the last chapter that this reliance on strength as the basis for citizenship claims can have implications for policy beliefs, sometimes leading black women to keep silent about their interests in an attempt to maintain the facade of strength that needs no assistance. To the extent that womanism is also rooted in the imperative of strength, it might also lead black women to silence their concerns within the church.

Unlike black liberation theologians, womanist scholars take black women's lived experience as their primary source material. They regularly point to literary, historical, and contemporary narratives of faith, strength, and struggle by black women.[10] These scholars draw from the historical accounts and mythology surrounding women like Harriet Tubman, Sojourner Truth, Ida B. Wells, Rosa Parks, Fannie Lou Hamer, and Ella Baker to make claims for the decisive revelation of God in the lives of poor black women. They may emphasize black women's survival through the story of Hagar, or they may link the undeserved suffering of someone like Fannie Lou Hamer to the redemptive suffering of Christ.

Although this scholarship is a positive contribution, it can be seductively celebratory. For example, womanist ethicist Katie Cannon writes, "untrammeled by external authority, Black female moral agents' intuitive faculties lead them toward a dynamic sense of moral reasoning. They designate the processes, the manners, and subtleties of their own experiences with the least amount of distortion from the outside."[11] We can read this as a claim that black women possess an innate capacity to straighten the angles of the crooked room. Cannon's description of the autonomous capacity for ethical reasoning and practice in the face of oppressive conditions represents the very best of what black women are capable of, but it describes only a fraction of the full experience of black women of faith. Womanist theologians articulate the brutality black women experienced during slavery and map the continuing injustices that mark contemporary black women's lives.[12] But they also highlight narratives of survival and triumph, often building on the legacy of extraordinary black women whose faith commitments led them to courageous acts of resistance. These stories are important to recover, but they can also engender a kind of forgetfulness. They encourage the false belief that black women always face adversity with strength and that their strength is always victorious. But for every Harriet Tubman there are hundreds of thousands of black women who died as slaves. For every Sojourner Truth there are hundreds of thousands who were never able to speak publicly about their experiences. For every black woman who remains an independent moral agent in the face of crushing oppression, there are many who are, in fact, crushed.

The efforts of womanist scholars to create space within black liberation theology for black women's experiences and concerns are emblematic of how ordinary black women have had to struggle for voice, opportunity, leadership, and equality within black religious communities. Far too frequently, the ideas, beliefs, concerns, and viewpoints of black men are assumed to represent the entire race. Because the battle for racial recognition has occupied a primary place in black political efforts, the complicating effect of gender inequality is often marginalized or left completely unaddressed. Womanists have tried to push to the center of the religious academy, arguing that a liberation theology that accounts implicitly and exclusively for black men is insufficient. Similarly, African American women of faith are often faced with religious images, themes, and practices that are not based in their stories, experiences, or self-understandings. They are forced to choose between accepting that God, like the American state, simply does not see them or creating new ways of understanding and communicating about God that make their own social, emotional, and political needs primary.

To uncover the complex process by which black women of faith engage in a search for recognition, we must acknowledge that black American Christianity contains both oppressive and liberating aspects for black women, whose faith expressions are constrained by the structures of white supremacy and patriarchy. Black Christianity has resisted racial domination, but it has perpetuated sexism and gender inequality. As the political scientist Frederick C. Harris has noted, "Patriarchy has operated through religiously sanctioned rules that exclude women from sharing power and authority with men, a practice that became especially entrenched in mainstream black religious institutions just as black men were excluded from the nation's political sphere in the late nineteenth century."[13] Even as theologians, historians, and social scientists assert the centrality of God in the lives of black women, the importance of black women's labor to the church, and the critical nexus between church and community life, we must be careful to question how religious faith and black church practices affect African American women themselves.

The Substance of Things Hoped For

The image of black churchwomen is ubiquitous. It is easy to picture an older black woman in a bodacious hat and white gloves sitting in the first wooden pew, waving her handkerchief and exclaiming, "Amen" and "Lord, have mercy" while sustaining a low, soft hum as a preacher brings forth the Word from the pulpit. Yet although this image contains important truths about black women of faith, it also obscures a great deal. It is surprisingly difficult to provide a brief and coherent narrative about African American women as religious persons, so I will not try to be comprehensive. Instead, I want to deal with a limited but important slice of black women, those who identify as Christian and understand themselves as connected to a black religious tradition, even if they do not regularly attend church.

African American women not only consume black religion but craft it. They are not only the mothers of the church who respond to the preacher, they are themselves preachers who send out the call. Most African Americans are Baptists, and most Baptists do not allow the ordination of women, but charismatic and Pentecostal traditions have long nurtured black women's preaching.[14] From slavery to the present, African American women have interpreted biblical texts in Sunday school, lectured from pulpits, and pastored unaffiliated religious bodies and informal, sometimes clandestine services.[15] Even when they are not in the pulpit, black women's ministries of music and service have been as important as men's tradition of preaching in shaping the character and direction of the church.[16]

African American women's religious lives reveal the important distinction between "the church" and the faith community. The institutional black church is represented by traditional African American congregations, but the invisible black church, the community of faith, is composed of shared beliefs, cultural practices, theological commitments, information networks, and associated institutions.[17] Black religious life is not confined to Sunday morning worship; it is a set of practices and beliefs that extends far beyond the pews and storefronts. Black women build, change, and express their religious commitments through song and music, literature and art, collective organizing and charitable endeavors. In the twenty-first century, new technologies have made it possible for black women who may never sit together in a pew to share videos, sermons, songs, and books. Worship is not confined by bricks and mortar.

Black women's religious commitments extend still further. For many women, faith in God, and in Christ in particular, is part of their identity. Being Christian feels to some like no more of a choice than being black or female. Some women with this strong sense of Christian identity are not regular churchgoers. As children they may have attended Sunday school in shiny shoes and starched skirts, but their adult lives may be too complicated, too busy, or too resource-deprived to permit regular church attendance. Still, they do not hesitate to call on Jesus to help them through the difficulties of their lives or to offer praise and gratitude to God when good things happen. Delores Williams argues that, like their biblical foremother Hagar, black women hear the voice of God in the wilderness of their difficulty.[18] Theologian Jacquelyn Grant distinguishes between the remote and heavenly Christ worshipped in mainline white churches and the immanent and intimate Jesus whom black women recognize as their friend.[19] For many black women, God is an omnipresent companion whom they may or may not visit in a formal, institutional setting.

Though this chapter deals exclusively with the Protestant tradition, not all black women of faith are Protestant Christians. Black Catholic women have a long and interesting tradition in the United States.[20] Though they are a racial minority in a church that does not ordain women, they have found that their faith inspires them to social action and personal healing. Many other black women practice Islam; others are ethnically or religiously Jewish; still others observe African diasporic religions including traditional Yoruba practices and voodoo.[21] What many of these women share is a commitment to using their faith actively to craft alternative images that do not conform to stereotypes of sisters. Emilie Townes describes this process as black women using womanist ethics to resist the cultural production of evil.[22]

Not only have faith communities helped black women counter negative images of themselves, African American churches have also been the primary site of black women's political organizing.[23] More than three decades of social science research have outlined the organizational resources that accrue to black churchgoers, mapped the psychological resources that contribute to the political actions of African American believers, and established the centrality of religious practice in black life.[24] Because black women constitute the majority of the church's regular membership and the vast majority of active participants, they have been the link between the black church and political action. Still, despite their numbers and activism, the work of black women in the church often goes unacknowledged. Both in popular imagination and in much social science research, the black church is imagined as a place where charismatic African American men offer stirring social commentary from the pulpit and bring about radical social and political change. From David Walker's Appeal to Martin Luther King's Dream to Jesse Jackson's Rainbow Coalition, the voices of male religious leaders symbolize the black church's prophetic moral politics. The role of African American women has been largely invisible to researchers.[25]

There are exceptions. The historian Evelyn Brooks Higginbotham has described how women in black Baptist congregations at the turn of the century organized to address pressing needs of their community that male church leaders left largely unaddressed from their pulpits. These women recognized the interconnection of racial and gender inequalities and confronted both the nation's racism and the sexism of their own places of worship.[26] Cheryl Townsend Gilkes directs attention away from the traditional Baptist church structure and toward the experience of black women in auxiliary organizations that inserted themselves into the center of the black religious and political struggle.[27] Religion scholar Judith Weisenfeld's investigation of YWCA activism at the turn of the century is another reminder that black women's religious work was not confined by traditional boundaries of the official church.[28] Through their churches, African American women throughout the twentieth century founded clubs, national political organizations, and local charitable institutions. Their work provided scholarships for students, meals for the hungry, training for the unemployed, and advocacy for the community.[29] This political and social action was most frequently undertaken on behalf of the larger community, not primarily for the benefit of the organizers. Recall my discussion of black club women from chapter 2. These women battled the stereotypes of sexuality with models of temperance, sought to protect black men from lynching, worked to provide safe communities for black families to live in, and pushed the political system to respond to the needs of the race. They operated under the directive "lifting as we climb." The image evoked by that line expresses the idea that black women of faith feel responsible for more than themselves: they see themselves as working with God to save and protect whole communities. It is a heavy burden for women with so few relative resources, yet they embrace the self-definition of strength and perseverance. The importance of black Christian women to political activism is not only a historic reality in the Jim Crow era and during the civil rights movement; it is a continuing marker of the black American experience.[30]

Even as women have served as the activist force of the black church, the black church has created institutional barriers to their political expression, prompting black women to level important critiques against it. At the turn of the century, antilynching advocate Ida B. Wells decried the black church as "corrupt" and "ignorant" and argued that black ministers, who resisted providing her support, encouragement, or even meeting space, were too timid in backing her work.[31] Jacquelyn Grant reminds us that while it may sound like a compliment to assert that women are the "backbone" of the church, "the telling portion of the word backbone is 'back.' It has become apparent to me that most of the ministers who use this term have reference to location rather than function."[32] While the black church provides a legacy of activism, institutional resources, and moral authority for doing political work, it also perpetuates a legacy of gendered inequality and patriarchal authority that discourages gendered political activism. Sociologist Cheryl Townsend Gilkes reminds us,

> Black women take seriously their own issues and problems, and they also pay special attention to the problems of black men in their conferences, national organizations, writings, and everyday lives. . . . Ironically, the concern that black women evince for the emergencies facing black men—criminalization, joblessness, poverty, hyperghettoization, and social isolation . . . —is not reciprocated by a similar concern for black women by the male leadership of black churches. The perception that black women have survived and succeed obscures the realities of poverty, welfare, social isolation, joblessness, and single parenting that create unparalleled stress in black women's lives.[33]

Willful ignorance and purposive silencing of black women's issues is not restricted to male clergy and laity. Evidence suggests that African American churchwomen also contribute to patriarchy-reinforcing political agendas. Analyzing data from the 1993 National Black Politics Study, Frederick Harris demonstrates that black women are less likely than black men to support an increase in the number of women clergy. Highly religious black women are less likely to support women clergy than their less religious counterparts, and black women who are frequent church attendees are more likely than their less churched counterparts to agree that "black women should not undermine black male political leadership" and that "black men's concerns deserve special attention."[34] Clyde Wilcox's analysis of General Social Survey (GSS) data from the 1980s shows that while black women are more supportive of government action to address gender inequality than are white women, this support is more linked to beliefs about the role of the state than to support for gender equity per se.[35] In fact, black women are not more supportive of gender equity in social or political realms. Although the black church has organized, mobilized, and radicalized black women around issues of race, it has largely failed to offer a similar mobilization on questions of gender. Many researchers of the black church point to its patriarchal structure as the primary cause of this dichotomy, but we should not overlook the role of religious ideas themselves. The women in my focus groups did not talk about the church; they talked about God. Their analysis of God's power in their life flowed from professions of faith and personal testimonies of lived experience. It is their religious ideas rather than church experiences that they pointed to as key to their capacity to survive difficult circumstances. These professions of faith raise questions about the connection between theology and practice.

Social scientists have largely treated the church as an institution that brings individuals into contact with organizational resources that are learned in a religious setting and then deployed in the political realm.[36] The scholarship of systematic theologians, meanwhile, has directly addressed the psychological and political consequences of religious belief. Although the work of womanist theologians is useful in delineating unique aspects of black women's religious experiences, its reliance on exceptional black women as source material is inherently limiting. In my first book I argued for the ability of ordinary people to develop political ideology through everyday conversational interactions.[37] This assertion counters the logic of scholars like Philip Converse, who understand political ideology as the purview of the elite and describe the attitudes of ordinary Americans as inconsistent and uninformed. Parallel arguments exist in the study of theology.[38] Some might argue that theology is exclusively the work of academic scholars who systematically derive theological precepts from agreed-upon source materials and canonical practices; but there is also an organic theology that emerges from shared understandings of God.

Womanists use a broad array of source materials for understanding black women's theology. The historiography of black women's lived experience; literary sources like Zora Neale Hurston, Toni Morrison, and Alice Walker; and the tradition of black women's preaching form the cornerstones in the womanist theological project.[39] Although these are crucial sources, womanist scholars rarely investigate the beliefs of ordinary black Christian women systematically. I attempt to address this shortcoming here using national survey data from the 1998 General Social Survey.[40] These data are dated, and they are limited in what they can tell us about black women as Christians, moral agents, and political activists, but they do open up new ways of seeing the intersections of black women's religious, emotional, and political experience. We can use these data to explore the content of black women's religious beliefs; to determine if black women differ from other groups in their religious beliefs or divine imaging; to question what difference these religious beliefs make for black women's emotional lives; and to show how these beliefs affect their political ideas.

What Black Women Believe

Womanist theologians frequently claim that African American women have a unique Christian faith marked by their race, gender, and class disprivilege. One way to test this claim is by comparing the professed religious beliefs of white women and men to those of black women and men. Using data from the General Social Surveys I considered four areas of religious belief: forgiveness, overall sense of connection with a divine presence, the extent to which religion influences other areas of life, and religious fundamentalism.[41] (For the data results, see Appendix, table 7.) It might seem strange to measure such deeply held personal commitments with public opinion surveys, but these metrics allow us to make comparisons across groups.

The results show that the group most unlike all other groups is not black women but white men, who score lower than all other race and gender categories on each of the four areas. Although this calls into question the normative practice of assuming that white men's experiences are universal, it hardly provides clear evidence that black women's religiosity represents a unique understanding of the divine. In each area of religious belief except forgiveness, black women's average score is higher than that of white women but indistinguishable from that of black men. African American women profess a stronger sense of divine connection, a greater commitment to religion guiding other areas of life, and greater fundamentalism than white women. But these appear to be racial differences within sex, not gendered differences within race. In each of these areas, black men and women share similar religious conceptions. These results provide evidence for what Lincoln and Mamiya call a "black sacred cosmos" derived from socialization in black churches and racialized cultural practices. They do not provide evidence for a distinctly gendered understanding of God within that black sacred cosmos.

The theological tradition of black liberation suggests that although black men and women understand themselves as American Christians, the content of black religiosity is so distinct as to constitute a separate religious expression. In short, black folks' God is not the same as white folks' God. This idea is best captured in the notion of the black Christ. The idea of a black Christ was first articulated by Albert Cleage, a theologian, preacher, and founder of the Shrine of the Black Madonna, in his book *The Black Messiah.*[42] Cleage uses a biblical genealogy that traces Jesus' maternal ancestry to provide evidence of an African bloodline and argue that Jesus of Nazareth was ethnically black. This notion of an ethnically black historical Jesus is not widely accepted in the terms Cleage outlined, but credible scholars of Christianity agree that the common iconography of Jesus as white, blond, and blue-eyed is highly unlikely given that he was a first-century Semitic Jew born in the Middle East. Still, the argument that Jesus was phenotypically "black" is less important to liberation theology than the argument that Christ is a God in solidarity with the concerns of African Americans. This idea of black Christ is central to James Cone's original articulation of black theology. For Cone, Jesus' blackness is ontological rather than biological. Cone reasons that Christ aligns himself with those who are struggling against oppression and takes on the position of the poorest and most despised in any historical moment. Thus in the American context, Christ must be understood as black.[43] Both Cleage and Cone see the Black Messiah as a necessary element of black religious thought. Each argues that African Americans can develop a full respect for their own humanity and dignity only if they see themselves as reflections of a black Jesus.

White feminist theologians make a parallel claim about the critical importance of alternative images of God. Pointing to the utter incomprehensibility of the divine, they assert that since no language can capture divine reality, the reliance on almost exclusively male language about God is deeply inaccurate and borders on heretical. Feminist theologian Anna Case Winters calls male images of God idolatrous, quoting feminist theologian Mary Daly's statement arguing that " 'If God is male, then the male is God.' "[44] Both black liberation and white feminist theologians also assert the emotional healing and politically subversive power of opening one's imagination of God beyond narrowly white and male representations.[45] One group wonders if a white God can save black people, and the other questions whether a male God can save women. Womanist scholars have built on both traditions, claiming that African American women have understood God, in the person of Jesus, to be a divine cosufferer. Womanist theologian Jacquelyn Grant writes, "For Christian Black women in the past, Jesus was their central frame of reference. They identified with Jesus because they believed that Jesus identified with them. As he was persecuted and made to suffer undeservedly, so were they."[46] By this understanding, black women are especially in need of an image of God that assumes divine presence is most available in the most difficult conditions. After all, they point out, it is black women who, like Jesus, bear the cross of racism, sexism, and poverty. It is black women's bodies that, like Jesus' body, were traditionally broken in service of white enslavers or black male abusers. It is black women who, like Jesus with the loaves and fish, manage to feed multitudes despite having few resources. It is black women who, like Jesus, form small groups of intimate friends who try to change to world against impossible odds. Womanists emphasize these similarities of the mission, ministry, and suffering of Jesus to the lived experiences of black women in order to claim that black women have a right and a need to imagine God as looking like and being like them.

The General Social Surveys offer an opportunity to learn more about just how black and white men and women picture God. The GSS asks respondents: "There are many ways of picturing God. We'd like to know the kinds of images you are most likely to associate with God. On a scale from 1 to 7 where would you place your image of God between the two contrasting images?" Respondents are then given a choice between mother or father, lover or judge, and friend or king. (For the data, see Appendix, table 8.) When it comes to imagining God, nearly everyone agrees. All four groups picture God much more as father than mother, and much more as judge than lover. For these two image pairs, the only real difference is that black women perceive God more as a lover than as a judge relative to white men.[47] Overall perceptions of God as friend or king are more balanced. Although all groups see God somewhat more as a king than a friend, the difference is not as strong as in the first two categories. Here black men differ from all other groups: they perceive God much more as king than friend.

This evidence challenges theological assertions of a unique racialized conception of God. For the most part, black women imagine the same God as other Americans. The God of black women is a father, judge, and king just as for other groups. Thus the evidence for an organic theology unique to black women is mixed. The GSS data tell us that although African American women largely picture the same God, they feel more closely connected to that God, more guided in their daily lives, and more fundamentalist in their belief than either white women or white men. The content of black women's religious beliefs appears to be more racialized than gendered. There may be a black sacred cosmos, but there may not be a unique female version of it. Given that within black churches, men have long dominated the role of preacher, and therefore of interpreter of religious symbols and texts, it is not surprising that they have not nurtured a more feminine and egalitarian imagination of God. The God of black men and women is still a judging father-king heading a hierarchal version of religious life.

Is There a Balm in Gilead?

Although the content of their belief is not unique, African American women are uniquely religiously committed. Of the four categories of GSS groupings, black women are the most likely to attend church, the most likely to be active members of church organizations, the most likely to report having a daily prayer life, the most likely to profess a belief in God, and the most likely to claim that they are guided in their daily decision making by their religious beliefs.[48] But if they do not hold an image of God that reflects themselves, what difference does this religiosity make for them as human beings? Research by psychologists Karen Lincoln and Linda Chatters shows that prayer and devotional life have a positive impact on black women's psychological well-being but do not mediate the life stressors they face. It seems that even as they draw nearer to God, sisters are still buffeted by the world.[49] How, then, does the content of black women's religious beliefs affect their emotional lives?

To answer this question we must return to the imperative of the strong black woman. Although the icon of strength encourages resiliency and independence, it also discourages black women from admitting weakness, sadness, and the need for help. The church has traditionally been the primary site for assistance in black communities. Black church women organize the clothing drives for the homeless; make the soup for the hungry; take meals to the shut-ins; fund scholarships for the youth; celebrate the pastor on his anniversary; and pray for everyone who has requests. But even as they give help, black women may feel discouraged from revealing the depths of their own needs.[50] The strong black woman is denied her sadness. Because she must serve, she cannot be broken, but black women do experience sadness and are perhaps uniquely vulnerable to it.[51] African Americans report the lowest levels of happiness, and one obvious reason lies in the depressing statistics regarding black women's poverty levels, unemployment status, and single parenthood.[52] But perhaps the unattainable goal of perfect independence also contributes. At the turn of the twenty-first century, mental health professionals and popular media outlets began taking a harder look at the consequences of the myth of strength.[53] These criticisms have forced African Americans to wonder whether the myth comes at the price of the health and sanity of black women.[54]

Their position within black communities and churches requires black women to maintain a facade of strength. Weakness, sadness, and depression are defined as necessarily alien to their experience. For some, the idea of being depressed is like being infected by white ideals and a sense of white privilege. In her text *Behind the Mask of the Strong Black Woman* sociologist Tamara Beauboeuf-Lafontant explores this challenge, writing, "Black women must struggle against the racialization of depression as a white illness even as they are encouraged to racialize struggle as a central manifestation of being authentically black."[55] To be true to the race, a black woman must not fall into depression or allow herself to be weak, pitiful, or needy —these are attributes of white women.[56] As the research of womanist theologian Monica Coleman convincingly demonstrates, the depressed or abused black woman may feel enormously guilty when her faith alone does not give her sufficient relief and consolation. She may believe that she has failed as a Christian as well as failing as a black woman.[57] Strength is the rent a black woman must pay for the room she takes up on the earth. In this sense, sadness, need, or victimization by abuse is not just a personal failure but a racial failure. These conditions render black women unable to serve as anyone's backbone, bridge, or rock. They are threatening because they rob black women of the strength that is the one positive attribute they are permitted. Without it, a black woman must discover a new standard against which to value her humanity, not just for herself but in relation to her family, church, race, and nation.

In the same way that strength is a racial imperative, suffering becomes understood as a Christian imperative. Discussing the religious beliefs of black Americans dating back to slavery, Monica Coleman writes, "The hermeneutic of sacrifice interprets Jesus' death on the cross to mean that personal sacrifice imitates Christ and demonstrates Christian character."[58] On one hand, this narrative may discourage black women from acknowledging depression or abuse as something for which they may need to seek help. Alternatively, suffering may bring black women closer to God, anchoring them in a belief that their pain is connected to Christ's passion in ways that are potentially empowering.

Because the passion and crucifixion of Jesus are foundational tenets of Christian faith, Christian black women may tend to assume that undeserved suffering is redemptive. Throughout this text we have seen the ways that social and political institutions act as abusive authorities that misrecognize black women's bodies, minds, talents, and spirits. We also know that African American women, as a group, lack the material resources to resist this subjugation effectively, but they nonetheless feel an imperative to be strong in the face of difficulty. Thus, many black women give meaning to experiences of suffering by seeking a divine purpose for agony. This can even manifest itself as a reluctance to feel consistent joy or self-love; these strong black women may worry that feeling good is an indication that they are not acting as soldiers on the battlefield for God.[59]

As a first step toward empirically mapping these processes, I again used the GSS to explore black women's religious coping mechanisms compared to other groups. (For data, see Appendix, table 9.) I wanted to see if black women are more likely to be positive, negative, or agnostic in their religious style when faced with difficulties. Positive coping is indicated by a respondent's agreement with two statements: "I work together with God as partners" and "I look to God for strength, support, guidance." Negative emotions associated with religious coping are indicated by agreement with the statements: "I feel that God is punishing me for my sins or lack of spirituality" and "I wonder whether God has abandoned me." Agnostic emotional coping is suggested by agreement with the statement, "I try to make sense of the situation and decide what to do without relying on God."

At first blush, religion seems to be a positive emotional tool for black men and women alike. African Americans have higher levels of positive religious emotions in the face of major problems than their white counterparts. There is some indication that more negative emotions are also present for both black men and women and that they are less likely to be agnostic in dealing with life problems. Black women turn to religion to help them cope, and their experience is generally positive. They are more likely to turn to God and more likely to feel like supported partners with God when facing life crises.

But while they see their religious coping style as positive, it is not clear whether religious coping is good for black women's overall emotional well-being. To address that question I used GSS data to test whether religious beliefs affect how black women feel in their daily lives.[60] (For data, see Appendix, table 10.) The results demonstrate that physical health is a powerful indicator of emotional health for black women. Their sense of physical well-being has a meaningful influence on their experience of negative emotions. Black women who rate their physical health as good or excellent are significantly less likely to experience sadness, anxiety, or worthlessness, or to feel overwhelmed. But even after we account for the powerful effect of physical health, religious belief and practice have substantive, independent effects on black women's emotions. African American women who pray frequently experience fewer negative emotions. Those who believe that major life crises are punishments for sin or reflections of God's absence in their lives are more likely to feel sadness, nervousness, hopelessness, and worthlessness. Although positive emotional coping does not provide a discernable protective effect, negative religious thoughts are associated with dramatic negative emotional states. When African American women suffer, their strong faith may not make them feel better.

Suffering is difficult terrain for feminist thinkers. The disobedience of Eve in the Genesis story has been used to justify women's inequality and suffering in many Christian traditions. Thus, what is understood as women's complicity with evil leads much traditional theological reflection on suffering to offer the "consequent admonition to 'grin and bear it' because such is the deserved place of women."[61] Similarly, when Jesus is seen as a divine co-sufferer, the potentially liberating narratives of Jesus as a revolutionary leader who takes the side of the poor and dispossessed can be ignored in favor of religious beliefs more interested in Jesus as a stoic victim. Christ's suffering is inverted and used to justify women's continued suffering in systems of injustice by framing it as redemptive. The myth of black women's strength functions in a similar way. It obscures suffering by defining endurance as natural.[62] Womanist Karen Baker-Fletcher points out that well-meaning religious communities can often convey to women that suffering and pain and loss are somehow the will of God.[63] Those who suffer often believe that their own suffering is somehow deserved or that by enduring it without complaint, they will win favor with God. These results support the conclusion that black women Christians are not necessarily made happier by their reliance on God. They actually feel worse if they interpret their suffering as punishment for sin. If black women fear that they might be sinful or inauthentic because they endure abuse, depression, or neediness, their sense of divine abandonment can significantly increase their suffering in already difficult circumstances. (For data, see Appendix, table 10.)

Although their religious beliefs do little to ameliorate black women's own suffering, they do have an important impact on African American women as moral agents. Remember that the ideal of the strong black woman is that she ignores her own emotional needs in order to meet the needs of those around her, especially her family and community. That religious beliefs have such little impact on black women's life satisfaction is initial evidence of the first element of the strong black woman identity; many sisters are not nurturing themselves emotionally through their faith. But what about the second element? Do they feel heightened responsibility for the world around them? The GSS asked individuals to respond to this statement: "I feel a deep sense of responsibility for reducing pain and suffering in the world." In the next test I wanted to observe the relationship between the religious ideas black women hold and this sense of responsibility for reducing pain and suffering in the world. (For data, see Appendix, table 11.)

The findings are interesting. Black women who are concerned with applying their religious beliefs to other aspects of their lives are also most likely to feel compelled to reduce suffering in the world. Fundamentalist black women are less likely than their liberal counterparts to feel called upon as moral agents. Surprisingly, there is no independent effect of prayer, church attendance, or religious coping mechanism on this measure of moral agency. Thus, it is not the traditional black church, in its fundamentalist and institutional form, that seems most responsible for developing black women's sense of moral agency. Instead, these results show that divine imagination is what has the real effect. Black women who perceive God more as mother than as father, and those who perceive God more as lover than as judge, are significantly more likely to feel called to reduce suffering and pain. This is powerful empirical evidence supporting the feminist claim that female imaging of God has an important influence on the creative possibilities of believers.[64] Those with a more womanist divine imagination are more likely to believe themselves responsible for moral and ethical action.

This empirical result is complicated because of what we know about the benefits and burdens of the strong black woman ideal. It seems that as black women embrace more womanist faith tenets, they become more likely to embrace the role of agent for moral change. On one hand, this is something to celebrate. It might be that this result is happily anticipated by womanist ethicist Emilie Townes in her book *Womanist Ethics and the Cultural Production of Evil.*

Townes argues that stereotypes, caricatures, and myths are the cultural tools of inequality. I have argued that the tilted images in America's crooked room create shame, suffering, and unequal policy outcomes for black women. In a similar way Townes explains that black women hold false images of themselves and that by failing to fully interrogate or challenge these images, African American women become unwittingly complicit in reproducing circumstances of inequality that Townes labels evil. Alternately, when black women develop the capacity to imagine themselves as something other than ugly stereotypes, they develop the power to challenge the structures that maintain inequality. Townes also says that challenging these evil ideas about the self allows black women to be more imaginative about ideas like God, government, and power. It is possible that this statistical analysis of GSS data underscores Townes's point; black women who imagine a different kind of God are more likely to feel responsible for reducing suffering in the world because they imagine a different and more just way of ordering the world.

However, we have already seen that celebrating black women's impervious strength can be double-edged. Perhaps womanist perspectives are simply another crooked image that encourages black women to take on yet another role of responsibility for others. Perhaps as they imagine a God who is like them, they see themselves as more like God, and although that imagining can bolster self-esteem, it might also encourage a level of sacrifice that is beyond what should be expected of a mere mortal. The evidence in the GSS is too scant to fully adjudicate this point. There is no way to be sure if these results mean that "the strong black woman" has just donned her religious vestments to take on yet another project (lessening suffering in the world) or if the power of divine imagination can prod black

women toward making institutional changes that can possibly liber-
ate them from the crooked room once and for all. To try to tease this
out more effectively, I decided to investigate just a bit more data.

On Whose Behalf?

This chapter has featured many statistical findings and much discussion of empirical results. Because it can be hard to keep track of all of
these ideas, let us pause for a moment and review what we have
learned so far about the connections between black women, their
faith claims, and their ideas about the political world.

• GSS data show that African American women profess a stronger
sense of divine connection, a greater commitment to religion guiding
other areas of life, and greater fundamentalism than white women. For
the most part they share these religious ideas with black men, which
leads me to conclude that Americans show race differences, but not
necessarily gender differences, in basic religious beliefs.

• GSS data show that black women imagine the same God as
other Americans. For the most part, they see God as a father, judge,
and king rather than as a mother, lover, and friend.

• GSS data show that black women are the most likely to turn to
God for assistance in their daily lives and more likely than other
groups to feel like supported partners with God when facing life
crises.

• GSS data also show that religious commitments do not make
black women generally more satisfied with their lives. In fact, when
black women have a negative religious coping style—that is, if they
interpret suffering as punishment for sin—then their religious beliefs
actually make them feel worse about their lives.

• Last, black women with more divine imagination are also more likely to feel compelled to social action. GSS data show that sisters who perceive God as more a mother than a father, and more as lover than as judge, are significantly more likely to feel called to reduce suffering and pain in the world.

Having established these patterns about black women's faith, divine imaginings, and sense of social commitment, I turn to a test of how religious belief affects black women's political action. Specifically, I wanted to know if religious belief and practice influence black women's support for a specifically gendered black political agenda. Although African American churches have a broadly developed political role, the gender dynamics of black churches seem to militate against feminist politics. There is significant evidence that religiosity and church activity provide psychological resources for black Christians that matter for political action. Frederick Harris uncovers both macro- and micro-level resources that support a variety of political activities by African Americans.[65] Christopher Ellison finds that religious involvement fosters self-esteem and a sense of personal empowerment among African Americans through networks, social and emotional support, and tangible aid.[66] At its best, the black church asserts African Americans' inherent uniqueness as individuals and emphasizes their spiritual qualities, such as wisdom and morality, over material possessions as a standard for self-evaluation. Noting the diversity within the black religious tradition, political scientist Allison Calhoun-Brown makes an important distinction between political and nonpolitical churches and finds little evidence to support a general connection between political sophistication and church attendance; but she does find an important link with political churches.[67]

These studies give us reason to believe that many African Americans encounter politics through their churches. In the 1993–1994 National Black Politics Study, nearly half of respondents reported engagement with some form of church-based political discussion. Thirty-four percent reported talking to people about political matters at church. Fifty percent heard a clergy member talk about the need for people to become involved in politics. Thirty-eight percent heard a political leader speak at church, and 23 percent heard a church official suggest voting for or against certain candidates. Nearly a quarter reported some involvement with church-based political action. Twenty-three percent helped in a voter registration drive; 25 percent gave people a ride to the polls on election day; 24 percent gave money to a political candidate; 27 percent attended a candidate fund-raiser; 23 percent handed out campaign materials; and 42 percent signed a petition supporting a candidate as a part of their regular religious duties in the past two years.[68] For the majority of African Americans, church is not a site of political conversation or action, but the religious life of a substantial portion of blacks includes political ideas and opportunities for political involvement. This gives us good reason to believe that religious life positively influences black women's political lives by providing the psychological and organizational resources for political actions such as voting, writing to public officials, and signing petitions.[69] We can also use the National Black Politics Study to uncover the relationship among political activity, religious beliefs, church attendance, church-based political action and charitable involvement, racial attitudes, and personal characteristics.[70] (For data, see Appendix, table 12.)

A statistical analysis of this study partly confirms earlier findings about African American political participation. Black women with a higher sense of black linked fate and those who support racial self-reliance are more likely to be politically involved. Those who attend churches that are politically active and who engage in frequent political discussion are much more likely to be politically involved. There is a strong and important connection between church-based political action and the likelihood of engaging in political activity outside the church. It is clear that the black church is an important site for gathering political resources that can be deployed elsewhere. Further, the results suggest that religious belief plays an independent role in influencing black women's political action. Even after we account for demographic variables, racial attitudes, and organizational resources, those who perceive Christ as a black messiah are significantly more likely to participate politically. This result confirms the 1998 GSS data. Black women who have a broader divine imagination also experience a greater calling to social and political engagement. If religious commitments and church life encourage black women to participate politically, on whose behalf do these women work?

The data from the National Black Politics Survey confirm these results. There is nothing terribly surprising here. Black women who have a strong sense of racial identity, who imagine Jesus as black messiah, and who partake in political discussion and actions in their church are more likely to be involved in politics beyond the church.

I also wanted to know how religious ideas and actions were associated with how black women think about their own position in American society and in the black community. These gender equality beliefs are measured by looking at how black women responded to the following statements: that the problems of racism, poverty, and sexual discrimination are all linked and must be addressed by the black community; that black feminist groups help the black community by working to advance the position of black women; that black women should share equally in the political leadership of the black community; and that black women have suffered from both sexism within the black community and racism within the women's movement. If a black woman responded to all of these statements very positively, then she would score at the top of the scale; if she disagreed with all of these statements, she would score at the bottom on this scale. A high score means strong support for gender equity, and a low score means little concern with women's leadership or issues.

Results from this second model are striking. No religious variable was significantly related to support for a gender-equitable black political agenda. African American women who attend church frequently, those who attend politically active black churches, those who are active in charitable actions in their churches, those for whom religion provides daily guidance, and those who believe Christ is black are indistinguishable from all other black women with respect to their support for a gender-equitable agenda within black politics. They are not any less likely to support black women's political issues, but neither are they more likely to support them. For black women, the black church is a site of tremendous political learning, and religious faith is the source of significant political motivation. The black Christ is a radicalizing figure encouraging political action. Divine imagination and religious service press black women into political action, but they do nothing to encourage black women to direct this action toward their own needs. Black women inhabit a religious life world that offers up their spirits, hearts, and labors on an altar of sacrifice for the larger community, but it is not clear that it always helps them to be fully citizens. These results show that although black women have engaged Jesus as their friend and ally in struggle, and though their faith might make them strong, it does not encourage them to turn that strength to their own political benefit.

These findings complicate social-scientific evidence about the political importance of black religious life. Researchers have found that the cultural practices and symbols of black church life are vital for shaping the form and content of black political life. Through ethnographic work in Chicago, Mary Pattillo illustrates how elements of religious worship, including prayer, gospel music, call-and-response leadership styles, and biblically based moral argument infuse the work of presumably secular black organizations laboring in urban communities.[71] These religious symbols and practices are cultural currency for black politics, both motivating and directing collective action. Sociologist Sandra Barnes finds that the black church is a cultural toolkit whose rituals and symbols foster community action.[72] Political scientist Frederick Harris offers convincing evidence that black churches nurture positive self-regard among black Americans and that churches thus improve the psychological resources available to African Americans for organizing and political action.[73] As believers, many Christian black women benefit from these cultural and psychological resources embedded in black religious practice, but even as they gain the general benefits of black religion, they fail to reap specifically gendered tools or motivation for action. Black women find a friend in Jesus, and through that friendship they find help in their quest to remain strong. Their religious beliefs also give them the motivation to try to engage in the public sphere and to address inequality. But for the most part, black Christian women's religious commitments appear to remain silent on the issues of gender fairness.

The Struggle Within

For much of this book I have discussed how American history, social institutions, policy initiatives, and popular culture have crafted negative images of black women that they have, in turn, attempted to resist or accommodate in order to gain full recognition as citizens. Because the American state is represented primarily by white people and institutions, if we are not careful, it is easy to interpret the story I have told as primarily a story of racial bias that just happens to affect women a little differently from men. But this analysis of religious beliefs reaffirms that the crooked room is not just a race story but a gender story. Black women find that they are second-class citizens even within the black church, an institution composed primarily of African Americans and operating relatively independently of white financial and political control. African American women are not only denied full citizenship by the institutional rules of many congregations that bar their ordination; they are also denied full citizenship in the image of God. For many, God is unlike them. They are mothers, workers, friends, but God is a father, a judge, and a king. Black women may enter the church seeking the recognition denied them in the American system, but even within the church they often find that they are valued to the extent that they remain strong—becoming a backbone on which the church can be built.

In the fall of 2010 the misrecognition of black women through the distorting lens of black, patriarchal forms of Christianity was evident in the much-anticipated film adaptation of Ntozake Shange's *for colored girls who have considered suicide / when the rainbow is enuf.* Earlier I discussed how Shange's choreopoem is a definitive artistic representation of the crooked room that has been embraced by at least two generations of black women. In 2010, the poem was produced as a feature-length film. The play was revised into a screenplay and then directed by Tyler Perry. Perry, a black man, is easily the most commercially successful contemporary African American filmmaker working in Hollywood. Having started as a wildly successful writer, producer, and actor of gospel stage plays, Perry has built his success primarily on the support of Christian, African American, female audiences who enjoy both the comedy and the moral lessons of his work. Perry's plays and films regularly center on female characters—the most popular of whom is actually Perry himself dressed as a woman—and he is a favorite artist among black female viewers, but his projects, arguably like the black church itself, are steeped in a narrow, Christian moralism that idealizes benevolent male leadership. Feminist writer Courtney Young describes Perry's "gender problem" writing,

> Each of his films advances nearly the same message to his audience (which is overwhelmingly African-American, female, devoutly Christian and over 30). Be demure. Be strong but not too strong. Too much ambition is a detriment to your ability to find a partner and spiritual health. Female beauty can be dangerous. Let a man be a "man." True female fulfillment is found in the role of wife and/or mother. To this effect, the black church plays a central role in Perry's vision.[74]

Perry's ownership of the *For Colored Girls* film ensured that it would be widely distributed and would attract large audiences, but it raised concerns about what would happen to Shange's original messages when filtered through Perry's lens. After all, when *for colored girls* was released in 1976, it was widely maligned, and Shange was broadly vilified by African American men who perceived the work as unnecessarily critical of embattled black men. Of this reaction Shange writes, "The reaction from black men to *for colored girls* was in a way very much like the white reaction to black power. The body traditionally used to power and authority interpreting through their own fear, my work celebrating the self-determination and centrality of women as a hostile act."[75] Shange's work is powerful in large part because of this insistence on self-determining black female characters written by a black feminist author. Shange's women are certainly not stereotypical strong black women, impervious to suffering. Her play is a direct challenge to the notion that black women's strength always trumps their anguish. Black women can and do feel the doubts, frustrations, pain, and depression that should rightfully accompany the hardships they often face. She indicts a world that leaves black women with no place to turn when the world is overwhelming and insists that black women can find comfort, and even God, in one another and in their authentic selves, rather than in the confines of traditional church membership.[76]

Perry's film distorts Shange's work of self-determination in ways that reinforce the crooked room imposed on black women by male-centered religion and resorts to tools of shaming that so often derive from the crooked room. Although the women in Shange's original work rely on spirituality and divine support, they are not beholden to any specific definition of God. In Perry's film the women are subjected to more dominating, moralistic, and constrained notions of morality. Perry creates a new character, played by Whoopi Goldberg, who is a religious fanatic. She serves as a tool of shaming surveillance in the film, interjecting her judgmental, mocking, dogmatic Christian ethics over Shange's original poetry. Perry also generates a homophobic story line that does not exist in Shange's play. In this subplot, one of the women learns she is infected with HIV by her closeted gay husband, whose philandering is caused by the woman's neglect of the relationship in favor of pursuing success in her career.[77] And in a particularly egregious revision of the original text, Perry conflates the Lady in Yellow monologue about sexual freedom and exploration with the Lady in Blue narrative about seeking an unsafe, illegal abortion. Feminist literary scholar Salamishah Tillet describes the violence that this revision causes to Shange's original intent.

> In the play, [the Lady in Yellow] delivers a lush monologue about her past experience of cruising, dancing and losing her virginity on graduation night. In the film, these same words are now recited by a teenage girl, Nyla (Tessa Thompson), whose bold act of sexual possession is eventually mocked by her mother, Alice (a new character introduced by Perry and played by Whoopi Goldberg). But even more violently, under Perry's disapproving directorial eye, Nyla is punished for her sexual curiosity. Her beautiful story of sexual awakening becomes merged with the original Lady in Blue's tale of a pre-*Roe v. Wade* back-alley abortion. The end result is a moralizing sermon against black women's promiscuity and sexual agency, and more subtly against choice itself.[78]

Tyler Perry's film adaptation of Shange's classic work is a harrowing example of how the gaze of black men can be just as crooked as that of white Americans when viewing African American women. African American religious life, whether in the traditional structure of the church or in religiously infused popular culture like the work of Tyler Perry, is fraught with distorted images that can be particularly difficult for black women to navigate because it is also a space that holds such potential for emotional healing and political organizing. The church, in the broadest and most plural sense, is a site of struggle for sisters.

When black liberation theology mounted its challenge to traditional Western theological traditions, it did so with a fierce and courageous willingness to name and refute racism; but this same tradition was nearly silent on gender. It took a second generation of liberation theologians, themselves black women, to fill in the missing testimony of black women's experiences and demand recognition within the discipline. But even as they recovered black women's faith experiences as the basis for a new theological tradition, many womanists did what black women so often do; they defined themselves in terms of strength. This self-image of strength resists the ugly lies of historic white racism, and it refuses to accept the silences of black male patriarchy, but it may still limit black women's ability to be fully citizens, fully vulnerable, and deserving of both recognition and support.

As Nadine talked with the other black women in the Chicago focus group, she mused on the meaning of being a strong black woman. "I think strength is measured by what you endure, what you have to take on. The things that have happened to me in my life, the next person may not be able to handle them. And it wasn't because I was so especially strong. I was just me and I dealt with the things as they came. With God's grace I made it." At face value, statements like Nadine's point to the ways that religious commitments have helped black women survive the oppressive conditions they encounter in America. But the evidence presented in this chapter calls us to reevaluate this seductive notion that faith in God helps black women to endure and is therefore good. African American women are profoundly religious. They use their experiences in church and their commitments to a present and loving God to motivate and direct social engagement and political action. But although black women provide much of the prophetic motivation and personal labor that makes struggle for racial liberation possible, their own needs as persons and political actors remain unmet.

In 1974, the women of the Combahee River Collective asserted that the "psychological toll of being a black woman and the difficulties this presents in reaching political consciousness and doing political work can never be underestimated."[79] The evidence I have presented bears out the ongoing relevance of this statement. Even as they seek a balm in Gilead, black women embrace a Christianity that gives them the comfort to endure suffering but fails to provide the tools to challenge patriarchy. But there is hope. Religious belief and practice have already created liberating racial reasoning and praxis for black women; they have simply failed to provide an adequately gendered analysis. With its broader divine imagination and insistence on specifically gendered understandings of God's justice, a black women's religiosity based in the precepts of womanism might have the potential to address a wider range of black women's spiritual needs. Womanism is an approach that may offer more opportunities for accurate recognition of black women.[80] By imagining a God more like themselves, black women might finally find a place to lay down the heavy mantle of impervious strength.

Toni Morrison offers a powerful image of this religious possibility in her novel *Beloved*. The novel is the complex and emotionally difficult tale that reveals the intergenerational human destruction wrought by slavery. At the heart of the story is Sethe, an enslaved woman who finds her way to freedom after being physically and sexually assaulted in nearly unimaginable ways. Through Sethe's experiences of infanticide, haunting, grief, and shame, Morrison hints at the excruciating choices black women have had to make in order to find and preserve freedom for themselves and their families. At the head of this family is Sethe's mother-in-law, Baby Suggs "Holy." During her decades of enslavement, Baby Suggs had eight children, and all but one were taken away from her. Though he dies enslaved, the one child she was allowed to keep eventually purchases her freedom. Years later, when Sethe escapes to freedom, she flees to Baby Suggs, who becomes a healing counselor for her.

In one of the book's few hopeful moments, before the most awful consequences of slavery reinvade their lives, Baby Suggs takes Sethe to a clearing in the woods where she preaches. In *Their Eyes Were Watching God,* Janie's grandmother laments that she had a great sermon to preach but no pulpit. In this novel the black grandmother as preacher becomes a reality. Baby Suggs has founded her own church, not in a building but in a small clearing, a hush arbor; there Baby Suggs serves as a minister ordained only by her own suffering and by her own great calling. Her words are the conduit of healing for an entire community of free blacks who are scarred by the world in which they find themselves. Rather than asking them to deny their pain or to bear it stoically in order to prove their strength, Baby Suggs encourages them to release it through song, dance, open weeping, and togetherness. She also asks the black people assembled in her clearing to embrace a new faith based on reimagining their own bodies as something beautiful and worthy of love.

In this here place, we flesh; flesh that weeps, laughs; flesh
that dances on bare feet in grass. Love it. Love it hard.
Yonder they do not love your flesh. They despise it. They
don't love your eyes; they'd just as soon pick em out. No
more do they love the skin on your back. Yonder they flay it.
And O my people they do not love your hands. Those they
only use, tie, bind, chop off and leave empty. Love your
hands! Love them. Raise them up and kiss them. Touch
others with them, pat them together, stroke them on your
face 'cause they don't love that either. *You* got to love it,
you![81]

This admonition to touch and love their own black flesh is Baby
Suggs's womanist contribution to a religious faith that can straighten
the shame-producing images of the crooked room. She points out
every crooked angle, every hateful assumption of racism, and every
policy that leaves black people unequal and vulnerable. Then she
reminds black people that they retain the power of self-love to rebuke
these crooked images. Baby Suggs promises that the fierce, genuine,
loving acceptance of one's own humanity is a path to freedom.
Through "Baby Suggs, holy," Morrison gives us a radically different
image of a black preacher and through this preacher a genuinely new
articulation of God. It is a glimpse into the possibilities represented
by black women's faith.

"Praise Song for the Day"

ELIZABETH ALEXANDER

On January 20, 2009, Barack Obama became the first black president of the United States of America. After taking the oath of office, he gave an inaugural address setting out a sweeping vision of hope and change for a country gripped by two foreign wars and spiraling into a deepening domestic economic crisis. When he took his seat, poet Elizabeth Alexander stood. Alexander is an accomplished African American poet and professor. Her writings and scholarship are deeply rooted in the history of black women in America. This is the poem she delivered on that day.

A Poem for Barack Obama's Presidential Inauguration

> Each day we go about our business,
> walking past each other, catching each other's
> eyes or not, about to speak or speaking.
>
> All about us is noise. All about us is
> noise and bramble, thorn and din, each
> one of our ancestors on our tongues.

Someone is stitching up a hem, darning
a hole in a uniform, patching a tire,
repairing the things in need of repair.

Someone is trying to make music somewhere,
with a pair of wooden spoons on an oil drum,
with cello, boom box, harmonica, voice.

A woman and her son wait for the bus.
A farmer considers the changing sky.
A teacher says, Take out your pencils. Begin.

We encounter each other in words, words
spiny or smooth, whispered or declaimed,
words to consider, reconsider.

We cross dirt roads and highways that mark
the will of some one and then others, who said
I need to see what's on the other side.

I know there's something better down the road.
We need to find a place where we are safe.
We walk into that which we cannot yet see.

Say it plain: that many have died for this day.
Sing the names of the dead who brought us here,
who laid the train tracks, raised the bridges,

picked the cotton and the lettuce, built
brick by brick the glittering edifices
they would then keep clean and work inside of.

Praise song for struggle, praise song for the day.
Praise song for every hand-lettered sign,
the figuring-it-out at kitchen tables.

Some live by *love thy neighbor as thyself,*
others by *first do no harm or take no more*
than you need. What if the mightiest word is love?

Love beyond marital, filial, national,
love that casts a widening pool of light,
love with no need to pre-empt grievance.

In today's sharp sparkle, this winter air,
any thing can be made, any sentence begun.
On the brink, on the brim, on the cusp,

praise song for walking forward in that light.

Seven

Michelle

O n the night he was elected president of the United States, Barack Obama told a story about an African American woman named Ann Nixon Cooper. Cooper was 106 years old and lived in Georgia, and vigorously supported his candidacy. She had been born in 1902, a time that President-Elect Obama described as "just a generation past slavery; a time when there were no cars on the road or planes in the sky, when someone like her couldn't vote for two reasons—because she was a woman and because of the color of her skin." During her life Cooper was a civil rights advocate, a community leader, a mother, and a wife. As he marked the moment of his historic victory, Barack Obama chose Cooper as the lens through which to tell the story of America. He tied her personal story both to the arc of the nation's history and to the future embodied in his own African American daughters. "America, we have come so far. We have seen so much. But there is so much more to do. So tonight, let us ask ourselves—if our children should live to see the next century; if my daughters should be so lucky to live as long as Ann Nixon Cooper, what change will they see? What progress will we have made?"[1]

Ann Cooper is the near namesake of a black feminist foremother,

Anna Julia Cooper, who was born in 1858 during slavery and became the fourth African American woman in history to earn a doctoral degree. She died in 1964, the year of the Civil Rights Act. This Anna Cooper also saw tremendous change in her life, as her people went from slavery to the brink of full citizenship. She famously wrote in her 1892 treatise, *A Voice from the South,* that the full freedom and equality of black women was critical to American democracy: "Only the BLACK WOMAN can say 'when and where I enter, in the quiet, undisputed dignity of my womanhood, without violence and without suing or special patronage, then and there the whole Negro race enters with me.' "[2] On November 4, 2008, it was of course a man who became the country's first black president, but through his invocation of Ann Nixon Cooper and, with her, Anna Julia Cooper, he made the experiences of black women central to the historical moment. Their importance was more than rhetorical. African American women voters had provided candidate Obama's margin of victory in many crucial primary wins, and they had helped him carry North Carolina, Virginia, Michigan, Maryland, and other states in the general election. Moments after concluding his speech, Barack Obama was joined onstage by his family: Michelle, Malia, Sasha, and his mother-in-law, Marian Robinson. It is a family of black women. Standing together in Chicago's Grant Park, these women served as a visual reminder that the election of Barack Obama had become a defining moment in black women's struggle for recognition.

Michelle's Crooked Room

There is much that one could write about Michelle Obama's role in the election of her husband and as a symbol of his administration. Political observers and authors have already written thousands of words about her and will spill a great deal more ink in the coming years about her role as first lady.[3] In this brief conclusion, I will not attempt a comprehensive analysis of Michelle Obama as a public figure or rehearse the contributions of other writers. Instead I want to employ her public persona as a way to summarize the claims I have made throughout this book. I have chosen Michelle Obama because she is the most visible contemporary example of an African American woman working to stand straight in a crooked room. The success and difficulty she has experienced in gaining accurate recognition is emblematic, if not typical, of black women's citizenship struggles.

Michelle Obama was introduced to the American public during her husband's Senate campaign. Barack Obama was invited to deliver a keynote address during the Democratic National Convention that nominated John Kerry in 2004. His performance that night was extraordinary; the tone and content of his address set forth the rhetorical strategy that would sweep him to a stunning presidential victory just four years later. His speech was carefully crafted to build a sense of shared identity with every person listening. He noted his connection to the American immigrant story through his father and his connection to the Greatest Generation through his grandparents. He could relate to those of African heritage as well as to white Midwesterners. He spoke of himself as a son and as a father. He talked of little league in liberal places and gay identity in conservative places. He rejected the notion of "red states" versus "blue states" in favor of a vision of the "United States" of America. His goal in this speech and throughout his presidential campaign was to encourage listeners from many different backgrounds to find their own story in his personal narrative.

This is a "green screen" political strategy.[4] Like television meteorologists who stand in front of a green screen backdrop so that they can appear onscreen in front of a changing array of maps and weather patterns, Barack Obama hoped to place himself in front of a blank space onto which Americans could project their own identities, political goals, and national hopes. In short, he perfected a kind of inverse politics of recognition. Identity politics is typically concerned with securing recognition of the specificity and unique experiences of a group, but this green screen strategy reverses that process. Candidate Obama used the compelling elements of his personal biography to encourage Americans to recognize themselves in him. It was a subtle but powerful shift in the use of recognition, and it was a strategy available to him because his biography is so encompassing. Given the vast racial gap in American public opinion, it is exceptional that he could so effectively cultivate this sense of shared identity with Americans from many different backgrounds. It is unlikely that any black American could have been elected president without this ability to elicit a sense of shared identity. The green screen strategy was a crucial aspect of his electability.

Michelle Obama did not put herself in front of a green screen. Her life, while exceptional, was a far more familiar story for a black American. She was raised on the South Side of Chicago, had opportunities to study at prestigious universities, returned to her hometown, where she worked for government and educational institutions, married, and raised a young family. Unlike Barack, Michelle has two black parents and a black sibling, and she comes from a city readily associated with black life and politics. She has a family tree that traces back to American slavery. While Barack Obama carefully cultivated the political value of his relatively unusual, even exotic, biography, Michelle was far more easily classified within America's existing racial framework. In the early months of the campaign, the *Chicago Sun-Times* wrote, "And although Obama is an adopted Chicagoan—born in Hawaii to a Kenyan economist father and a Kansas-bred cultural anthropologist mother—his wife is pure Chicago."[5] Just a month before the presidential election, the *Washington Post* agreed, "While Barack Obama's provenance—his black Kenyan father, white Kansas-born mother and Hawaiian childhood—has been celebrated as a uniquely American example of multicultural identity, Michelle Obama's family history—from slavery to Reconstruction to the Great Migration north—connects her to the essence of the African American experience."[6] Even the international press weighed in the day after the election: the *Times* of London commented, "Michelle Obama's ancestors suffered slavery, segregation and humiliation. Her heritage embodies a dark past many would rather forget."[7]

Because Michelle Obama seemed to fit neatly within the American racial framework, she was readily subjected to the distorting images of the crooked room. For example, there were attempts to frame her with the common trope of hypersexuality. In the heat of the general election fight, Fox News referred to her as "Barack's baby mama."[8] *Baby mama* is a derogatory term for the mother of children born outside of marriage; it usually implies that the woman is difficult and bothersome to the children's father—thus the slang phrase "baby mama drama." Many commentators found this reference to Mrs. Obama appalling, denounced Fox News, and elicited an apology.[9] While Fox News has earned a reputation as particularly virulent on issues involving the Obama family, their characterization of Michelle Obama was not motivated by political opposition alone: it was rooted in the specific history of shaming black women as sexually immoral. In reality, of all the major players in the 2008 presidential campaign, the Obamas had the most traditional, least controversial sexual history. Hillary Clinton, Barack Obama's rival in the primaries, still labors under the shadow of her husband's public infidelity. John McCain's relationship with his second wife caused a scandal in Washington, DC, after his first marriage abruptly ended. Sarah Palin's teenage daughter was unmarried and pregnant during the campaign. Even Joe Biden is in his second marriage, though the story of his first wife's death was far more tragic than scandalous. Only Michelle and Barack were in a scandal-free, traditional first marriage, raising the biological children born of and in that marriage. Yet it was Michelle who was derided as a "baby mama." It is the negative myths surrounding black women in America that allowed some commentators to feel they were licensed to deploy such a wildly inaccurate term.

Other observers comfortably framed Michelle Obama as an angry Sapphire figure. She earned the label "angry black woman" at several points during the campaign.[10] One key moment occurred when the content of her Princeton University senior thesis was made public. In 1985, a young Michelle Robinson had written a senior research project for the Princeton sociology department in which she explored the social and personal difficulties many African American students experienced at the university. The thesis also revealed her own sense of alienation on campus. In the introduction she wrote, "My experiences at Princeton have made me far more aware of my 'blackness' than ever before. I have found that at Princeton, no matter how liberal and open-minded some of my white professors and classmates try to be toward me, I sometimes feel like a visitor on campus; as if I really don't belong. Regardless of the circumstances under which I interact with whites at Princeton, it often seems as if, to them, I will always be black first and a student second."[11] Her analysis, though unsophisticated, is compelling and steeped in her frustrated effort to gain recognition. It resonates with the struggle we have seen as representative for black women throughout American history. Yet when this paper was made public, many in the media questioned whether Michelle Obama harbored resentments and hatred toward white people, white institutions, and America in general. Few questioned the veracity of her claims; instead, her complaint alone was enough to label her as angry. Some clearly believed that as a black girl from "inner city" Chicago, she should have been unreservedly grateful for the opportunity to study at Princeton, and any discomfort or criticism must necessarily be irrational and angry. The results that have emerged throughout this book suggest that Michelle Robinson was most likely responding to Princeton University as a crooked room where securing recognition was difficult.

The angry black woman label was most severely applied after Michelle Obama said, during a campaign stop in Milwaukee, that "for the first time in my adult life I am proud of my country because it feels like hope is finally making a comeback."[12] This comment became fodder for opposition speculation about her latent anger. She was a forty-four-year-old mother of two who earned a significant salary and held degrees from Princeton and Harvard—yet she was never previously proud of her country? Again, her critique was taken as evidence of her irrational anger. If her criticism of Princeton University was seen as revealing an inappropriately racialized psychology rather than the university's institutionally discriminatory practices, her pride comment was received as evidence of her lack of patriotism rather than as cause for reconsidering the nation's racial history. Every time she pointed out that the angles of the room were crooked, the nation seemed to shout back that she, not the room, was askew.

The July 21, 2008, cover of the *New Yorker* captured the growing characterization of Michelle Obama as an angry black woman. It depicted Barack and Michelle Obama as fist-bumping terrorists. An American flag burned in the fireplace of the oval office, Osama bin Laden's picture hung over the mantel, and Barack was dressed in traditional North African apparel. Michelle was shown in military gear and combat boots with an AK-47 slung across her back and her hair in a large, curly Afro. The cover outraged many, but magazine spokespersons repeatedly denied that their depiction was anything other than a satirical jab at those who had inaccurately characterized the couple as a radical threat to American democracy.[13] Whatever the intent, it captured a particular sentiment about Michelle. Although Barack Obama had been photographed in similar attire during a trip to Africa, Michelle has never styled her hair in a large Afro, been heavily armed, or worn military gear. The *New Yorker*'s representation of her was not derived from visual evidence but from an ideological perspective about her. As is often the case in the crooked room, anger was an easy default framework for interpreting Michelle.

I was in the midst of writing this book during the 2008 campaign. As the hypersexualized and angry characterizations of Michelle emerged, I anticipated that I would conclude by explaining how she had been vilified as a result of the crooked images deployed against black women. Then something unexpected happened. In the months leading up the election, Michelle Obama's favorability ratings rose steadily. By the time she appeared with Oprah Winfrey on the cover of *O Magazine* in April 2009, she enjoyed 68 percent approval among whites generally and 78 percent among American women. A look at national polls beginning in February 2008, when she first made the "pride" statement, and ending in April 2009 shows that favorable opinions of her increased by 30 percentage points among all groups in just over a year. As this book went to press, she continued to enjoy more robust favorability than her husband. How Michelle effected such a dramatic reversal in public opinion is an interesting study in black women's resistance and accommodation of stereotypes. (For survey data, see Appendix, table 13.)[14]

Michelle Obama most forcefully encountered the myths about black women in three areas: conversations about her body, discussions about her role as mother, and speculations about her marriage. Each area maps onto one of the three primary myths about black women. Issues of hypersexuality lurk in the media obsession with Michelle's body; the specter of the angry black woman shadows discussions about her marriage; and national yearnings to depict black women as Mammy are embedded in public discourse about her role as mother. In each case, she made a number of choices to deflect, resist, redirect, or accommodate these anxieties about her black womanhood. Because her efforts were so public, they provide insight into the efforts of one African American woman to stand straight in a crooked room. They also suggest the limitations of individual strategies to challenge deeply embedded myths.

Jezebel and Michelle's Body

As the married mother of two young daughters, Michelle Obama was not a particularly good candidate for the projections about immoral hypersexuality. Except for the "baby mama" episode, the licentious discussions about Michelle centered not on her sexual behavior but on her physical body. Interestingly, one of the most profane came from Erin Aubry Kaplan, an African American woman writing for *Salon* who gushed with ecstatic familiarity, "First Lady Got Back!" Kaplan wrote of the First Lady's posterior, "It is a solid, round, black, class-A *boo-tay*. Try as Michelle might to cover it with those Mamie Eisenhower skirts and sheath dresses meant to reassure mainstream voters, the butt would not be denied."[15] Only because it was written by an African American woman, whose identity shielded her from being labeled racist or sexist, was this article publishable in the mainstream media. But it still set off a firestorm, particularly among black feminist writers, who denounced the piece as both derogatory and irrelevant. One black woman blogger commented, "My problem is that articles about Michelle Obama's wardrobe, booty, and mom duties are what is fit to publish, what is seen as relevant to a mass audience."[16]

One such article was a March 2009 *New York Times* op-ed by Maureen Dowd titled "Should Michelle Cover Up?"[17] The piece was written in response to Michelle's having worn a sleeveless purple dress to President Obama's first address to a joint session of Congress. Dowd's article rehearses some familiar American anxieties about black women's bodies. She expresses a sort of terror that Michelle is a symbol of overt sexuality that should be covered and shrouded so as not to distract men of power. In the piece Dowd claims that it is David Brooks, her fellow editorial writer, who suffers these anxieties, not her, but Dowd does seem irritated about the stimulating effect Michelle's dress had on the congressmen. Dowd echoes the white women of antebellum plantations who fretted about maintaining the virtue of their husbands and sons in the presence of scantily clad enslaved women, who were thought to be sexually insatiable.

Even as Dowd replays the Jezebel anxiety, she employs the pervasive misrepresentation of the strong black woman. She revels in the idea of Michelle as a powerful superwoman who could easily "wind up and punch out Rush Limbaugh, Bernie Madoff and all the corporate creeps who ripped off America." Dowd is tapping her own racial imagination when she perceives the First Lady as capable of engaging in a street brawl with grown men. This fantasy of the super-strong, masculine black woman who could easily best a man in a physical altercation is a crooked image perpetrated in black popular culture by comedians like Martin Lawrence, Tyler Perry, and the Wayans brothers—all black men who dress as women in comic routines that portray black women as masculine and outrageously pugnacious.[18]

The public dissection of Michelle Obama into body parts—first her butt and then her arms—is reminiscent of the treatment of Saartjie Baartman, the so-called Hottentot Venus. Recall that Baartman was a Khoikhoi woman from southern Africa who became an exhibit in London's Piccadilly Circus as a result of her supposedly abnormal sexual organs. In his discussion of the dissection of Baartman, Sander Gilman writes, "The antithesis of European sexual mores and beauty is embodied in the black, and the essential black, the lowest rung on the great chain of being, is the Hottentot. The physical appearance of the Hottentot is, indeed, the central nineteenth-century icon for sexual difference between the European and the black."[19] By Gilman's reading, this Khoikhoi woman's body becomes the icon of savagery and difference marking the scientific projects of the twentieth century. It is impossible to ignore this history when a black woman's body is rhetorically dissected, observed, and displayed as remarkable. Yet Michelle Obama's choice of the sleeveless dress (and her later decision to wear shorts in public) can be understood as an attempt to straighten the images in the crooked room. I take her wardrobe choices as evidence that Michelle Obama is actively using her role as First Lady to cultivate a particular representation of femininity that is meant to push back against a number of racialized gender stereotypes.

Michelle Obama is capturing a particular (though arguably narrow) definition of femininity that is often denied to black women. For example, she chose President Thomas Jefferson's portrait as the backdrop for her official White House photo. There she is, the first black, First Lady, in a sleeveless dress, and behind her is Thomas Jefferson, who raped a teenage bondswoman, Sally Hemings (the half-sister of his wife), and enslaved his own children.[20] Michelle's photo executes a self-conscious taunting that reaches across the span of history to repudiate the violence and brutality suffered by so many enslaved women. Michelle stands boldly in a White House where she is mistress, not slave. Her body is for her. She is not reduced to a mule or a breeder. Her children belong to her, and she is free to love and protect them. It is an act of resistance for a black woman to demand that her body belong to herself for her pleasure, her adornment, even her vanity, because in the United States, black women's bodies have often been valued only to the extent that they produce wealth and pleasure for others. When Michelle insists on audacious, sleeveless femininity, she strikes back against the reduction of black women to hypersexual breeders or asexual laborers. Hers is an important departure from the dissemblance strategies of twentieth-century club women who sought to prove their respectability through prim sexual ethics. Michelle refuses to be ashamed of her distinctive black woman's body and all the attributes and anxieties it evokes. Rather than shrouding herself in shame, she shows her body with surprising, self-confident ease.[21]

First Lady Michelle Obama. Photo: White House/Joyce N. Boghosian

Mammy and Michelle's Children

Throughout this book I have discussed the problematic ways that black motherhood has been understood in the United States. Recall, for example, that black pregnancy has often been a source of public shaming and public policy efforts to control fertility. Toni Morrison used the stories of enslaved black mothers to depict the most horrifying effects of American slavery. Her novel *Beloved* reveals the unimaginable pain some black mothers experienced because their children were profitable for their enslavers. Enslaved black women did not birth children; they produced merchandisable units of labor. Despite the patrilineal norm that governed free society, enslaved mothers were forced to pass their slave status on to their infants; the first inheritance black mothers gave to black children in America was chattel bondage.

When they became free citizens, black women's reproduction was no longer directly tied to profit. In this new context, black mothers became the object of fierce eugenics efforts. In *Killing the Black Body,* Dorothy Roberts explains how the state employed involuntary sterilization, pressured women to submit to long-term birth control, and restricted state benefits for large families as a means to control black women's reproduction.[22] Black mothers were again blamed as the central cause of social and economic decline in the early 1990s, when news stories and popular films took up the theme of "crack babies." Crack babies were the living, squealing, suffering evidence of pathological black motherhood, and American citizens were going to have to pay the bill for the children of these bad mothers. Susan Douglas and Meredith Michaels, authors of *The Mommy Myth,* explain that media created the "crack baby" phenomenon as a part of a broader history that understands black motherhood as inherently pathological. They write: "It turned out there was no convincing evidence that use of crack actually caused abnormal babies, even though the media insisted this was so. . . . Media coverage of crack babies serves as a powerful cautionary tale about the inherent fitness of poor or lower-class African American women to be mothers at all."[23]

This long tradition of pathologizing black motherhood is the backdrop against which Michelle Obama announced that she planned to serve as mom-in-chief. Many progressive feminists, who had hoped for a more aggressive policy agenda, were distressed with her assertion of motherhood as her primary role. Michelle Obama is a graduate of Princeton University and Harvard Law School who has spent her career as an effective advocate for urban communities in their fraught relationship with powerful institutions. She is smart, capable, and independent. She maintained her own career and ambitions throughout her husband's early forays into politics and even during his election to the US Senate. While no one expected her to commute to a nine-to-five job from the White House, many hoped that she would take on an independent political role in the Obama administration. These people were disappointed when she chose to focus on supporting her daughters through their school transition and providing companionship to her husband as he governs. White feminists in particular saw this as Michelle conforming to restrictive gender norms.

I see it differently. Michelle Obama is surprisingly thwarting expectations of black women's role in the family and representing a different image of black women than we are used to encountering in this country. As Mom-in-Chief Michelle Obama, she subverts a deep, powerful, and old public discourse on black women as bad mothers. Enslaved black women had no control over their children. Their sons and daughters could be sold away without their consent and brutally disciplined without their protection. When a black woman claims public ownership of her children, she helps rewrite this ugly history. In the modern era, black mothers have been publicly shamed as crack mothers, welfare queens, and matriarchs of fatherless families. Black single motherhood is blamed for social ills ranging from crime to drugs to urban disorder. Michelle Obama is an important corrective to this distorted view. She and her own mother, Grandma Robinson, are kind, devoted, loving, and firm parents who challenge the negative images of black motherhood that dominate the public discourse.

Michelle Obama's insistence on focusing on her children is also a sound repudiation of the Mammy role. Mammy is a symbol of black women as competent, strong, and sassy, yet she is beloved among white people because she uses all of her skills and talents to serve white domestic interests. Mammy makes sure that white children are well fed, that white women are protected from the difficulties of household labor, and that white men have a safe and comfortable home to return to at the end of the day. She ensures order in the white world by ignoring her own family and community. Her devotion and attention are for others, not for herself or her family. Calling on Michelle Obama to take a more active policy role while her children are still young is in a way requesting that she use her role as First Lady to serve as the national Mammy. Michelle refused. Instead of assuming that the broader public sphere was necessarily more important than the needs of her own children, she made a choice that has been denied to generations of black women.

There is a danger in this strategy. Michelle Obama's traditionalist public persona could be used as a weapon against women who do not conform to this domestic ideal. The majority of black mothers are working women who struggle to raise their children without husbands and often without adequate financial support from partners or the state. It would be easy to use Michelle Obama's choice, a choice fostered by a unique circumstance of privilege, to reassert that black women who labor for pay outside the home are inadequate parents. Given the pervasive myths of black women as bad mothers, this narrative could easily be deployed to undercut support for public policies focused on creation of a just and equal political and economic structure and to focus instead on "marriage" and "family values" as solutions to structural barriers facing black communities. At the same time, these conservative discourses have never needed any particular excuse to exist. Michelle Obama's framing herself as mom-in-chief does not make her complicit in the demonization of black mothers that began long before she became First Lady. Her decision does, however, deliver a blow to the Mammy image that many might have preferred that she embody.

Sapphire and Michelle's Marriage

In his second book, *The Audacity of Hope,* Barack Obama recounts the story of the night he delivered the keynote address at the 2004 Democratic National Convention. After he told Michelle that his stomach felt queasy, she hugged him, looked him in the eye and said, "Just don't screw it up, buddy!"[24] This gentle teasing of her "rock star" husband was a hallmark of Michelle Obama's self-presentation early in the presidential primary season. She talked about how Barack did not pick up his dirty socks, laughed about how their daughters complained about his snoring, and was honest about how she sometimes felt abandoned in the early years of child rearing. She explicitly refused to worship her husband solely for political purposes but instead insisted that they were equal partners. "And Barack is very much human. So let's not deify him, because what we do is we deify, and then we're ready to chop it down. People have notions of what a wife's role should be in this process, and it's been a traditional one of blind adoration. My model is a little different—I think most real marriages are."[25] For some, Michelle's honest assessment of Barack made him seem more human and likeable; it allowed many to believe that the Obamas would be models of gender equity in the White House.[26] Others saw Michelle's unwillingness to take on a traditional spousal role as evidence that she was a dominating, overpowering black woman.

This specter of the dominating black matriarch is a riff on the angry Sapphire character. As I discussed earlier in this book, the black matriarch first entered the national policy discussion with Daniel Patrick Moynihan's 1965 report *The Negro Family: The Case for National Action,* which designated black mothers as the principal cause of a culture of pathology that kept black people from achieving equality. Moynihan's research reported the assumed deviance of black families. This deviance was obvious, he opined, because women seemed to have the primary decision-making roles in black households.[27] Michelle Obama has the same Ivy League educational pedigree as her husband, throughout their marriage she was an independent wage earner—sometimes drawing a higher salary than he—and because of her husband's political responsibilities, she often took on the role of primary parental caretaker as well. Thus when she teased her husband, pointed out his faults, and declined to worship him, she did so as an equal partner. For those inclined to see

black women through the angles of the crooked room, this independence easily read as deviant and domineering matriarchy.

Remember that the crooked room is not only set askew by the
racial inequality of broader society; it is also a problem of sexism
within black communities. Black women struggle for recognition
both within and outside their own racial group. The belief that black
women make inadequately submissive wives is not the exclusive
creation of white prejudice. African Americans embraced the image
of the strong black woman, and this image figures prominently in the
idea of black women as overpowering. For example, during the 2008
campaign, African American comedian Chris Rock added a new
joke to his routine. Its premise is that African American women are
dominating shrews unable to allow their husbands to lead in the
domestic sphere. His humor assumes both that men are the rightful
leaders of the home and that black women's inability to submit to
this leadership is pathological.

> Barack has a handicap the other candidates don't have: Bar-
> ack Obama has a black wife. And I don't think a black
> woman can be first lady of the United States. Yeah, I said it!
> A black woman can be president, no problem. First lady?
> Can't do it. You know why? Because a black woman cannot
> play the background of a relationship. Just imagine telling
> your black wife that you're president? "Honey, I did it! I
> won! I'm the president" "No, we the president! And I want
> my girlfriends in the Cabinet. I want Kiki to be secretary of
> state! She can fight!"[28]

Rock's comic imagination is fueled by widely held assumptions
about who black women are in relation to black men: that African

American women are strong, unyielding, and uncompromising while black men are endangered and emasculated. The image of aggressive black women dominating their male partners persists despite empirical evidence that African American women are more likely to be victims than aggressors in heterosexual partnerships. Black women suffer higher rates of domestic assault and homicide than women of other racial and ethnic groups.[29] Their romantic attachments are also linked to their growing incarceration rates: black women's crimes tend to be ancillary to those of their male partners.[30] Black women are also the women most likely to face unassisted child rearing and the vulnerability to poverty that single parenthood entails. The reality is that black women's political, social, and economic marginalization ensures that they nearly always "play the background," but Rock can get an easy laugh by evoking the familiar stereotype of the domineering black woman.

In contrast to her repudiation of Jezebel and Mammy, Michelle Obama more readily accommodated to the anxieties produced by the strong black woman stereotype. She flouted attempts to shame her about her body. She refused the role of Mammy by turning her efforts toward her own hearth. But she found it necessary to defuse the dangerous image of the angry black matriarch by consciously embracing a softer image. After her pride comment and the Princeton thesis were used to frame her effectively as an "angry black woman," she noticeably softened her spousal image. While the couple's mutual respect remained evident, Michelle was more frequently photographed with her head on Barack's shoulder, grasping his hand at public events, or evading reporters by stealing brief, romantic walks on the White House grounds. The outspoken Michelle Obama who made many bristle with anxiety earlier in the campaign was replaced largely by a woman who evokes a warm feeling when we see her with her husband, her children, and even her dog. Many reporters and scholars expressed anxiety about the ascendance of this kinder, gentler Michelle. They worried that she was being packaged in a way that thwarts her authenticity and undermines the efforts of feminists committed to the notion of women as equal partners in their marriages.[31] Although this worry is not groundless, it is important to remember that as an African American woman, Michelle Obama is constrained by different stereotypes from those that inhibit white women. After she was depicted as irrationally angry and potentially unpatriotic, the public space for her as an independent but loving wife shrank considerably.

As First Lady, Michelle has crafted a more traditional role for herself. She is highly visible, but she has taken on relatively safe issues like childhood literacy, ending childhood obesity, advocacy for women and girls, and support of military families. Even her White House garden is framed more as an initiative for healthy eating than as a commitment to local foods in an effort against global climate change. White, middle-class gender norms in the United States have generally asserted that women belong in the domestic sphere. These norms have limited white women's opportunities for education and employment. But the story has been different for women of color and those from poor or working-class origins. These women have had to work, and they have shouldered the extreme burden of being effective parents while providing financially for their families. Black women were full participants in agricultural labor during slavery, in the backbreaking work of sharecropping, and in the domestic services of Jim Crow. Even middle-class and elite black women have typically worked as teachers, journalists, entrepreneurs, and professionals. At every level of household income and at every point in American history, black women have been much more likely to engage in paid labor than their white counterparts.[32] In exchange for their labor and independence, they have been labeled with ugly terms like Sapphire and matriarch, told that they are emasculating their men, and punished by a public discourse that sees them as insufficiently feminine. It was within this crooked room that Michelle Obama attempted to embrace a wifely traditionalism that is unusual for black women in the public sphere.

Michelle's choice to accommodate this demand for traditionalism is also dangerous for black women, who have so little space in which to speak back against patriarchy and sexism among black men. Black men face tremendous structural and personal challenges caused by racial inequality. Many of them believe that black women have a responsibility to silence their own concerns so as to ensure that black men not be given any additional burdens. Further, to the extent that Michelle Obama's apparent embodiment of traditional submission is connected to her position as First Lady, her "success" as a woman can be used as a rhetorical weapon against the majority of African American women who are unmarried. If only they, like Michelle, would submit to the authority of a husband, perhaps they, too, could live a life of wealth and comfort. Michelle Obama's traditionalism could encourage the discourse that establishing appropriately patriarchal families will offer solutions to the social ills facing black communities.

A glimpse of this trajectory in public discourse occurred during a *Nightline* special that aired April 9, 2010. The program, titled "Why Can't a Successful Black Woman Find a Man?" insisted that a crisis exists because 70 percent of professional black women are without husbands. It began with the assumption that marriage is an appropriate and universal goal for women and that any failure to achieve it must therefore be pathological. Panelists were encouraged to offer solutions without needing to articulate exactly why low marriage rates are troubling. Furthermore, given the distortions or absence of black women in most mainstream media outlets, I am skeptical that the *Nightline* special was motivated primarily by a desire to address the needs of African American women. More likely, marriage is a trope for other anxieties about respectability, economic stability, and the maintenance of patriarchy. Which social issue appears on the public agenda is never accidental. In this moment of economic crisis, social change, and racial transformation, black women are being encouraged to embrace traditional models of family and to view themselves as deficient if their lives do not fit neatly into these prescribed roles.

The solution offered most frequently by the *Nightline* panelists was that professional black women need to scale back their expectations. Black female success, the panelists concluded, is an impediment to finding and cultivating black love. Despite advertising itself as a news program, *Nightline* failed to call on any sociologist, psychologist, historian, or therapist who could have contributed context, statistics, or analysis about the "marriage crisis" among African Americans. Instead, these delicate and compelling issues were addressed by comedians, actors, bloggers, and journalists. Without structural analysis or evidence-based reasoning, the panel relied on personal experience. The three male participants have all written books on the black marriage and partnership crisis.[33] To varying degrees, all of these books frame the issue as a black female problem rather than a community issue. They encourage women to conform to a more sanitized ideal of femininity that doesn't compete with socially sanctioned definitions of masculinity. Each of these male participants was allowed to pontificate about how black women should behave without being challenged on his own relationship history and status. None of them can boast a lifetime marriage to one black woman. This personal information is relevant because personal narrative was the sole basis of the conversation. The women participating in the panel were subjected to public scrutiny of their supposed shortcomings, while the men's biographies were shielded by an assumption that their maleness alone made them worthy. The discussants on the show cited Michelle Obama as an example of a black woman who knew how to catch and keep a good black man. In that moment, Michelle was used as a weapon against other black women.

Straightening the Crooked Room

The week after Barack Obama was elected president, *Newsweek* ran an article by Allison Samuels titled "What Michelle Means to Us." Samuels, an African American woman, expressed enthusiasm about the possibilities inherent in Michelle Obama's impending tenure in the White House. She suggested that Michelle had a unique opportunity to straighten the angles of the black women's crooked room. "The new First Lady will have the chance to knock down ugly stereotypes about black women and educate the world about American black culture more generally. But perhaps more important—even apart from what her husband can do—Michelle has the power to change the way African-Americans see ourselves, our lives and our possibilities."[34]

Here Samuels is drawing on the fictive kinship that ties African Americans to one another. I have written here about how this fictive kinship can lead to collective shaming; Samuels is suggesting that greater acceptance of Michelle Obama could have residual effects for black women in America. If she can find a way to stand straight, perhaps she will expose the angles of the room as ugly myths rooted in racist and sexist history. Perhaps Michelle Obama's efforts could ease other black women's task of securing recognition.

Newsweek is the same publication whose cover image of a black woman Katrina survivor and her two children reduced white Americans' willingness to support government spending for rebuilding New Orleans. Less than five years later, Michelle Obama and her children replaced Katrina victims as America's default image of black women and children. But it is not clear that this substitution constitutes a meaningful or permanent shift in our national understanding of African American women. Few episodes more clearly illustrate the limitations of a Michelle-led recognition revolution than the July 2010 firing of the US Department of Agriculture's Georgia director of rural development, Shirley Sherrod.

Sherrod, an African American woman living and working in rural Georgia, was forced to resign her position with the USDA after conservative blogger Andrew Breitbart posted highly edited excerpts of her address at a March 2010 local branch meeting of the NAACP. Breitbart posted the inflammatory segment of Sherrod's speech to goad the NAACP, which had passed a resolution at its national conference denouncing racist elements within the conservative Tea Party movement. Breitbart's goal was to reveal NAACP hypocrisy by uncovering a "reverse" racist in its midst. In the clip, Sherrod seems to say that because she harbored racial animus, she refused to use her full authority as a USDA representative to assist a white farm family. When the clip became public, the national NAACP publicly condemned her. Executive Director Benjamin Jealous used his Twitter account to say that Sherrod "should be ashamed of herself." Rather than receive the accusations of a conservative blogger with judicious skepticism, Jealous's immediate response to an apparently rogue black woman was to publicly shame her. Within hours, Secretary of Agriculture Tom Vilsack, with approval of the White House, requested her resignation. Neither Vilsack nor Jealous bothered to watch the entire tape of her lecture or discuss the incident with Sherrod directly. In a symbolic violation of her citizenship, they denied Shirley Sherrod due process.

Within hours, a more complete picture of Sherrod's speech began to emerge. The full tape denies every assumption evoked in the short clip. Sherrod was not discussing an episode that occurred during her time as a federal government official; rather, her story was about her work for a private organization in the 1980s. She did not deny the white family her advocacy; in fact, she became a highly effective partner with them and ultimately helped them save their farm. Her speech to the NAACP had not been about racial hatred: in the minutes immediately following the clip, Sherrod talks about the path that led to her aggressive advocacy of the white family. She goes on to describe this moment of interracial cooperation as a turning point in her personal and political ideology, and she concludes with a powerful moral lesson about the need for Americans to work together across the color line.

The interracial cooperation continued as the white farm family against whom she had supposedly discriminated jumped to her immediate and vigorous defense. While others were saying she should be ashamed of herself, they loudly declared her an ally and a friend for life. The defense of Sherrod came most effectively and fully from the white farming community.

The Sherrod episode caught fire during the slow summer news cycle and dominated political news for several days. The NAACP and the White House issued immediate apologies, and the USDA made her a new job offer. But Sherrod was not quick to accept these attempts to appease her. Rather than slink off into the shadows, bruised and ashamed, she instead stepped up to the national microphone and spoke forcefully on her own behalf. She made the rounds on television, appeared on dozens of radio broadcasts, and began to accept high-profile speaking engagements throughout the country. She denounced Breitbart, the NAACP, and the White House for so casually, publicly vilifying her. The more she spoke, the more compelling her story became. Shirley Sherrod, it turns out, was not an obscure Southern bureaucrat. Instead, she was a woman with an impeccable civil rights pedigree. Her father was murdered by a white supremacist, but no one was ever charged or prosecuted in his murder. She is also the wife of civil rights icon Charles Sherrod. Charles Sherrod was an early member of the Student Nonviolent Coordinating Committee (SNCC). He served as SNCC's first field secretary, led the Albany movement for the desegregation of Georgia, founded the Southwest Georgia Independent Voters Project, and sat on the Albany City Council for more than a decade. That Sherrod's wife could be publicly shamed by the nation's preeminent civil rights organization without regard for his decades of contributions to the movement is an indication that Shirley Sherrod was literally unrecognized by the NAACP. She was misrecognized as racist, misrecognized as unimportant, misrecognized as unconnected to the organization's own history. This misrecognition had immediate personal consequences for Sherrod and longer-term political reverberations for the country.

The Sherrod incident was surprisingly discordant with Michelle Obama's trajectory. Many in the American media, federal government, and even a national civil rights organization readily believed the profound distortion of Sherrod's words and character. Such cavalier disdain is hard to attribute to anything other than very deep, persistent assumptions about black women as unsavory and ultimately disposable. Yet the vilification of Sherrod occurred amid wide acceptance of and support for Michelle Obama. For years, Michelle had been working hard to straighten the crooked angles of the national stage where black women are attempting to gain accurate recognition as women, wives, mothers, and, most important, citizens. She had successfully turned the tide of public opinion in her own favor, but there was not enough residual goodwill to stay the executioner's hand from falling on Shirley Sherrod. For Sherrod, the old assumptions, not the new realities, were most powerful. Yet like Michelle Obama, Shirley Sherrod did not stoop in the crooked room but battled to stand straight. Throughout the episode she was a fierce advocate for herself. She gave unflinching testimony about her own experiences of American racism, called on those who attacked her to be responsible for their actions, and refused to accept empty rhetoric in response to the real suffering that the events had caused her and her family.

Watching Sherrod in mid-July 2010 I was reminded of another Southern black woman who worked to organize poor, rural Americans: Fannie Lou Hamer. Like Charles Sherrod, Hamer was affiliated with SNCC. She led the fight to organize black sharecroppers for voter registration in Mississippi. In 1964 she was one of the organizers of the Mississippi Freedom Democratic Party, which challenged the all-white Mississippi delegation at the 1964 Democratic National Convention. Hamer testified before the credentials committee at the convention about the extreme violence and intimidation she and others faced in their attempts to register to vote. Plainspoken and riveting, she retold her story of being beaten, physically violated, and exiled from her home under threat of death. She and her fellow organizers had endured these abuses out of a deep yearning to be full citizens able to freely participate in and change America. Her leadership was rooted in her own struggle as a poor black woman laboring as a sharecropper in the Jim Crow South. Her race, womanhood, poverty, and lack of formal education made her claim on citizenship particularly subversive within the context of American apartheid. Her efforts were met with brutal repression by the state, ignored by the Democratic Party, and even compromised by members of the mainstream civil rights establishment. Her demand for first-class citizenship is one chapter in the difficult and uneven progress toward full inclusion for African American women. Shirley Sherrod's is another chapter in the same story.

Fannie Lou Hamer's testimony before the Democratic National Committee was a landmark event in American political history. Her forthright demand for first-class citizenship was an audacious claim for an African American woman. Despite having been born poor, black, and female in the segregated South, Hamer insisted that she had an equal right to choose her representatives in the American government. Facing the microphones in a room full of hostile, powerful white men, she rejected their definitions of her as unequal and unworthy. Her testimony was a watershed in a centuries-old struggle by black women who first came to America as slaves but who were nonetheless determined to carve out a place in the American public sphere. Hamer's testimony was not about ordinary barriers to participation; it is about systematic, state-sponsored violence and intimidation. She revealed the brutality of the white police who detained and beat her after she tried to register to vote. To solidify her sense of helplessness and isolation, these police coerced African American men into helping brutalize her. When she attempted to shield her dignity as a woman, these police shamed her by lifting up her skirt. Their goal was not only to batter her, not only to keep her from the polls, but also to dehumanize and humiliate her. Shirley Sherrod's story has some of the same elements. She, too, was an African American woman vulnerable to abuse by a conservative, white power structure and found that black men were complicit in her public shaming. When Hamer boldly and honestly told her story before a national audience, she was refusing to succumb to the crushing weight of terror. Charles Sherrod was with Fannie Lou Hamer in 1964 when she testified. He was among the few civil rights leaders who supported her attempts to reject the coopting compromise offered by the national party. Thus it was stunning when, more than forty-five years later, his own wife was also forced to assert her humanity as well as her citizenship as she rebuked the ugly lies told about her by a white man and believed by black men.

Final Thoughts

We began this book looking at the late summer of 2005 when the levee breach in New Orleans unleashed a disaster of misrecognition for African American women. We end five years later, in the late summer of 2010. Dramatic changes have been wrought on the land-scape of those five years. America has its first black president and, with him, its first black woman serving as First Lady. Defying genera-tions of stereotypes and shame, she has managed to become one of the most popular individuals in the country. Michelle Obama is the living, breathing possibility of sister citizenship. But this is not an easy or triumphant story. For most black women, America is still a crooked room filled with distorted images, presenting many oppor-tunities for shame and disaster. In response to these continuing realities, many black women continue to feel that the only viable strategy is to cultivate impervious strength and that their only consis-tent ally is a loving but distant God. But this strategy leaves them without the material resources or earthly allies necessary to effec-tively challenge institutional inequality on their own behalf.

I have used empirical evidence to suggest that the myth of the strong black woman has measurable consequences. The realities of black women's lives militate against achieving the mythical position of unwavering strength, and the resulting disillusionment and sense of failure have real effects on their emotional and physical well-being. Framing black women's citizenship around notions of strength also encourages undue self-sacrifice in the political realm. Seeking to sustain their position as backbones of communities and pillars of strength, African American women too often hesitate to demand resources to meet their individual needs. Similarly, the silences in black political agendas and in national partisan organizing are in areas where black women have the most critical needs. African American women not only struggle at the intersection of multiple forms of marginalization; they also find that their political labor often leaves them mentally and physically less well.

And yet somehow, stunningly, they continue to fight for recognition. Many are emotionally injured in the process, but the irrepressible desire to be seen—truly seen and understood as human and as a citizen—compels individual and collective efforts to achieve gender and racial equality. I leave you, not with my words, but with those of Shirley Chisholm, the first African American woman elected to the US Congress and the first to run for president. Chisholm said, "I want history to remember me not just as the first black woman to be elected to Congress, not as the first black woman to have made a bid for the presidency of the United States, but as a black woman who lived in the 20th century and dared to be herself."

Appendix

SURVEY DATA

A note on reading tables containing data from regression analysis: *In most of the tables presented below, you will see three kinds of numbers: (1) whole numbers, representing the percentage of individuals who answered each question with the response on the left; (2) fractions (decimals) measured from 0 to 1, in which 0 indicates complete disagreement and 1 indicates complete agreement with each question; and (3) numbers in parentheses, or standard errors, a statistical measure that simply indicates the amount of noise or spread in the responses to each question.*

Regression allows researchers to estimate the relationship between answers to several questions on a survey. Sometimes we find we do not have enough information to determine if answers to two different questions really are related. We call this a nonsignificant finding. Every entry in these tables without an asterisk (*) next to it is a nonsignificant finding. Because I cannot be sure about those relationships, I have chosen not to say much about them. But where you see an asterisk, I am reasonably confident that there is a discernable relationship between a person's answer on one question and his or her answers on other questions. For example, in table 5, the first cell shows

us that black women's overall health self-rating has a positive relationship to their sense of overall life satisfaction. Each time you see an
asterisk, you know that there is an effect worth noting.

Once you see an asterisk, the next thing you want to know is how
big the effect is. To determine this, look at the first number in the cell:
you do not need to worry about the number in the parentheses, since
that number is the one I used to determine whether to give the cell an
asterisk; instead, look at the number without parentheses. Every question is measured on a scale from 0 to 1. This allows us to read the
results almost like a percentage. Scoring 0 means answering a question at the bottom of the scale, and scoring 1 means answering a
question at the top of the scale (100%). In table 5, for instance, the .08
under "Black women" for "Overall health self-rating" means moving
up the scale of 8 steps from 0 toward 100. This is not a perfect or
complete description of regression analysis, but it should help you
review the charts more easily.

Table 1. Black women who report particular emotions when asked to think about black women (percentage)

	Proud	Hopeful	Inspired	Angry	Afraid	**Discouraged**
Yes, extremely	45	29	37	8	7	7
Yes, very	27	40	37	14	10	7
Somewhat	23	23	19	41	25	27
No, not really	2	4	6	24	32	34
Not at all	2	3	1	14	26	26

Source: 2005 Expo for Today's Black Woman Survey.
Notes: N=135; percentages may not add up to 100 due to rounding.

Table 2. Mean scores on emotion items for white and black respondents in the weeks following Hurricane Katrina

In the weeks since the Hurricane Katrina disaster how often have you felt . . .	Average for whites N=615	Average for blacks N=355	t-test score
So sad that nothing cheers	.39	.45	−7.2
Nervous	.44	.48	−4.7
Restless	.43	.47	−4.2
Hopeless	.35	.40	−5.8
Everything is an effort	.45	.54	−9.5
Worthless	.31	.34	−3.6
Difficulties too high to overcome	.45	.52	−8.2
Unable to control life	.49	.56	−7.1
Overall emotional distress scale	.41	.48	−8.8

Source: University of Chicago Center for the Study of Race, Politics, and Culture Racial Attitudes and Katrina Disaster Study.
Notes: Computed mean on a 0–1 scale; t-test scores estimated using a difference of means test; all items significant at p<.01.

Table 3. Black women's most common descriptions of race and gender categories (percentages)

Black women		Black men		White women		White men	
Description	Responses	Description	Responses	Description	Responses	Description	Responses
Strong	21%	Strong	17%	Passive	12%	Aggressive	9%
Beautiful	14%	Smart	7%	Stupid	5%	Rich	8%
Smart	8%	Powerful	5%	Dishonest	5%	Arrogant	8%
Independent	6%	Handsome	4%	Arrogant	4%	Dishonest	6%
Kind, loving	6%	Kind, loving	4%	Privileged	4%	Mean	6%
		Determined	4%			Powerful	6%
Responses in top categories	54%		39%		30%		42%
Total responses (N)	388		344		276		238

Source: 2005 Survey of Chicago's Expo for Today's Black Woman.
Notes: N=125; total of 52 unique response categories.

Table 4. Comparison of race and gender categories on physical health, emotional contentment, life stressors, and self-reliance

	Black women N=401	White women N=309	Black men N=185	White men N=244
Assessment of physical health				
Excellent or very good	41%	56%	54%	59%
Good	30%	27%	23%	28%
Fair or poor	26%	18%	13%	13%
Overall life satisfaction				
Completely/very satisfied	42%	67%	50%	60%
Somewhat satisfied	51%	29%	43%	35%
Not very or not at all satisfied	8%	5%	7%	5%
General sadness[a]				
Feel so sad nothing can cheer me	.41	.41	.38	.34
Often feel nervous	.45	.47	.40	.43
Often feel restless	.47	.49	.44	.48
Often feel hopeless	.31	.31	.28	.29
Total general sadness scale	.39 (.17)	.39 (.17)	.36 (.16)	.36 (.15)
Family support and demands[a]				
How much do your family members make you feel loved and cared for?	.88 (.22)	.89 (.16)	.86 (.20)	.86 (.18)
How much do your friends make you feel loved and cared for?	.77 (.23)	.83 (.18)	.74 (21)	.76 (.19)
Do you feel your family members make too many demands on you?	.54 (.29)	.49 (.25)	.49 (.27)	.44 (.21)
Do you feel your friends make too many demands on you?	.39 (.21)	.35 (.18)	.40 (.24)	.36 (.18)
Assumed self-reliance				
I can do just about anything I set my mind to	73%	55%	69%	57%
What happens to me in the future mostly depends on me	77%	73%	71%	72%
When things don't go the way I want them to it just makes me work harder	51%	38%	51%	31%
Sometimes I feel that if anything is to be done right, I have to do it myself	59%	45%	48%	37%
Total self-reliance scale[a]	.65 (.28)	.53 (.30)	.59 (.30)	.49 (.29)

Source: 1995 Detroit Area Study.

Notes: [a] Computed mean on a 0–1 scale; numbers in parentheses indicate standard errors.

Table 5. Model of overall life satisfaction in each race/gender category

	Black women r²=.18	White women r²=.22	Black men r²=.24	White men r²=.31
Overall health self-rating	.08 (.04)*	.12 (.05)*	.08 (.06)	.05 (.06)
Assumed self-reliance	−.01 (.08)	.08 (.08)	−.02 (.10)	.10 (.09)
Socioeconomic status				
Education	−.01 (.004)*	.0001 (.04)	−.004 (.005)	.008(.005)
Income	.003 (.002)	.0002 (.02)	.004 (.003)	.006 (.002)*
Wealth	.01 (.003)*	.001 (.004)	.01 (.006)*	.007 (.004)
Family of origin	−.02 (.04)	.07 (.05)	.09 (.06)	.11 (.05)*
Personal connection				
Religiosity	.03 (.06)	.11 (.05)*	−.01 (.07)	.08 (.05)
Married	.01 (.02)	.04 (.02)	−.02 (.03)	−.002 (.03)
Children	.02 (.02)	.04 (.03)	−.03 (.03)	.03 (.03)
Feel loved by family	.09 (.04)*	.12 (.07)	.02 (.08)	.16 (.06)*
Feel loved by friends	.03 (.04)	.15 (.06)*	.15 (.07)*	.12 (.06)*
Race important sense of self	.03 (.04)	.05 (.04)	−.20 (.06)	.03 (.04)
Personal stressors				
Family demand	−.13 (.04)*	−.04 (.05)	−.01 (.07)	−.06 (.06)
Friends demand	−.05 (.05)	−.02 (.06)	−.15 (.06)*	.04 (.04)
Political ideas				
Political ideology	.06 (.05)	.04 (.07)	.01 (.08)	.01 (.07)
Social/economic ideology	−.01 (.04)	.02 (.06)	−.02 (.06)	.06 (.07)
Democrat	−.004 (.02)	−.006 (.02)	.03 (.03)	−.03 (.03)
Proud to be American	.02 (.02)	.04 (.03)	.03 (.03)	.05 (.03)
Constant	.53 (.10)	.13 (.12)	.65 (.14)	−.02 (.11)

Source: 1995 Detroit Area Study.

Notes: Computed mean on a 0–1 scale; numbers in parentheses indicate standard errors; * denotes significance at p<.05.

Table 6. Model of "get over it" in each race and gender category

	Black women	White women	Black men	White men
Average score on scale	.53 (.16)	.68 (.14)	.52 (.16)	.67 (.15)
General health	.02 (.04)	.01 (.04)	.04 (.06)	.01 (.06)
Assumed self-reliance	.17 (.07)*	.09 (.07)	.07 (.09)	.04 (.07)
Socioeconomic status				
Education	−.003 (.004)	−.02 (.004)*	−.007 (.005)	−.02 (.004)
Income	−.005 (.002)	−.002 (.002)	−.001 (.003)	.001 (.002)
Wealth	−.002 (.003)	.004 (.004)	.004 (.006)	−.002 (.004)
Family of origin	.10 (.004)*	−.01 (.04)	−.02 (.06)	−.03 (.05)
Personal connection				
Religiosity	−.05 (.05)	.06 (.04)	.09 (.07)	−.07 (.05)
Married	.02 (.02)	.04 (.02)*	.02 (.03)	.01 (.02)
Children	−.02 (.02)	−.02 (.02)	−.04 (.03)	.05 (.02)*
Feel loved by family	.04 (.04)	−.02 (.06)	−.03 (.08)	.04 (.06)
Feel loved by friends	.02 (.04)	.02 (.05)	−.03 (.06)	−.01 (.06)
Race important to sense of self	−.11 (.04)*	−.05 (.03)	−.05 (.06)	−.03 (.03)
Personal stressors				
Family demand	.05 (.03)	.01 (.04)	.02 (.06)	.05 (.05)
Friends demand	−.11 (.05)	.06 (.05)	−.10 (.06)	−.02 (.06)
Political ideas				
Political ideology	−.11 (.05)*	−.09 (.06)	−.21 (.07)*	.01 (.07)
Social/economic ideology	.01 (.04)	−.07 (.06)	.04 (.06)	−.18 (.06)*
Democrat	−.04 (.02)	−.04 (.02)*	.002 (.03)	.01 (.02)
Proud to be American	.06 (.02)*	.07 (.02)*	.04 (.02)*	.09 (.03)*
Constant	.54 (.11)	.87 (.12)	.66 (.13)	.91 (.11)
	$r^2 = .17$	$r^2 = .24$	$r^2 = .17$	$r^2 = .26$

Source: 1995 Detroit Area Study.
Note: Computed mean on a 0–1 scale; numbers in parentheses indicate standard errors; * denotes significance at $p < .05$.

Table 7. Religious belief scales by race and gender category

	Forgiveness	Strong sense of divine connection	Religious belief guides other areas	Fundamentalism
Black women N=120	.88 (.14)	.76 (.17)*	.82 (.19)*	.81 (.26)*
White women N=588	.86 (.14)	.65 (.21)	.75 (.21)	.66 (.25)
Black men N=77	.88 (.14)*	.73 (.19)*	.79 (.21)*	.79 (.27)*
White men N=515	.81 (.17)	.57 (.23)	.68 (.22)	.64 (.26)

Source: 1998 General Social Survey.
Notes: Computed mean on a 0–1 scale; numbers in parentheses indicate standard errors; * represents significance at $p < .05$ for a racial effect within the same sex category using a difference of means t-test.

Table 8. Images of God by race and gender categories

	Mother/Father	Lover/Judge	Friend/King
Black women N=207	.80 (.26)	.75 (.29)	.56 (.33)
White women N=1,010	.81 (.24)	.73 (.27)	.54 (.31)
Black men N=117	.82 (.24)	.73 (.31)	.63 (.33)
White men N=835	.80 (.23)	.69 (.27)	.57 (.30)

Source: 1998 General Social Survey.
Note: Computed mean on a 0–1 scale; numbers in parentheses indicate standard errors; scores below .5 represent greater agreement with the image on the left, and scores above .5 represent greater agreement with the image on the right.

Table 9. Religious coping mechanisms by race and gender categories

	Positive religious effect in hard times	Negative religious effect in hard times	Agnostic effect in hard times
Black women N=120	.82 (.19)*	.32 (.11)	.37 (.19)*
White women N=588	.70 (.23)	.30(.10)	.49 (.25)
Black men N=77	.79 (.21)*	.32 (.12)	.44 (.24)*
White men N=515	.60 (.24)	.31 (.12)	.57 (.26)

Source: 1998 General Social Survey.
Notes: Computed mean on a 0–1 scale; numbers in parentheses indicate standard errors; * represents significance at p<.05 for a racial effect within the same sex category.

Table 10. Model of negative emotions scale as a function of religious beliefs among African American women

	Coefficient	Standard errors
Physical health assessment	−.21**	.08
Religious beliefs		
Forgiveness	.17	.14
Strong sense of divine connection	−.05	.11
Religious belief guides other areas	−.10	.11
Fundamentalism	.01	.02
Coping in difficult times		
Positive effect	.15	.12
Negative effect	.43**	.17
Agnostic effect	.01	.09
Imaging of God		
God more father than mother	−.09	.06
God more judge than lover	.01	.05
God more king than friend	−.0002	.05
Religious practice		
Frequency of prayer	−.02*	.01
Frequency of church attendance	.001	.01
Demographics		
Age	−.0003	.001
Income	−.01	.01
Education	−.01	.01
Married	−.01	.03
Children	−.01	.01

Source: 1998 General Social Survey.
Notes: N=112; coefficients and standard errors are derived from an ordinary least squares regression; r^2 = .32; * denotes significance at p<.10; ** denotes significance at p<.05.

Table 11. Model of need to reduce suffering as a function of religious belief among African American women

	Coefficient	Standard errors
Religious beliefs		
Forgiveness	1.97	1.95
Strong sense of divine connection	.37	1.5
Religious belief guides other areas	5.30**	1.64
Fundamentalism	−.52*	.29
Coping in difficult times		
Positive effect	.93	1.5
Negative effect	−1.1	2.2
Agnostic effect	−.10	1.2
Imaging of God		
God more father than mother	−1.5*	.84
God more judge than lover	−1.2*	.69
God more king than friend	.88	.67
Religious practice		
Frequency of prayer	−.19	.10
Frequency of church attendance	−.05	.09
Demographics		
Age	−.03*	.02
Income	.07	.07
Education	−.02	.09
Married	.44	.53
Children	−.02	.12

Source: 1998 General Social Survey.

Notes: N=112; coefficients and standard errors are derived from an ordered logit estimate; log likelihood = −93.53; LR chi^2 (17) = 63.60; pseudo r^2= .17; * denotes significance at p<.10; ** denotes significance at p<.05.

Table 12. Political action and gender equity as a function of religious belief and action among African American women

	Political action as a function of religious belief and action		Gender equity beliefs as a function of religious belief and action	
	Coefficient	Standard errors	Coefficient	Standard errors
Religious variables				
Jesus is black	.06*	.02	.02	.02
Political action in church	.45*	.03	.02	.03
Political discussion in church	.08*	.04	−.04	.04
Active church service	.06*	.02	.002	.02
Frequency of church attendance	.02	.04	−.02	.04
Religious guidance in daily life	−.03	.03	−.02	.02
Baptist	.02	.02	.01	.01
Racial variables				
Racial self-reliance	.08*	.03	−.001	.03
Attitudes toward whites	.02	.02	−.04*	.02
Black linked fate	.02	.02	−.02	.03
Black women linked fate	.08*	.03	.08*	.03
White women linked fate	−.01	.02	−.01	.02
Demographics				
Age	.0001	.0001	−.001*	.0005
Married	.01	.02	.002	.02
Income	.01*	.003	.01*	.004
Education	.004	.003	.01*	.002

Source: 1993 National Black Politics Study.
Notes: Coefficients are derived from ordinary least squares regressions; * denotes significance at p<.05.

Table 13. Opinions of Michelle Obama by race and gender, February 2008 to April 2009 (percentage)

Survey date	Whites Favor-able	Whites Unfavor-able	Blacks Favor-able	Blacks Unfavor-able	Men Favor-able	Men Unfavor-able	Women Favor-able	Women Unfavor-able
February 2008	36	8	60	0	35	5	41	9
April 2008	22	20	51	3	23	19	26	18
June 2008	39	34	84	5	49	28	44	29
October 2008	34	20	81	1	30	20	43	17
December 2008	39	14	70	2	35	14	46	11
January 2009	45	9	74	3	40	9	52	8
February 2009	51	7	79	0	46	6	57	6
March 2009	70	18	96	1	72	16	74	15
April 2009a	54	7	70	0	44	7	63	5
April 2009b	68	4	90	0	65	3	78	3

Sources: June 2009 and March 2009, ABC News/Washington Post; all others CBS News/New York Times.

Notes

Introduction

1. Julie Roemer, "Reclaiming the Canon: Celebrating the Black Female Self: Zora Neale Hurston's American Classic," *English Journal* 78, no. 7 (1989): 79.

2. Sharon Davie writes, "Hurston's text not only inverts the terms of accepted hierarchies (black over white, female over male) but—more significantly—allows readers to question, if only for a moment, the hierarchal mode itself." "Free Mules, Talking Buzzards, and Cracked Plates: The Politics of Dislocation in *Their Eyes Were Watching God,*" *PMLA* 108 (1993): 447.

3. Missy Dehn Kubitschek, " 'Tuh de Horizon and Back': The Female Quest in *Their Eyes Were Watching God,*" *Black American Literature Forum* 17, no. 3 (1983): 109.

4. Zora Neale Hurston, *Their Eyes Were Watching God* (Philadelphia: J. B. Lippincott), 29.

5. This reading of Janie as a heroic quester is at odds with an older literary tradition that discounted Hurston's novel as entirely romantic and lacking any political relevance. In his article "Between Laughter and Tears," *New Masses* (October 1937), Hurston's contemporary Richard Wright famously attacked the work, writing, "The sensory sweep of [Hurston's] novel carries no theme, no message, no thought" (25).

6. Hurston, *Their Eyes Were Watching God,* 150–151.

7. Louisiana governor Kathleen Blanco declared a state of emergency on Friday, August 26, 2005. Mayor Ray Nagin did not issue a mandatory order to evacuate until 9:30 a.m. on Sunday, August 28, 2005. The first report that levees in New Orleans had been breached came at 7:30 a.m. on Monday, August 29, 2005.

8. Susan Cutter, "The Geography of Social Vulnerability: Race, Class and Catastrophe," in *Understanding Katrina: Perspectives from the Social Sciences* (Social Science Research Council, 2005).

9. Robert C. Lieberman, " 'The Storm Didn't Discriminate': Katrina and the Politics of Color Blindness," *Du Bois Review* 3 no. 1 (2006): 8–22.

10. John Lewis and Michael D'Orso, *Walking with the Wind: A Memoir of the Movement* (New York: Mariner Books, 1999).

11. John McCain with Mark Salter, *Why Courage Matters: The Way to a Braver Life* (New York: Random House, 2004).

12. Michael Eric Dyson, *Come Hell or High Water: Hurricane Katrina and the Color of Disaster* (New York: Basic Civitas, 2006).

13. Data from the "2006 Hurricane Katrina and America's Racial Attitudes Study" conducted by Michael Dawson, Melissa Harris-Lacewell, and Cathy Cohen show that 91 percent of African Americans believed that Kanye West's comments were justified. Only 44 percent of white Americans agreed.

14. Immediately following the congressional elections in November 2010, American media spent several days reporting on the publication of President George W. Bush's memoir, *Decision Points* (Crown). One of the most controversial aspects of the book was the president's assertion that Kanye West's comments about Hurricane Katrina were both "disgusting" and a "low point" for President Bush.

15. On September 2, New Orleans mayor Ray Nagin made an angry and anguished plea for federal assistance during an interview with a New Orleans radio station (WWL-AM). His interview became a defining moment for the disaster and for his political career. By openly pleading for assistance and expressing his frustration with the lack of action, Mayor Nagin implied that the victims of the flooding had been unfairly abandoned by the government. "We're getting reports and calls that [are] breaking my heart from people saying, 'I've been in my attic. I can't take it anymore. The water is up to my neck. I don't think I can hold out.' And that's happening as we speak. . . . You mean to tell me that a place where you probably have thousands of people that have died and thousands more that are dying every day, that we can't figure out a way to authorize the resources that we need? Come on man. . . . I need reinforcement. I need troops, man. I need 500 buses, man. This is a national disaster."

16. The Hurricane Katrina Survey, sponsored by the Pew Research Center for the People and the Press, obtained telephone interviews with a nationally representative sample of one thousand adults living in continental US telephone households. The survey was conducted by Princeton Survey Research International. Interviews were done in English by Princeton Data Source, LLC, September 7–8, 2005. Statistical results are weighted to correct known demographic discrepancies. The margin of sampling error for the complete set of weighted data is ±3.5 percent.

17. D'Ann R. Penner and Keith C. Ferdinand have collected a series of first-person accounts of African American survivors of Hurricane Katrina in their text *Overcoming Katrina: African American Voices from the Crescent City and Beyond* (New York: Palgrave Macmillan, 2009). Several informants tell compelling stories

of how the military personnel deployed to New Orleans to assist in rescue and evacuation treated survivors as enemy combatants rather than as citizens in need of relief.

18. African American political leaders, including several members of the Congressional Black Caucus, openly rejected the term *refugee* during live televised broadcasts on CNN and MSNBC. For more on this issue, see "Calling Katrina Survivors 'Refugees' stirs debate: Jesse Jackson, Other Critics Say Word Carried Racist Implications," Associated Press, September 7, 2005.

19. Elizabeth Fussell, "Leaving New Orleans: Social Stratification, Networks, and Hurricane Evacuation," in *Understanding Katrina: Perspectives from the Social Sciences* (Social Science Research Center, 2006), available at http://understand ingkatrina.ssrc.org/Fussell/.

20. See "New Orleans Evacuations Under Way: Health Emergency Declared; Thousands May Be Dead," CNN.com, September 1. It is interesting to note that this article was published under the "weather" section of the news website: http://www.cnn.com/2005/WEATHER/08/31/katrina.impact/index.html.

21. For a more complete treatment of these issues, see Dyson, *Come Hell or High Water*.

22. Havidán Rodríguez, Joseph Trainor, and Enrico L. Quarantelli, "Rising to the Challenges of a Catastrophe: The Emergent and Prosocial Behavior Following Hurricane Katrina," *Annals of the American Academy of Political and Social Science* 604 (2006): 82–101.

23. Some examples of this research include: Jeanette Covington, "Racial Classification in Criminology: The Reproduction of Racialized Crime," *Sociological Forum* 10 (1995): 547–568; Mark Peffley and Jon Hurwitz, "The Racial Components of 'Race-Neutral' Crime Policy Attitudes," *Political Psychology* 23, no. 1 (2002): 59–75; Vincent Sacco, "Media Constructions of Crime," *Annals of the American Academy of Political and Social Science* 539 (1995): 141–154; and Lincoln Quillian and Devah Pager, "Black Neighbors, Higher Crime? The Role of Racial Stereotypes in Evaluations of Neighborhood Crime," *American Journal of Sociology* 107 (2001): 717–767.

24. Sociologists Kathleen Tierney, Christine Bevc, and Erica Kuligowski argue that this crime framework is not only racial, it also has roots in "disaster myths," in their article "Metaphors Matter: Disaster Myths, Media Frames, and Their Consequences in Hurricane Katrina," *Annals of the American Academy of Political and Social Science* 604 (2006): 57–81. They show that there are several prominent disaster myths that influence how they are framed by media. "Following Hurricane Katrina, the response of disaster victims was framed by the media in ways that greatly exaggerated the incidence and severity of looting and lawlessness."

25. Rodríguez, Trainor, and Quarantelli, "Rising to the Challenges of a Catastrophe."

26. Penner and Ferdinand, *Overcoming Katrina.*

27. Anna Julia Cooper, *A Voice from the South* (1892; New York: Oxford University Press, 1990).

28. Combahee River Collective, "A Black Feminist Statement" [1977], reprinted in *Words of Fire: An Anthology of African American Feminist Thought,* ed. Beverly Guy-Sheftall (New York: New Press, 1995). The Combahee River Collective was a black, feminist lesbian organization active 1974–1980. They were founded during the 1973 National Black Feminist Organization meeting in New York. For more, see Duchess Harris, "The Kennedy Commission to the Combahee Collective," in *Sisters in the Struggle: African American Women in the Civil Rights–Black Power Movement,* ed. Bettye Collier-Thomas and V. P. Franklin (New York: New York University Press, 2001).

29. Evan Thomas, "Pray for Us," *Newsweek,* September 12, 2005, 43–52.

30. "Very few critics, however, recognize in Janie the independence and strength of the archetypal quester. Rather, they diminish her, denying her an independent sphere of action and being." Kubitschek, " 'Tuh de Horizon and Back,' " 109.

31. Henry Louis Gates, *The Signifying Monkey: A Theory of African-American Literary Criticism* (New York: Oxford University Press, 1988), 195.

32. Carlene Young, "Psychodynamics of Coping and Survival of the African-American Female in a Changing World," *Journal of Black Studies* 20 (1989): 208–223.

33. Hurston, *Their Eyes Were Watching God.*

Chapter 1. Crooked Room

Epigraph: Audre Lorde, "The Master's Tools Will Never Dismantle the Master's House," in Cherríe Moraga and Gloria Anzaldúa, eds., *This Bridge Called My Back: Writings by Radical Women of Color* (New York: Kitchen Table Press, 1983), 94–101.

1. H. A. Witkin et al., "Field-Dependent and Field-Independent Cognitive Styles and Their Educational Implications," *Review of Education Research* 47, no. 1 (1977): 1–64.

2. I am the black woman educator in this scenario. In 2008, I appeared on a panel for the television show *Hip Hop v. America* on Black Entertainment Television. Though I am normally quite calm during televised political debates, one member of the panel consistently goaded me during the taping of this show. I lost

my temper, became angry, and yelled during the taping. The spectacle became a lead-in teaser for the show and erupted into a minor debate on several African American political websites. During the incident and in the responses afterward I was often referred to as an "angry black woman." The experience was useful in helping me to think through the challenging stereotypes that black women face despite relative class privilege.

3. An enduring example of accommodating negative images of the self is the Clark doll study. Conducted during the same post-WWII era as the field dependence studies, African American psychologist Kenneth Clark demonstrated that African American children in segregated schools preferred white dolls to black ones. Black children also described the white dolls as nicer and smarter. The Supreme Court cited Clark's evidence in *Brown v. Board of Education of Topeka Kansas* (1954). The justices argued that the clear distortion of black children's self-concept, as evidenced in their choice of white dolls over black ones, was a meaningful reason to end educational segregation in primary schools. It seems that the Court could see just how crooked the room was, and they intervened to try to straighten it. For brief review of doll studies, see Kenneth Clark and Mamie Clark, "Racial Identity Preference in Negro Children," in *Readings in Social Psychology,* ed. Theodore Mead Newcomb and Eugene L. Hartley (New York: Holt, Reinhart and Winston, 1947), 169–178. For the Court's decision, see Brown v. Board of Education of Topeka, 347 US 483 (1954).

4. Salamishah Tillet, "Black Feminism, Tyler Perry Style," *theRoot.com,* November 11, 2010. Shange's reflections are printed in the introduction to a 2010 edition of her choreopoem released by Simon and Schuster in anticipation of the film adaptation of her piece. Ntozake Shange, *for colored girls who have considered suicide/ when the rainbow is enuf* (1975; New York: Simon and Schuster, 2010).

5. Novelist Sandra Hollin Flowers describes *for colored girls* as "an important work which ranks with Ellison's *Invisible Man,* Wright's *Native Son,* and the handful of other black classics—it is an artistically successful female perspective on a long-standing issue among black people." Sandra Hollin Flowers, "*Colored Girls:* Textbook for the Eighties," *Black American Literature Forum* 15, no. 2 (1981): 51.

6. Shange, *for colored girls who've considered suicide,* 10.

7. Evelyn Brooks Higginbotham, *Righteous Discontent: The Women's Movement in the Black Baptist Church, 1880–1920* (Cambridge, MA: Harvard University Press, 1994).

8. Tera W. Hunter, *To 'Joy My Freedom: Southern Black Women's Lives and Labors After the Civil War* (Cambridge, MA: Harvard University Press, 1997).

9. Three focus groups were conducted in August 2003 at the Center for the

Study of Race, Politics, and Culture at the University of Chicago. Each group lasted approximately two hours and consisted of eight or nine participants. Participants received fifty dollars for their participation. Two additional groups were conducted in New York at Focus Suites and participants received a seventy-five-dollar incentive. Participants represented a variety of households and socioeconomic groups. All had at least a GED, and participants with a professional degree were excluded. None of the participants worked in marketing, advertising, market research, health care, counseling, or higher education. All of the residents lived in their respective urban areas. Two additional groups were conducted in Oakland, California, on the campus of Laney Community College. Precious Issues Research in Chicago and Linda Tischler Market in New York and the author (formerly Melissa Harris-Lacewell) in Oakland did recruitment. Lisa McDonald of Research Explorers moderated and coordinated the groups in conjunction with Melissa Harris-Lacewell.

10. My focus group respondents mirror concerns that have animated recent research. In 2004 a group of Chicago researchers developed a quantitative scale of black women stereotypes. Their study is the first attempt to quantify how African American women subscribe to the common race and gender stereotypes of Mammy, Jezebel, and Sapphire. They conclude that internalizing these myths is negatively correlated with self-esteem among black women. In 2005 another group of researchers used experimental techniques to examine how stereotypical portrayals of African American women influenced assessments of black women in social situations. Participants in this study were exposed to film clips of Jezebel and Mammy. After viewing these stereotypic portrayals, the participants more quickly associated black women with negative terms and showed stereotype-influenced assessments of their employment abilities. Jennifer L. Monahan, "Priming Welfare Queens and Other Stereotypes: The Transference of Media Images into Interpersonal Contexts," *Communication Research Reports* 22, no. 3 (2005): 199–205.

11. Charisse Jones and Kumea Shorter-Gooden, *Shifting: The Double Lives of Black Women in America* (New York: HarperCollins, 2003), 6.

12. Jones and Shorter-Gooden describe the phenomenon of shifting, writing: "Shifting is what she does when she speaks one way in the office, another way to her girlfriends, and still another way to her elderly relatives. It is what may be going on when she enters the beauty parlor with dreadlocks and leaves with straightened hair, or when she tries on five outfits every morning looking for the best camouflage for her ample derriere. And shifting is often internal, invisible. It's the chipping away at her sense of self, at her feelings of wholeness and centeredness—often as a consequence of living amidst racial and gender bias." Jones and Shorter-Gooden, *Shifting,* 7.

13. See Iris Marion Young, *Justice and the Politics of Difference* (Princeton, NJ: Princeton University Press, 1990); Amy Gutman, ed., *Multiculturalism: Examining the Politics of Recognition* (Princeton, NJ: Princeton University Press, 1994); and Alex Honneth, "Integrity and Disrespect: Principles of a Conception of Morality Based on a Theory of Recognition," *Political Theory* 20, no. 2 (1992): 187–201.

14. For a review of Hegel's key works on recognition, particularly *Philosophy of Right* and *Phenomenology of Spirit,* see Robert R. Williams, *Hegel's Ethics of Recognition* (Berkeley: University of California Press, 1998).

15. Hannah Arendt, *The Human Condition* (1958; Chicago: University of Chicago Press, 1998), 41.

16. Thomas Hobbes, *Leviathan* (1651; Oxford University Press, 2009).

17. Arendt, *Human Condition,* 51, 71.

18. Young, *Justice and the Politics of Difference.*

19. W. E. B. Du Bois, *The Souls of Black Folk* (1903; New York: Bantam Books, 1989).

20. Ralph Ellison, *Invisible Man,* 2nd ed. (New York: Vintage International, 1995), 3.

21. bell hooks, *Black Looks: Race and Representation* (New York: Routledge, 1992), 7.

22. Patchen Markell, *Bound by Recognition* (Princeton, NJ: Princeton University Press, 2003), 3, 18, 154.

23. Nancy Fraser and Axel Honneth, *Redistribution or Recognition: A Political-Philosophical Exchange* (New York: Verso, 2003).

24. Charles Taylor, "The Politics of Recognition," in Taylor, *Multiculturalism: Examining the Politics of Recognition,* ed. Amy Gutmann (Princeton, NJ: Princeton University Press, 1994), 25–73.

25. Suzanne Lebsock, *The Free Women of Petersburg: Status and Culture in a Southern Town, 1784–1860* (New York: W. W. Norton, 1984), 88.

26. Chana Kai Lee, *For Freedom's Sake: The Life of Fannie Lou Hamer* (Urbana: University of Illinois Press, 1999).

27. Chana Kai Lee in Deborah Gray White, ed., *Telling Histories: Black Women Historians in the Ivory Tower* (Chapel Hill: University of North Carolina Press, 2008), 212.

28. Professor Lee describes her experience of returning to class: "I heard my own voice. I had tried out my badly slurred speech in front of students, and it had taken so long to say so few words. I was horrified. I broke down and cried. I could not finish. In tears, I dismissed the class by telling them that we would discuss how to resume the course. (We had about six weeks left in the semester.) I noticed some

students crying as they left the classroom. I felt so vulnerable, so weak and embarrassed. I hate crying in front of anybody, even my own mother. That I cried in front of students was deeply disturbing to me. My embarrassment soon turned to rage." Ibid., 211.

29. About one of every four blacks lived below the poverty level, compared with about one of every ten non-Hispanic whites. Blacks have a lower median income and are more likely to rent their homes. American Community Survey of the U.S. Census Bureau, 2004.

30. T. J. Mathews and Marian F. MacDorman, "Infant Mortality Statistics from the 2004 Period Linked Birth/Infant Death Set," *National Vital Statistics Reports* 55, no. 14 (May 2, 2007).

31. American Community Survey of U.S. Census Bureau, 2004.

32. Ibid.

33. In 2007 about 17 percent of black women had a bachelor's degree or more education, compared with about 32 percent of non-Hispanic white men and about 28 percent of non-Hispanic White women. Ibid.

34. For an account of racial and gendered health disparities and their influence on black women's wellness, see Amy J. Schulz and Leith Mullings, eds., *Gender, Race, Class, and Health: Intersectional Approaches* (New York: Jossey-Bass, 2007).

35. The current rate is 149 women per 100,000 persons in the US resident black population. Matthew Cooper, William J. Sabol, and Heather C. West, *Prisoners in 2008,* Bureau of Justice Statistics, US Department of Justice, Office of Justice Programs, NCJ 228417, December 8, 2009.

36. Overall, African Americans were victimized by intimate partners at significantly higher rates than persons of any other race between 1993 and 1998. Black females experienced intimate partner violence at a rate 35 percent higher than that of white females and about twenty-two times the rate of women of other races. Black males experienced intimate partner violence at a rate about 62 percent higher than that of white males and about twenty-two times the rate of men of other races. Callie Marie Rennison and Sarah Welchans, *Intimate Partner Violence,* US Department of Justice, NCJ 178247, 2000.

The lifetime rates of rape and attempted rape for women, by race, are: all women: 17.6%; white women: 17.7%; black women: 18.8%; Asian Pacific Islander women: 6.8%; American Indian/Alaskan women: 34.1%; and mixed race women: 24.4%. National Institute of Justice and Centers for Disease Control and Prevention, *Prevalence, Incidence and Consequences of Violence Against Women Survey* (1998).

37. Here is sociologist Karyn Lacy's description of Jack and Jill: "Founded by a group of upper middle-class mothers in 1938, *Jack and Jill*'s mission was to provide middle-class black children with the educational, cultural, and social

experiences traditionally reserved for middle-class white children. Membership in *Jack and Jill* is by invitation only (unless your mother held a membership), although this screening process is far less restrictive now than it was at the organization's founding. Early on, the organization acquired a reputation for snobbery." Lacy, "Black Spaces, Black Places: Strategic Assimilation and Identity Construction in Middle-Class Suburbia," *Ethnic and Racial Studies* 27 (2004): 923.

38. Harriet A. Washington, *Medical Apartheid: The Dark History of Medical Experimentation on Black Americans from Colonial Times to the Present* (New York: Doubleday, 2006).

39. Michelle van Ryn and Jane Burke, "The Effect of Patient Race and Socio-Economic Status on Physicians' Perceptions of Patients," *Social Science and Medicine* 50 (2000): 813–828.

40. Deborah Gray White, *Ar'n't I a Woman: Female Slaves in the Plantation South* (New York: W. W. Norton, 1985).

41. Dorothy Roberts, *Killing the Black Body: Race, Reproduction, and the Meaning of Liberty* (New York: Vintage, 1998).

42. See E. Frances White, *Dark Continent of Our Bodies: Black Feminism and the Politics of Respectability* (Philadelphia: Temple University Press, 2001); K. Sue Jewell, *From Mammy to Miss America and Beyond: Cultural Images and the Shaping of US Social Policy* (New York: Routledge, 1993); Leith Mullings, "Images, Ideology, and Women of Color," in *Women of Color in U.S. Society,* ed. Maxine Baca Zinn and Bonnie Thornton Dill (Philadelphia: Temple University Press, 1994), 265–289; Angela Y. Davis, *Women, Race, and Class* (New York: Vintage, 1981); Patricia Hill Collins, *Black Feminist Thought: Knowledge, Consciousness, and the Politics of Empowerment* (New York: Routledge, 1991); hooks, *Talking Back;* Ange-Marie Hancock, *The Politics of Disgust: The Public Identity of the Welfare Queen* (New York: New York University Press, 2004); Roberts, *Killing the Black Body;* Dána-Ain Davis, *Battered Black Women and Welfare Reform: Between a Rock and a Hard Place* (Albany: SUNY Press, 2006); Rupe Simms, "Controlling Images and the Gender Construction of Enslaved African Women," *Gender and Society* 15 (2001): 879–897; and Ivy Kennelly, "'That Single-Mother Element': How White Employers Typify Black Women," *Gender and Society* 13, no. 2 (1999): 168–192.

Chapter 2. Myth

Epigraph: Patricia Hill Collins, *Black Feminist Thought: Knowledge, Consciousness, and the Politics of Empowerment* (New York: Routledge, 1991), 69.

1. Ntozke Shange, *for colored girls who have considered suicide/ when the rainbow is enuf* (1975; New York: Simon and Schuster, 2010), 48, 49–50, 61.

2. Casey Gane-McCalla, "Tavis Smiley Draws 'Child Rape' Criticism for Publishing R. Kelly's Book," *News One for Black America,* December 16, 2009.

3. See Anita Hill and Emma Coleman Jordan, eds., *Race, Gender, and Power in America: The Legacy of the Hill-Thomas Hearings* (New York: Oxford University Press, 1995).

4. Kimberlé Crenshaw, "Whose Story Is It, Anyway? Feminist and Antiracist Appropriations of Anita Hill," in *Race-ing Justice, En-Gendering Power: Essays on Anita Hill, Clarence Thomas, and the Construction of Social Reality,* ed. Toni Morrison (New York: Pantheon Books, 1992), 402–440.

5. See Aaron Baker and Todd Boyd, eds., *Out of Bounds: Sports, Media and the Politics of Identity* (Bloomington: Indiana University Press, 1997).

6. Suzanne Lebsock, *The Free Women of Petersburg: Status and Culture in a Southern Town, 1784–1860* (New York: W. W. Norton, 1985).

7. Deborah Gray White, *Ar'n't I a Woman: Female Slaves in the Plantation South* (New York: W. W. Norton, 1985).

8. Thomas Jefferson, *Notes on the State of Virginia,* ed. Frank Shuffelton (1785; New York: Penguin Classics, 1998), 145.

9. Louis Agassiz as quoted in Harriet A. Washington, *Medical Apartheid: The Dark History of Medical Experimentation on Black Americans from Colonial Times to the Present* (New York: Doubleday, 2006), 46.

10. E. Frances White, *Dark Continent of Our Bodies: Black Feminism and the Politics of Respectability* (Philadelphia: Temple University Press, 2001), 34.

11. Paula Giddings, "The Last Taboo," in Morrison, *Race-ing Justice, En-Gendering Power,* 441–470.

12. Edward Said, *Orientalism* (New York: Vintage Books, 1978); Lee Baker, *From Savage to Negro: Anthropology and the Construction of Race, 1896–1954* (Berkeley: University of California Press, 1998).

13. Patricia Hill Collins writes: "The treatment of women within each respective nation-state as well as within the colonies were important to national identity. Ideas of pure White womanhood that were created to defend women of the homeland required a corresponding set of ideas about hot-blooded Latinas, exotic Suzy Wongs, wanton jezebels, and stoic native squaws. Civilized nation-states required uncivilized and backward colonies for their national identity to have meaning, and the status of women in both places was central to this endeavor. In this context, Black women became icons of hypersexuality." *Black Sexual Politics: African Americans, Gender, and the New Racism* (New York: Routledge, 2004), 30.

14. See the discussion of the dissection of Baartman by the French anatomist Georges Cuvier in Sander L. Gilman, "Black Bodies, White Bodies: Toward an

Iconography of Female Sexuality in Late Nineteenth-Century Art, Medicine, and Literature," *Critical Inquiry* 12 (1985): 204–242.

15. One of the most powerful engines of this transmission is Edward Livingston Youman's *Popular Science Monthly,* founded in 1872. For a discussion of this periodical's influence in nineteenth-century American racial discourse, see White, *Dark Continent of Our Bodies.*

16. Gilman traces the work of the Comte de Buffon, whose nineteenth-century scientific observations of black Africans included characterizations of the apelike sexuality of black women, including "that this animallike sexual appetite went so far as to lead black women to copulate with apes." "Black Bodies, White Bodies," 212.

17. Darlene Clark Hine, "Rape and the Inner Lives of Black Women in the Middle West," *Signs* 14 (1989): 912–920.

18. Paul Laurence Dunbar, "We Wear the Mask," in *Lyrics of Lowly Life* (New York: Dodd, Mead, 1896).

19. Hine, "Rape and the Inner Lives of Black Women," 915.

20. Ibid., 920.

21. Evelyn Brooks Higginbotham, *Righteous Discontent: The Women's Movement in the Black Baptist Church, 1880–1920* (Cambridge, MA: Harvard University Press, 1993); Stephanie Shaw, *What a Woman Ought to Be and to Do: Black Professional Women Workers During the Jim Crow Era* (Chicago: University of Chicago Press, 1996).

22. Darlene Clark Hine, *Hine Sight: Black Women and the Re-Construction of American History* (Bloomington: Indiana University Press, 1997), 45.

23. Hazel Carby, "Policing the Black Woman's Body in an Urban Context," *Critical Inquiry* 18 (1992): 738–755.

24. Evelynn M. Hammonds, "Toward a Genealogy of Black Female Sexuality: The Problematic of Silence," in *Feminist Theory and the Body: A Reader,* ed. Janet Price and Margrit Shildrick (New York: Routledge, 1999), 93–104. Political scientist Cathy Cohen describes this phenomenon as secondary marginalization. In her book *Boundaries of Blackness: AIDS and the Breakdown of Black Politics* (Chicago: University of Chicago Press, 1999), Cohen explains that African American political leaders mounted little initial response to AIDS crisis in black communities because doing so would have meant acknowledging and working with gay black men, intravenous drug users, and incarcerated persons. Traditional civil rights leaders shunned such work because it threatened their position in mainstream politics.

25. "Yet what seems so clear to many present-day feminists was not apparent to the club leaders: the need to attack the ideology behind the good woman/bad woman dichotomy. They struggled to have black women reclassified as good

women rather than expose the bankruptcy of the entire system." White, *Dark Continent of Our Bodies*, 35.

26. Farah Jasmine Griffin, *If You Can't Be Free Be a Mystery: In Search of Billie Holiday* (New York: Free Press, 2001).

27. Shayne Lee, *Erotic Revolutionaries: Black Women, Sexuality, and Popular Culture* (Lanham, MD: Hamilton Books, 2010).

28. Nataki Goodall, "Depend on Myself: T.L.C. and the Evolution of Black Female Rap," *Journal of Negro History* 79 (1994): 85–94.

29. Beretta E. Smith-Shomade, " 'Rock-a-Bye, Baby!': Black Women Disrupting Gangs and Constructing Hip-Hop Gangsta Films," *Cinema Journal* 42, no. 2 (2003): 25–40.

30. Ellis Cashmore, *The Black Culture Industry* (New York: Routledge, 1997). Several good sources analyze the central issues of black women's representation in hip-hop music and culture. See Tricia Rose, *Black Noise: Rap Music and Black Culture in Contemporary America* (Hanover, NH: Wesleyan University Press, University Press of New England, 1994); Rana A. Emerson, " 'Where My Girls At?': Negotiating Black Womanhood in Music Videos," *Gender and Society* 16, no. 1 (2002): 115–135; Joan Morgan, *When Chickenheads Come Home to Roost: My Life as a Hip-Hop Feminist* (New York: Simon and Schuster, 1999); Goodall, "Depend on Myself"; and Nghana Lewis, " 'You Sell Your Soul Like You Sell a Piece of Ass': Rhythms of Black Female Sexuality and Subjectivity in MeShell Ndegeocello's *Cookie: The Anthropological Mixtape*," *Black Music Research Journal* 26, no. 1 (2006): 111–130.

31. Lewis, " 'You Sell Your Soul Like You Sell a Piece of Ass,' " 114.

32. For a discussion of the role of reality television in promoting inaccurate and sexist images of and to women, see Jennifer L. Pozner, *Reality Bites Back: The Troubling Truth About Guilty Pleasure TV* (Berkeley, CA: Seal Press, 2010). There is an established feminist literature discussing the negative psychological effects of sexualized culture on white women. A foundational and accessible text in this area is Mary Pipher, *Reviving Ophelia: Saving the Selves of Adolescent Girls* (New York: G. P. Putnam's Sons, 1994).

33. Cathy J. Cohen, *Democracy Remixed: Black Youth and the Future of American Politics* (New York: Oxford University Press, 2010).

34. Martin Gilens, *Why Americans Hate Welfare: Race, Media, and the Politics of Antipoverty Policy* (Chicago: University of Chicago Press, 2000).

35. Ange-Marie Hancock, *The Politics of Disgust: The Public Identity of the Welfare Queen* (New York: New York University Press, 2004).

36. Dorothy Roberts, *Killing the Black Body: Race, Reproduction, and the Meaning of Liberty* (New York: Vintage, 1998).

37. For a more complete discussion of the political implications associated with the moral judgments about black youth sexuality, see Cohen, *Democracy Remixed.*

38. For an interesting example of how "mammy" was reported in academic historiography before the civil rights movement, see Jessie W. Parkhurst, "The Role of the Black Mammy in the Plantation Household," *Journal of Negro History* 23 (1938): 349–369.

39. K. Sue Jewell, *From Mammy to Miss America and Beyond: Cultural Images and the Shaping of US Social Policy* (New York: Routledge, 1993), 38.

40. Gilman, "Black Bodies, White Bodies."

41. Jo-Ann Morgan, "Mammy the Huckster: Selling the Old South for the New Century," *American Art* 9, no. 1 (1995): 86–109.

42. Micki McElya, *Clinging to Mammy: The Faithful Slave in Twentieth Century America* (Cambridge, MA: Harvard University Press, 2007).

43. Joan Marie Johnson, " 'Ye Gave Them a Stone': African American Women's Clubs, the Frederick Douglass Home, and the Black Mammy Monument," *Journal of Women's History* 17, no. 1 (2005): 62–86.

44. Cecil Elliot, "Monuments and Monumentality," *Journal of Architectural Education* 18, no. 4 (1964): 51–53. "A monument does not really function as a means of explicit communication. It is predicated upon the assumption that the viewer already knows pertinent facts about it and its subject, and the monuments are customarily overlaid with minutiae and subtleties of symbolism which are meaningless without the viewer's previous knowledge" (53). Thus the proposed Mammy monument of 1923 was not intended to create the myth of mammy but is a reflection of the broad acceptability of the stereotype already in existence.

45. Tera W. Hunter, *To 'Joy My Freedom: Southern Black Women's Lives and Labors After the Civil War* (Cambridge, MA: Harvard University Press, 1997).

46. Although the national monument movement was defeated, some states managed to memorialize Mammy in a number of ways. An enduring example is Georgia's Black Mammy Memorial Institute, discussed in June O. Patton, J. Strickland, and E. J. Crawford, "Moonlight and Magnolias in Southern Education: The Black Mammy Memorial Institute," *Journal of Negro History* 65 (1980): 149–155.

47. White, *Ar'n't I a Woman,* 189.

48. Morgan, "Mammy the Huckster," 87–88.

49. Jill Watts, *Hattie McDaniel: Black Ambition, White Hollywood* (New York: HarperCollins, 2005).

50. "When celebrating the figure of the black mother, whites never referred to her own family, a deliberate silence that allowed them to ignore the coercion that

helped make possible this intimate relationship between black female caretakers and their white charges. It also showed a fundamental lack of concern for black women's private emotions, their families, and the maternal work they performed outside the white domestic sphere." Micki McElya, *Clinging to Mammy: The Faithful Slave in Twentieth-Century America* (Cambridge, MA: Harvard University Press, 2007), 80–81.

51. Morgan, "Mammy the Huckster," 94.

52. Kim Euell, "Signifyin(g) Ritual: Subverting Stereotypes, Salvaging Icons," *African American Review* 31 (1997): 667–675.

53. Patton, Strickland, and Crawford, "Moonlight and Magnolias."

54. McElya, *Clinging to Mammy.*

55. Greg Braxton, "Buddy System," *Los Angeles Times,* August 29, 2007. Reflecting on the role of Black Best Friends (BBF) in movies and television, Braxton writes, "They are gorgeous, independent, loyal and successful. They live or work with their friend but are not really around all that much except for well-timed moments when the heroine needs an eating companion or is in crisis. BBFs basically have very little going on, so they are largely available for such moments. And even though they are single or lack consistent solid relationships, BBFs are experts in the ways of the world, using that knowledge to comfort, warn or scold their BFF."

56. Collins, *Black Sexual Politics,* 171.

57. As recorded by McElya, *Clinging to Mammy.*

58. "Rather than take care of her white owners like her Mammy predecessor, the Black superwoman now withstands adversity for the sake of her own family and community. However, many of the characteristics of fortitude and caretaking ascribed to strong Black women are an inversion of the Mammy myth and a continuation of the extreme selflessness that the Mammy role expected of Black women." Tamara Beauboeuf-Lafontant, "Strong and Large Black Women? Exploring Relationships Between Deviant Womanhood and Weight," *Gender and Society* 17, no. 1 (2003): 114.

59. Claudine Gay and Katherine Tate, "Doubly Bound: The Impact of Race and Gender on the Politics of Black Women," *Political Psychology* 19, no. 1 (1998): 182.

60. Melissa Harris-Lacewell, "Hillary's Scarlett O'Hara Act," *theRoot.com,* February 8, 2008.

61. Lori Ginzberg, *Elizabeth Cady Stanton: An American Life* (New York: Hill and Wang, 2009).

62. Barbara Hilkert Andolsen, *"Daughters of Jefferson, Daughters of Bootblacks": Racism and American Feminism* (Macon, GA: Mercer University Press, 1986).

63. For a useful source on contemporary African American women's compli-

cated relationship with feminism, see Duchess Harris, *Black Feminist Politics from Kennedy to Clinton* (New York: Palgrave Macmillan, 2009).

64. www.theangryblackwoman.wordpress.com/2008/02/14/a-black-woman-contemplates-breaking-up-with-feminism/.

65. www.foxnews.com/story/0,2933,367601,00.html.

66. A. Mitchell and K. Herring, *What the Blues Is All About: Black Women Overcoming Stress and Depression* (New York: Berkley, 1998); Jewell, *From Mammy to Miss America and Beyond.*

67. Marcyliena Morgan and Dionne Bennett, "Getting Off of Black Women's Backs: Love Her or Leave Her Alone," *Du Bois Review* 3 (2006): 490.

68. Charisse Jones and Kumea Shorter-Gooden, *Shifting: The Double Lives of Black Women in America* (New York: HarperCollins, 2003), 207.

69. Ivy Kennelly, " 'That Single-Mother Element': How White Employers Typify Black Women," *Gender and Society* 13, no. 2 (1999): 168–192.

70. Lynn Weber and Elizabeth Higginbotham, "Black and White Professional-Managerial Women's Perceptions of Racism and Sexism in the Workplace," in *Women and Work: Exploring Race, Ethnicity and Class,* ed. Elizabeth Higginbotham and Mary Romero (Thousand Oaks, CA: Sage, 1997), 153–175.

71. "Catalyst Women of Color in Corporate Management: Opportunities and Barriers–Executive Summary. New York," reported in Jones and Shorter-Gooden, *Shifting.*

72. James Scott, *Weapons of the Weak: Everyday Forms of Peasant Resistance* (New Haven: Yale University Press, 1985).

73. For a poignant and ironic take on this stereotype, see Denene Millner, Angela Burt-Murray, and Mitzi Miller, *The Angry Black Woman's Guide to Life* (New York: Plume, 2004). The authors both embrace and reject the stereotype, offering semiserious advice about how to deal with the stressors that cause black women to be angry. The authors also have a popular website: theangryblackwoman.com.

74. African Americans also took offense at the September 23, 2004, firing of the lone black female contestant on the *Apprentice* the season after Omarosa became famous. Stacie J. was a small business owner in Harlem. She was fired by Donald Trump when the women on her team suggested that she was "crazy" and expressed fear of her. Critics and journalists immediately pointed to how the firing of Stacie J. reinforced negative images of black women as scary and angry. For a more complete accounting of how race and gender stereotypes are used in reality television programming, see Pozner, *Reality Bites Back.*

75. Elsie J. Smith, "Mental Health and Service Delivery Systems for Black Women," *Journal of Black Studies* 12 (1981): 126–141.

76. Diagnosis is always a difficult matter and part of the harried territory of the

social construction of mental health and illness. The prevalence and causes of black mental health disorders has often been motivated by the racist intentions of those studying it. For black people, mental health is always politicized. An important source is Nancy Krieger, "Shades of Difference: Theoretical Underpinnings of the Medical Controversy on Black/White Differences in the United States, 1830–1870," *International Journal of Health Services* 17 (1987): 259–278. Krieger traces the political and ideological motivations for differential rates of diagnosis of both physical and mental ailments among black populations in the waning decades of slavery. For example, proslavery physicians claimed that the correlation between insanity rates and living in the North showed that freedom drove black people crazy. For more on this, see A. Deutsch, "The First US Census of the Insane (1840) and Its Use as Pro-Slavery Propaganda," *Bulletin of the History of Medicine* 15 (1944): 469–482.

77. James Patterson, *Freedom Is Not Enough: The Moynihan Report and America's Struggle over Black Family Life* (New York: Basic Books, 2010).

78. Hancock, *Politics of Disgust;* Julia Jordan-Zachery, "Black Womanhood and Social Welfare Policy: The Influence of Her Image on Policy Making," *Sage Race Relations Abstract* 26, no. 3 (2001): 5–24; Nikol G. Alexander-Floyd, *Gender, Race, and Nationalism in Contemporary Black Politics* (New York: Palgrave, 2007).

79. Morgan and Bennett, "Getting Off of Black Women's Backs," 499.

80. A brief history of the first decade of post-Moynihan social science inquiry on black women is available in Patricia Bell Scott, "Debunking Sapphire: Toward a Non-Racist and Non-Sexist Social Science," in *All the Women Are White, All the Blacks Are Men, But Some of Us Are Brave: Black Women's Studies,* ed. Gloria T. Hull, Patricia Bell Scott, and Barbara Smith (New York: Feminist Press, 1982), 85–92. For oppositional research, see Robert Staples, "The Myth of Black Matriarchy," *Black Scholar* 1 (1970): 8–16; and Andrew Billingsley, *Black Families in White America* (Englewood Cliffs, NJ: Prentice-Hall, 1969).

81. Michele Wallace, *Black Macho and the Myth of the Superwoman* (New York: Dial Press, 1979).

82. Alexander-Floyd, *Gender, Race, and Nationalism in Contemporary Black Politics,* 71.

83. Barbara Ransby, *Ella Baker and the Black Freedom Movement: A Radical Democratic Vision* (Chapel Hill: University of North Carolina Press, 2005).

84. Clayborne Carson, *In Struggle: SNCC and the Black Awakening of the 1960s* (Cambridge, MA: Harvard University Press, 1995), 148.

85. Tracey Matthews, " 'No One Ever Asks, What a Man's Place in the Revolution Is': Gender and Politics in the Black Panther Party, 1966–1971," in *The

Black Panther Party [Reconsidered], ed. Charles E. Jones (Baltimore: Black Classic Press, 1998), 267–304.

86. For a discussion of black feminist responses to the Million Man March, see Melissa Victoria Harris-Lacewell, *Barbershops, Bibles, and BET: Everyday Talk and Black Political Thought* (Princeton, NJ: Princeton University Press, 2004).

87. Toni Cade, ed., *The Black Woman: An Anthology* (New York: New American Library, 1970), 162–163.

88. Anthropologists Marcyliena Morgan and Dionne Bennett explain, "Stereotypes do not merely tell us how a culture 'sees' a group of people; they also tell us how a culture *controls* that group, how it bullies them into submitting to or evading the representations that haunt them." Morgan and Bennett, "Getting Off of Black Women's Backs," 490.

89. "The 'Angry Black Woman' [is] cultural ideology rather than social or psychological reality, an ideology that serves to silence and dehumanize Black women by blaming them for experiences of racist sexism that affect them in personal and political ways." Ibid., 486.

90. W. E. B. Du Bois, *The Souls of Black Folk* (1903; New York: Bantam Books, 1989), 3.

Chapter 3. Shame

Epigraph: Zora Neale Hurston, *Dust Tracks on a Road: An Autobiography* (1942; New York: Harper and Row, 1995), 177.

1. Psychologists Kumea Shorter-Gooden and N. Chanell Washington report data from their study of adolescent African American girls indicating that young black women often spoke about role models of strength. "Strength appears to refer to being tough, determined, and able to deal with the adversity one meets because of being Black, as well as to having a strong sense of self that is not overrun by others. Most of the participants conveyed that they either felt they had these qualities, that they were working to develop these qualities, or that they admired these characteristics in those people who had had the most impact on their identity development." Shorter-Gooden and Washington, "Young, Black and Female: The Challenge of Weaving an Identity," *Journal of Adolescence* 19 (1996): 470.

2. E. J. Barnes, "The Black Community as the Source of Positive Self-Concept for Black Children: A Theoretical Perspective," in *Black Psychology,* 2nd ed., ed. R. L. Jones (New York: Harper and Row, 1980), 106–130.

3. T. A. Parham and J. E. Helms, "Attitudes of Racial Identity and Self-Esteem of Black Students: An Explanatory Investigation," *Journal of College Stu-*

dent Personnel 26 (1985): 143–147; J. S. Phinney, "Stages of Ethnic Identity Development in Minority Group Adolescents," *Journal of Early Adolescence* 9 (1985): 34–39.

4. The survey question wording was as follows: "We would like to know how you feel when you think about black women in general. When you think about today's black woman, what emotions do you have? There is no right or wrong way to feel. Now, thinking about black women today, please consider each of the emotions that are listed below. To what extent do you have each of the following emotions?"

5. Meyer Fortes, *Kinship and the Social Order: The Legacy of Lewis Henry Morgan* (Chicago: Aldine, 1969); Julian Pitt-Rivers, "The Kith and Kin," in *The Character of Kinship,* ed. J. Goody (Cambridge: Cambridge University Press, 1973); Carol Stack, *All Our Kin: Strategies for Survival in a Black Community* (New York: Harper and Row, 1974).

6. Michael C. Dawson, *Behind the Mule: Race and Class in African-American Politics* (Princeton, NJ: Princeton University Press, 1994).

7. Melissa Victoria Harris-Lacewell, *Barbershops, Bibles, and BET: Everyday Talk and Black Political Thought* (Princeton, NJ: Princeton University Press, 2004).

8. Helen Block Lewis, *Shame and Guilt Neurosis* (New York: International Universities Press, 1971); Susan Miller, *The Shame Experience* (Hillsdale, NJ: Analytic Press, 1985); Gershen Kaufman, *The Psychology of Shame: Theory and Treatment of Shame-Based Syndromes* (New York: Springer, 1989). For a review on shame as a research topic, see June Price Tangney and Kurt W. Fischer, eds., *Self-Conscious Emotions: The Psychology of Shame, Guilt, Embarrassment, and Pride* (New York: Guilford, 1995).

9. One notable exception is the field of queer studies, where shame has played a central role in theorizing for two decades. A terrific resource for understanding how scholars in the field have approached the issues of shame is the volume edited by David M. Halperin and Valerie Traub, *Gay Shame* (Chicago: University of Chicago Press, 2009). The contributors to this volume explore the role of gay pride and gay shame in shaping contemporary political efforts in LGBT communities.

10. Sally S. Dickerson et al., "Immunological Effects of Induced Shame and Guilt," *Psychosomatic Medicine* 66 (2004): 124–131.

11. Shorter-Gooden and Washington, "Young, Black, and Female"; Bonnie Moradi, Janice D. Yoder, and Lynne L. Berendsen, "An Evaluation of the Psychometric Properties of the Womanist Identity Attitudes Scale," *Sex Roles* 50 (2004): 253–266.

12. Tangney and Fischer, *Self-Conscious Emotions.*

13. Nita Lutwak, Ben Razzino, and Joseph Ferrari, "Self-Perceptions and Moral Affect: An Exploratory Analysis of Subcultural Diversity in Guilt and Shame Emotions," *Journal of Social Behavior and Personality* 13 (1998): 333–348.

14. Tangney and Fischer, *Self-Conscious Emotions.*

15. "Consequently, repeated experiences of shame have been found to be associated to a number of negative cognitive-behavioral experiences, including depression, self-derogation, shyness, interpersonal anxiety, perfectionism, and a diffuse-oriented identity." Lutwak, Razzino, and Ferrari, "Self-Perceptions and Moral Affect," 334.

16. Janice Lindsay-Hartz, "Contrasting Experiences of Shame and Guilt," *American Behavioral Scientist* 27 (1984): 696.

17. A. Browne and D. Finkelhor, "Impact of Childhood Sexual Abuse: A Review of the Research," *Psychological Bulletin* 99 (1986): 66–77.

18. Helen Block Lewis, "The Role of Shame in Depression over the Life Span," in *The Role of Shame in Symptom Formation,* ed. Lewis (Hillsdale, NJ: Lawrence Erlbaum, 1987), ch. 2; Hartmut B. Mokros, "Suicide and Shame," *American Behavioral Scientist* 38 (1995): 1091–1103; Paul Gilbert, "The Evolution of Social Attractiveness and Its Role in Shame, Humiliation, Guilt and Therapy," *British Journal of Medical Psychology* 30 (1997): 113–147.

19. "Implicit in the idea of the self and self boundaries is the fact that we are also accustomed to an automatic localization of the self in the field, including the field of space. Localization of the self in the field involves the literal localization of the body in space. It also involves the localization of experience as originating within the integument (within the body) or originating 'out there.' The self is a necessary reference point for this localization of the source of experience. In the experience of shame, the source of blame or negative valuation of the self is localized as 'out there.'" Block, *Shame and Guilt in Neurosis,* 32.

20. Thomas Jefferson, *Notes on the State of Virginia,* ed. Frank Shuffelton (1785; New York: Penguin Classics, 1998), 145.

21. J. P. Tangney et al., "Are Shame, Guilt, and Embarrassment Distinct Emotions?" *Journal of Personality and Social Psychology* 70 (1996): 1256–1269; P. Gilbert, "Varieties of Submissive Behavior as Forms of Social Defense: Their Evolution and Role in Depression," in *Subordination and Defeat: An Evolutionary Approach to Mood Disorder and Their Therapy,* ed. Leon Sloman and Paul Gilbert (Mahwah, NJ: Lawrence Erlbaum Associates, 2000), 3–48.

22. Dickerson et al., "Immunological Effects of Induced Shame and Guilt"; C. Kirschbaum and D. H. Hellhammer, "Salivary Cortisol in Psychoneuroendocrine Research: Recent Developments and Applications," *Psychoneuroendo-*

crinology 19 (1994): 313–333; Michael Lewis and Douglas Ramsey, "Cortisol Response to Embarrassment and Shame," *Child Development* 73 (2002): 1034–1045.

23. "We randomly assigned participants to conditions in which they wrote about an experience of self-blame or a neutral topic on three separate days over a week period. Participants in the self-blame condition wrote about a variety of stressful situations, including experiences of rejection and failing to live up to parental expectations. The self-blame induction elicited greater increases in shame and guilt than other emotions measured, and this increase was observed on each of the three experimental days. In addition, the reception for TNF- α(sTNF-RII), a marker of pro-inflammatory cytokine activity, significantly increased from pre- to post-writing across the three days among the individuals in the self-blame condition, while there were no changes for those in the control condition. Furthermore, among the participants in the self-blame condition, those who reported the greatest increases in shame also showed the greatest increases in pro inflammatory cytokine activity, but anger, guilt, anxiety, sadness and general negative emption were unrelated to this parameter. Together these findings suggest that the experience of self-blame and self-related emotions can elicit changes in pro-inflammatory cytokine activity, and that there could be a specific relationship between shame and inflammatory markers." Tara Gruenewald, Sally Dickerson, and Margaret Kemeny, "A Social Function for Self-Conscious Emotions," in *The Self-Conscious Emotions: Theory and Research* ed. Jessica Tracy, Richard Robins, and June Tangney (New York: Guilford, 2007), 77–78.

24. "Shame and accompanying physiology are integral component of a coordinated psychobiological response to threats to social self preservation, just as fear and its physiological correlates are components of the response to threats to physical self preservation." Sally S. Dickerson, Tara L. Gruenewald, and Margaret E. Kemeny, "When the Social Self Is Threatened: Shame, Physiology, and Health," *Journal of Personality* 72 (2004): 1193.

25. Dickerson et al., "Immunological Effects of Induced Shame and Guilt."

26. Some researchers have been particularly interested in how shame is implicated in the progression of HIV-AIDS. Because HIV-AIDS is both an immune disorder and a socially stigmatized condition, researchers are particularly interested in how shame affects the quality of health and immune functioning in AIDS patients. See, e.g., T. T. Lewis et al., "Perceived Interpersonal Rejection and CD4 Decline in a Community Sample of Women Infected with HIV," *Journal of Personality* (2004): 1191–1216.

27. Lisa Silberstein, Ruth Striegel-Moore, and Judith Rodin, "Feeling Fat: A Woman's Shame," in Lewis, *Role of Shame in Symptom Formation,* 89–108.

28. Carolyn West, "Mammy, Sapphire, and Jezebel: Historical Images of

Black Women and Their Implications for Psychotherapy," *Psychotherapy* 32 (1995): 458–466; N. Boyd-Franklin, *Black Families in Therapy: A Multisystems Approach* (New York: Guilford, 1989). See also Beverly Greene, Judith White, and Lisa Whitten, "Hair Texture, Length and Style as a Metaphor in the African American Mother-Daughter Relationship: Considerations in Psychodynamic Psychotherapy," in *Psychotherapy with African American Women: Innovations in Psychodynamic Perspectives and Practice,* ed. Leslie C. Jackson and Beverly Greene (New York: Guilford, 2000), 166–193; and M. Okazawa-Rey, T. Robinson, and J. V. Ward, "Black Women and the Politics of Skin Color and Hair," *Women and Therapy* 6 (1987): 89–102.

29. Erving Goffman, *Interaction Ritual* (New York: Anchor, 1967).

30. John Braithwaite, *Crime, Shame and Reintegration* (Melbourne: Cambridge University Press, 1989).

31. Sheldon X. Zhang, "Measuring Shaming in an Ethnic Context," *British Journal of Criminology* 35 (1995): 248–261.

32. For discussion of the adaptive purposes of shame, see John Braithwaite, "Shame and Modernity," *British Journal of Criminology* 33 (1933): 1–18.

33. Braithwaite, *Crime, Shame and Reintegration.*

34. Ibid.

35. Martha C. Nussbaum, *Hiding from Humanity: Disgust, Shame, and the Law* (Princeton, NJ: Princeton University Press, 2004), 174.

36. Paul Gilbert, "The Evolution of Social Attractiveness," *British Journal of Medical Psychology* 70 (1997): 113–147; M. Daly and M. Wilson, "Evolutionary Psychology of Male Violence," in *Male Violence,* ed. John Archer (London: Routledge, 1994), 253–288; Melvin Lansky, "Shame and Domestic Violence," in *The Many Faces of Shame,* ed. Donald L. Nathanson (New York: Guilford, 1987), 335–362.

37. Nussbaum argues that states should not only refrain from shaming their own citizens but should also refrain from shaming their opponents. Pointing to the example of abuses by American military personnel of Muslim prisoners at Abu Ghraib prison, she contends that prisoners there were treated as though their very bodies and lives were criminal, rather than being held for any given act that they committed. Nussbaum, *Hiding from Humanity.*

38. June Price Tangney, Patricia Wagner, and Carey Fletcher, "Shamed into Anger? The Relation of Shame and Guilt to Anger and Self-Reported Aggression," *Journal of Personality and Social Psychology* 62 (1992): 669–675.

39. Nussbaum, *Hiding from Humanity.*

40. W. E. B. Du Bois, *The Souls of Black Folk* (1903; New York: Bantam Books, 1989), 1.

41. Elizabeth Abel, "Bathroom Doors and Drinking Fountains: Jim Crow's Racial Symbolic," *Critical Inquiry* 25 (1999): 435–481.

42. The Cook thirty-item scale, called the Internalized Shame Scale (ISS), is consistently negatively correlated with various measures of self-esteem, including the Coopersmith Self-Esteem Inventory Scale, Tennessee Self Concept Scale, and the Janis-Field Feelings of Inadequacy Scale. David R. Cook, "Measuring Shame: The Internalized Shame Scale," *Alcoholism Treatment Quarterly* 4 (1987): 197–215; Cook, "Shame, Attachment, and Addictions: Implications for Family Therapists," *Contemporary Family Therapy* 13 (1991): 405–418; Christopher J. Rybak and Beverly Brown, "Validity and Reliability of the Internalized Shame Scale," *Alcoholism Treatment Quarterly* 14 (1996): 71–83.

43. Stéphane D. Dandeneau and Mark W. Baldwin, "The Inhibition of Socially Rejecting Information Among People with High Versus Low Self-Esteem: The Role of Attentional Bias and the Effects of Bias Reduction Training," *Journal of Social and Clinical Psychology* 23 (2004): 584–602.

44. C. Vann Woodward, *The Strange Career of Jim Crow* (1955; New York: Oxford University Press, 2001).

45. Glenda Elizabeth Gilmore, *Defying Dixie: The Radical Roots of Civil Rights, 1919–1950* (New York: W. W. Norton, 2008), 15.

46. Philip Alexander Bruce, "Evolution of the Negro Problem" [1911], in *The Development of Segregationist Thought,* ed. I. A. Newby (Homewood, IL: Dorsey, 1968).

47. Jennifer Ritterhouse, *Growing Up Jim Crow: The Racial Socialization of Black and White Southern Children, 1890–1940* (Chapel Hill: University of North Carolina Press, 2006).

48. Abel, "Bathroom Doors and Drinking Fountains."

49. Norbert Elias, *The Civilizing Process: The History of Manners and State Formation and Civilization,* trans. Edmund Jephcott (Oxford: Blackwell, 1978).

50. Earlier theorists have argued that because shame is related to power it is class-structured and profoundly gendered. Braithwaite provides an example, "White-collar workers will shamelessly indulge inconsiderate behaviour in the gaze of their secretary that they would never indulge in the presence of their boss." Braithwaite, "Shame and Modernity," 4–5.

51. Glenda Elizabeth Gilmore, *Gender and Jim Crow: Women and the Politics of White Supremacy in North Carolina, 1896–1920* (Chapel Hill: University of North Carolina Press, 1996).

52. Stephanie J. Shaw, *What a Woman Ought to Be and Do: Black Professional Women Workers During the Jim Crow Era* (Chicago: University of Chicago Press, 1996).

53. Blair Kelley, *Right to Ride: Streetcar Boycotts and African American Citizenship in the Era of Plessy v. Ferguson* (Chapel Hill: University of North Carolina Press, 2010).

54. Joe William Trotter Jr., ed., *The Great Migration in Historical Perspective: New Dimensions of Race, Class, and Gender* (Bloomington: Indiana University Press, 1991). See also the classic text on African American urban life in the interwar period: St. Clair Drake and Horace R. Cayton, *Black Metropolis: A Study of Negro Life in a Northern City* (Chicago: University of Chicago Press, 1946).

55. Hazel Carby, "Policing the Black Woman's Body in an Urban Context," *Critical Inquiry* 18 (1992): 738–755.

56. Judith Weisenfeld, *African American Women and Christian Activism: New York's Black YWCA, 1905–1945* (Cambridge, MA: Harvard University Press, 1998).

57. Carby, "Policing the Black Woman's Body." See also Davarian L. Baldwin, *Chicago's New Negroes: Modernity, the Great Migration, and Black Urban Life* (Chapel Hill: University of North Carolina Press, 2007).

58. "Experiences of the Race Problem by a Southern White Woman," *Independent* 56 (March 17, 1904), quoted in Beverly Guy-Sheftall, *Daughters of Sorrow: Attitudes Toward Black Women, 1880–1920* (New York: Carlson, 1991), 46.

59. James Patterson, *Freedom Is Not Enough: The Moynihan Report and America's Struggle over Black Family Life* (New York: Basic Books, 2010).

60. Ange-Marie Hancock, *The Politics of Disgust: The Public Identity of the Welfare Queen* (New York: New York University Press, 2004).

61. Susan Douglas and Meredith Michaels, *The Mommy Myth: The Idealization of Motherhood and How It Has Undermined Women* (New York: Free Press, 2004), 190.

62. Dorothy Roberts, *Killing the Black Body: Race, Reproduction, and the Meaning of Liberty* (New York: Pantheon, 1997), 226.

63. Jennifer Nelson, *Women of Color and the Reproductive Rights Movement* (New York: New York University Press, 2003); Roberts, *Killing the Black Body*.

64. Suezanne Orr et al., "Psychosocial Stressors and Low Birthweight in an Urban Population," *American Journal of Preventive Medicine* 12(1996): 459–466; J. P. Harrell, S. Hall, and J. Taliaferro, "Physiological Response to Racism and Discrimination: An Assessment of the Evidence," *American Journal of Public Health* 93 (2003): 243–248.

65. Suezanne Orr, Sherman A. James, and Cheryl Blackmore Prince, "Maternal Prenatal Depressive Symptoms and Spontaneous Preterm Births Among African-American Women in Baltimore, MD," *American Journal of Epidemiology* 156 (2002): 797–802.

66. Clinical researchers have established that stress, like shame, is implicated in elevated cortisol and depressed immunity. Kenneth Rosenberg, Rani Desai, and Jinali Kan, "Why Do Foreign-Born Blacks Have Lower Infant Mortality than Native-Born Blacks? New Directions in African-American Infant Mortality Research," *Journal of National Medical Association* 94 (2002): 770–778; James Collins et al., "Very Low Birthweight in African American Infants: The Role of Maternal Exposure to Interpersonal Racial Discrimination," *American Journal of Public Health* 94 (2004): 2132–2138.

67. These effects were independent of medical and socioeconomic variables. James Collins et al., "Low-Income African-American Mothers' Perception of Exposure to Racial Discrimination and Infant Birth Weight," *Epidemiology* 11 (2000): 337–339.

68. On self-esteem, see M. Hughes and D. H. Demo, "Self-Perceptions of Black Americans: Self-Esteem and Personal Efficacy," *American Journal of Sociology* 95 (1989): 132–159; and Parham and Helms, "Attitudes of Racial Identity and Self-Esteem in Black Students." On mental health, see Robert M. Sellers et al., "Racial Identity, Racial Discrimination, Perceived Stress, and Psychological Distress Among African American Young Adults," *Journal of Health and Social Behavior* 44 (2003): 302–317. On political activity, see Richard Shingles, "Black Consciousness and Political Participation: The Missing Link," *American Political Science Review* 75 (1981): 76–91.

69. Lutwak, Razzino, and Ferrari, "Self-Perceptions and Moral Affect," 333.

70. Andrew Delbanco, "The Political Incorrectness of Zora Neale Hurston," *Journal of Blacks in Higher Education* 18 (Winter 1997–1998): 103–108. See also David Krasner, "Migration, Fragmentation, and Identity: Zora Neale Hurston's *Color Struck* and the Geography of the Harlem Renaissance," in *Beautiful Pageant: African American Theatre, Drama, and Performance in the Harlem Renaissance, 1910–1927* (New York: Palgrave Macmillan, 2002), 113–130.

71. Signithia Fordham, "Racelessness as a Factor in Black Students' School Success: A Pragmatic Strategy or Pyrrhic Victory?" *Harvard Educational Review* 58 (1988): 54–85.

72. Stephen Dale Jefferson, "The Role of Shame in African American Racial Identity: A Bridge to Negative Affect" (PhD diss., Michigan State University, 2001), 17.

73. Nita Lutwak and Joseph R. Ferrari, "Moral Affect and Cognitive Processes: Differentiating Shame from Guilt Among Men and Women," *Personality and Individual Differences* 21 (1996): 891–896.

74. Ibid.

75. Suzanne Lebsock, *The Free Women of Petersburg: Status and Culture in a Southern Town, 1784–1860* (New York: W. W. Norton, 1984).

76. See above, ch. 1, n. 28.

77. Catherine Lu, "Shame, Guilt and Reconciliation After War," *European Journal of Social Theory* 11 (2008): 367–383; Gaines Foster, *Ghosts of the Confederacy Defeat, the Lost Cause, and the Emergence of the New South, 1865–1913* (New York: Oxford University Press, 1988).

78. Halperin and Traub, *Gay Shame.*

79. Jefferson, "Role of Shame in African American Racial Identity," 16.

80. Rose Weitz, "Women and Their Hair: Seeking Power Through Resistance and Accommodation," *Gender and Society* 15 (2001): 667–686.

81. For a review of these arguments, see Bill Cosby and Alvin F. Poussaint, MD, *Come On, People: On the Path from Victims to Victors* (New York: Thomas Nelson, 2007); and Michael Eric Dyson, *Is Bill Cosby Right? Or Has the Black Middle Class Lost Its Mind?* (New York: Perseus Books, 2006).

82. Fordham, "Racelessness as a Factor in Black Students' School Success."

83. Nina Parikh et al., "Shame and Health Literacy: The Unspoken Connection," *Patient Education and Counseling* 27 (2996): 33–39.

84. Bruce McEwen, "Protective and Damaging Effects of Stress Mediators," *New England Journal of Medicine* 338 (1998): 171–179.

85. Thomas J. Scheff, "Interminable Quarrels: Shame-Rage as a Social and a Psychological Spiral," in Lewis, *Role of Shame in Symptom Formation.* See also Thomas J. Scheff and Suzanne M. Retzinger, *Emotions and Violence: Shame and Rage in Destructive Conflicts* (Lexington, MA: Lexington Books, 1991).

86. Gershen Kaufman, *The Psychology of Shame: Theory and Treatment of Shame-Based Syndromes,* 2nd ed. (New York: Springer, 2004), 97.

87. Ibid.

88. Robert Joseph Taylor, Bogart R. Leashore, and Susan Toliver, "An Assessment of the Provider Role as Perceived by Black Males," *Family Relations* 37 (1988): 426 431.

89. Scheff and Retzinger, *Emotions and Violence.*

90. There is a rich tradition of literary criticism engaging Morrison's *The Bluest Eye.* Several pieces specifically bring a psychoanalytic lens to the text or deal directly with issues of depression or shame. See Cat Moses, "The Blues Aesthetic in Toni Morrison's *The Bluest Eye,*" *African American Review* 33 (1999): 623–637; Cynthia Davis, "Self, Society, and Myth in Toni Morrison's Fiction," *Contemporary Literature* 23 (1982): 323–342; and Jane Kuenz, "*The Bluest Eye:* Notes on History, Community, and Black Female Subjectivity," *African American Review* 27 (1993): 421–431. For me the most useful article in thinking through the specific arguments of shame in the text is Kathleen Woodward, "Traumatic Shame: Toni Morrison, Televisual Culture, and the Cultural Politics of the Emotions," *Cultural Critique* 46 (2000): 210–240.

91. For more on the meanings of Morrison's style and form in this text, see Linda Dittmar, 'Will the Circle Be Unbroken?' The Politics of Form in *The Bluest Eye*," *Novel: A Forum on Fiction* 23, no. 2 (1990): 137–155.

92. A similar argument about Claudia's function as a child narrator is made by Woodward, "Traumatic Shame."

93. Toni Morrison, *The Bluest Eye* (New York: Plume, 1970), 11–12, 12.

94. Ibid., 36, 72.

95. Ibid., 39.

96. Ibid., 107, 112, 127. Pauline does retain some agency and independence from her role as domestic servant for the white family. Though she shows them little affection, she does live with her own family. This decision to "live-out" is a choice that Pauline makes early on in her life as a domestic. At her first job, a wealthy white woman she worked for tried to convince her to leave Cholly after he comes to the house and abuses Pauline. The white woman tells Pauline that she can't return unless she divorces Cholly, but Pauline thinks, "it didn't seem none too bright for a black woman to leave a black man for a white woman." As much as Pauline has embraced the role of mammy, she still resists being entirely defined by her relationship to white domestic space. Ibid., 120.

97. Ibid., 148, 150.

98. Ibid., 190.

99. Kuenz, "*The Bluest Eye*."

100. Morrison, *Bluest Eye*, 210.

101. For a description of the cognitive science that undergirds these claims, see Alan Schore, "Early Shame Experiences and Infant Brain Development," in *Shame: Interpersonal Behavior, Psychopathology, and Culture,* ed. Paul Gilbert and Bernice Andrews (New York: Oxford University Press, 1998), ch. 3.

102. Michael Lewis, *Shame: The Exposed Self* (Detroit: Free Press, 1995).

103. Kaufman, *Psychology of Shame,* 2nd ed.; Schore, "Early Shame Experiences and Infant Brain Development."

Chapter 4. Disaster

Epigraph: Denise Roubion-Johnson's extraordinary narrative of her experiences in New Orleans during and after the Hurricane Katrina disaster is recorded in D'Ann R. Penner and Keith C. Ferdinand, *Overcoming Katrina: African American Voices from the Crescent City and Beyond* (New York: Palgrave Macmillan, 2009), 79.

1. *When the Levees Broke: A Requiem in Four Acts* premiered at the New Orleans Arena on August 16, 2006. The television premiere aired in two parts on

August 21 and 22, 2006, on HBO. The film was shown in its entirety on August 29, 2006, the one-year anniversary of Katrina's landfall. The film had wide-reaching consequences for American understandings of the disaster through its curriculum component "Teaching the Levees." "Teaching the Levees" is an official curriculum that includes supporting materials and web-based resources. The curriculum, funded by the Rockefeller Foundation and created by educators from Teachers College, Columbia University, takes the film as the basis for a pedagogical intervention for discussions of race and national politics in schools, colleges, and community organizations.

2. Phyllis Montana-Leblanc, *Not Just the Levees Broke: My Story During and After Hurricane Katrina* (New York: Atria, 2008).

3. Ibid., 5, 46.

4. Portions of this chapter come from my article "Do You Know What It Means . . . : Mapping Emotion in the Aftermath of Katrina," *Souls* 9, no. 1 (2007): 28–44.

5. The Hurricane Katrina Survey, sponsored by the Pew Research Center for the People and the Press, obtained telephone interviews with a nationally representative sample of one thousand adults living in continental US telephone households. The survey was conducted by Princeton Survey Research International. Interviews were done in English by Princeton Data Source, LLC, September 7–8, 2005. Statistical results are weighted to correct known demographic discrepancies. The margin of sampling error for the complete set of weighted data is ±3.5 percent.

The oversample of African Americans is designed to allow a sufficient number of interviews for reporting results of this demographic group. The national sample of telephone households was supplemented with an additional 103 interviews with African Americans whose households had been recently contacted for past Pew Research Center national surveys. Demographic weighting was used to ensure that the survey results reflect the correct racial and ethnic composition of national adults, based on US Census information.

6. Kimberly Gross and Marcie Kohenak, "Race, Poverty, and Causal Attributions: Media Framing of the Aftermath of Hurricane Katrina" (Unpublished ms, presented at Midwest Political Science Association, April 2007).

7. Daniel Hopkins, "Flooded Communities: Explaining Local Reactions to the Post-Katrina Migrants" (Unpublished ms, presented at American Political Science Association, 2009).

8. News sources mattered for the conclusions that Americans drew about the efficiency of presidential response. Seventy-three percent of CNN watchers reported that the president could have done more, but only 50 percent of Fox News

viewers agreed. Forty-six percent of those whose primary source of Katrina coverage was Fox News believed that the president had done all he could.

9. This Pew survey reports a 50 percent approval rating for President Bush in January 2005 and a 40 percent approval rating immediately following Katrina.

10. Jonathan Weisman and Michael Abramowitz, "Many See Storm as President's Undoing," *Washington Post,* August 26, 2006.

11. Montana-Leblanc, *Not Just the Levees Broke,* 90–91, 101, 171.

12. Ibid., 81, 111.

13. Ibid., 102.

14. One such story comes from Harold Toussaint and is recorded in Penner and Ferdinand, *Overcoming Katrina.* He reports, "All these federal police saw was that I was black, and blacks are criminal. That's what I got from them when we needed them most. It was very discouraging to be treated as an enemy combatant rather than someone who needed to be rescued" (53). Toussaint goes on to describe this misrecognition as shaming experience: "The military people that came from the outside treated us like we were diseased or contaminated" (54). Psychologists describe shame as the feeling of being a malignant self. This sense of contamination is a description of shame.

15. Ibid., 74.

16. Hurricane Katrina Survey.

17. The Center for the Study of Race, Politics, and Culture at the University of Chicago supported a national survey of Americans to gauge political and racial attitudes in the aftermath of Hurricane Katrina. Principal investigators were Michael Dawson, Melissa Harris-Lacewell, and Cathy Cohen. The data were collected by Knowledge Networks, October 28–November 17, 2005. Knowledge Networks employs a Random Digit Dialing (RDD) telephone methodology to develop a representative sample of households for participation in its panel. Once a Knowledge Networks household is selected, members are contacted first by an express delivery mailing and then by telephone for enrollment in the Knowledge Networks panel. The panel structure enables clients to conduct surveys of low-incidence populations, such as African Americans, more efficiently and inexpensively than would otherwise be possible. Every participating Knowledge Networks household receives free hardware, free Internet access, free e-mail accounts, and ongoing technical support. Participants receive a short multimedia survey about once a week. Surveys are delivered by e-mail on the same standardized hardware, through the television set. The data include responses from 1,252 Americans. The racial composition of the respondents is as follows: White, 703; Black, 487; Hispanic, 52; Other, 10. Interviews were conducted in person by Melissa Harris-Lacewell in various locations in New Orleans, November 11–18, 2005. Interviews

include twenty-eight personal discussions with local residents and hours of transcripts from three community meetings about rebuilding efforts.

18. The difference in emotional response exists for respondents who have the most extreme responses and those who have more average emotional responses to the Katrina disaster (see Appendix, table 2). The racial differences in emotional states remain when we consider the average of white and black survey respondents. Each item in the table is coded on a unit scale so that higher numbers reflect greater emotional distress. Although the absolute difference between blacks and whites is dampened when we consider average scores, the racial disparity remains statistically significant for each item. Black respondents are significantly more distressed in the weeks following Katrina than are whites.

19. Paul B. Amato, "Parental Absence During Childhood and Depression During Later Life," *Sociological Quarterly* 32 (1991): 543–556; N. Breslau et al., "Trauma and Posttraumatic Stress Disorder in the Community: The 1996 Detroit Area Survey of Trauma," *Archives of General Psychiatry* 55 (1998): 626–623; Linda George and Scott Lynch, "Race Differences in Depressive Symptoms: A Dynamic Perspective on Stress Exposure and Vulnerability," *Journal of Health and Social Behavior* 44 (2003): 353–369.

20. William Cockerman, "A Test of the Relationship Between Race, Socioeconomic Status and Psychological Distress," *Social Science and Medicine* 31 (1990): 321–331; Ronald C. Kessler and Harold W. Neighbors, "A New Perspective on the Relationships Among Race, Social Class, and Psychological Distress," *Journal of Health and Social Behavior* 27 (1987): 107–115.

21. Research shows that in the days and weeks following September 11, Americans experienced elevated stress and signs of probable post-traumatic stress disorder. In the two months following the attack, 17 percent of respondents in a national sample reported post-traumatic stress symptoms. The National Opinion Research Center (NORC) at the University of Chicago conducted the National Tragedy Study September 13–27, 2001. NORC interviewed 2,126 Americans and with an oversample of residents in New York City and Washington, DC. The National Tragedy Study replicated a series of questions used to gauge the emotional state of Americans in the days following the assassination of President Kennedy in 1963. The Kennedy Assassination Survey Symptom Checklist (KA-SSC) measures fifteen physical and emotional reactions to traumatic shock. Research from these data reports that New York residents (both black and white) have elevated negative emotion scores compared with their counterparts in the general population. These data further show that when negative emotions are modeled as a function of race, gender, age, education, income, and employment and estimated with an ordinary least squares regression, the results demonstrate that in the days

immediately following September 11, there was no statistically significant differ-
ence in KASSC scores among blacks and whites in either the national or the New
York samples. In the case of September 11, proximity to the disaster was much
more important than race in predicting initial emotional responses. See Kenneth
Rasinski et al., "The 9/11 Terrorist Attacks: Ethnic Differences in Emotional
Response and Recovery" (National Opinion Research Center, University of Chi-
cago, 2002); M. A. Schuster, B. D. Stein, and L. Jaycox, "A National Survey of
Stress Reactions After the September 11, 2001, Terrorist Attack," *Journal of the
American Medical Association* 345 (2001): 1507–1512; W. E. Schlenger et al., "Psy-
chological Reactions to Terrorist Attacks: Findings from the National Study of
Americans' Reactions to September 11," *Journal of the American Medical Associa-
tion* 288 (2002): 581–588; Roxane Cohen Silver et al., "Nationwide Longitudinal
Study of Psychological Responses to September 11," *Journal of the American
Medical Association* 288 (2002): 1235–1244.

22. N. Breslau, G. C. Davis, and P. Andreski, "Risk Factors for PTSD-
Related Traumatic Events: A Prospective Analysis," *American Journal of Psychiatry* 152 (1995): 529–535.

23. Quotations cited in Melissa Harris-Lacewell, "Do You Know What It
Means . . . : Mapping Emotion in the Aftermath of Katrina," *Souls: A Critical
Journal of Black Politics, Culture, and Society* 9, no. 1 (2007): 28–44.

24. To test the hypothesis that Americans' affective responses to Katrina were
primarily rooted in a particular understanding of America's racial history, the
following analysis estimates a model of emotional distress among black Americans
in the weeks following Katrina as a function of personal, political, and racial
variables. This estimation is performed using data from the University of Chicago
Center for the Study of Race, Politics, and Culture Racial Attitudes and Katrina
Disaster Study.

Researchers normally do not think of an individual's mental or emotional state
as resulting primarily from world political events. Decades of epidemiological
work have convincingly demonstrated that we can make predictions about the
likelihood that an individual will feel depressed, angry, or fragile based on a
number of personal characteristics and proximate life circumstances. Even in the
days and weeks following Katrina we should expect that most emotional variability
between individuals is directly related to durable and personal patterns that have
been explicated in previous research. We should expect that poorer and less
educated Americans should generally feel more psychological distress than their
more affluent counterparts. We should expect women to express more sadness
than men and for the very young and very old to express more sadness than those
who are middle-aged. In light of these expectations, the equations estimated below
control for education, income, sex, and age.

Acknowledging that a significant proportion of the variation in individual emotional responses can be accounted for by these variables, the goal of this analysis is to determine whether there is an independent relationship between negative emotions and political variables after accounting for the demographic variables. To explore this question, the model uses three categories of variables. The partisan variables used in the equation include partisan self-identification and agreement with the statement that President George W. Bush represents the concerns of people like you. The second set of questions taps respondents' attitudes toward America. Respondents were asked to rank their level of agreement with the statement, "I am proud to be an American," and the statement, "America is the land of opportunity. If a person works hard in America, he or she can accomplish almost anything." The survey respondents were also asked to assess which statement is truer: "America's economic system is fair to everyone" or "America's economic system is unfair to poor people."

The model tested the hypothesis that Americans' emotional responses to Hurricane Katrina were intimately linked to their beliefs about race and America's racial history. Several measures of racial attitudes were used to capture this idea. Blacks were asked if they believed that what happens to black people will affect their lives, and whites were asked if they believe what happens to whites will affect their lives. These racially linked fate attitudes are included in the model. Respondents also indicated if they believed that blacks in America have achieved racial equality, will soon achieve racial equality, will not achieve equality in your lifetime, or will never achieve racial equality. Responses to this question serve as a measure of racial pessimism.

Finally, respondents were asked a series of questions about their support for federal reparations for African Americans as compensation for a number of historic injustices. Blacks and whites were asked: "Do you think the federal government should or should not pay money to African Americans whose ancestors were slaves as compensation for that slavery?" "Do you think the federal government should or should not pay money to African Americans as compensation for the system of antiblack violence and legal segregation known as 'Jim Crow'?" and "Do you think that reparations should or should not be paid to survivors and their descendants of large, violent, twentieth-century antiblack riots such as those that occurred in Tulsa, Oklahoma, and Rosewood, Florida?" Responses to these three items were combined in a single scale indicating overall support for reparations to Black Americans.

The dependent variable is a scale derived from a factor of eight emotional response variables that asked respondents, "In the past five weeks since the Hurricane Katrina disaster how often have you felt: so sad that nothing could cheer you up; nervous; restless or fidgety; hopeless; that everything was an effort; worthless;

that difficulties were piling up so high you could not overcome them; and that you are unable to control the important things in your life." The scale is computed as a factor and is constrained to a unit scale where 1 represents the highest presentation of symptoms on all indicators and 0 represents having none of these negative emotions. For the estimated coefficients and standard errors from an ordinary least squares regression on black respondents, see Appendix, table 2.

25. Montana-Leblanc, *Not Just the Levees Broke*, 100.

26. Melissa Harris-Lacewell, Kosuke Imai, and Teppei Yamamoto, "Racial Gaps in the Responses to Hurricane Katrina: An Experimental Study" (Unpublished manuscript, 2007, available at http://imai.princeton.edu/research/files/katrina.pdf).

27. For a full discussion of the technical aspect of the estimation, see ibid.

28. National Fair Housing Alliance (NFHA), *No Home for the Holidays: Report on Housing Discrimination Against Hurricane Katrina Survivors* (Washington, DC: National Fair Housing Alliance, 2005). NFHA conducted sixty-five tests in five states, all with two white callers and one African American caller. In forty-three of these tests, white testers were favored over African American testers. With limited resources and a short time-frame, NFHA was able to conduct five in-person tests at apartment complexes for which we had identified differential treatment on the initial phone test. These in-person tests were matched pair tests with one white tester and one African American tester. In these site visit tests, differential treatment that favored white testers was detected in three of the five tests, or 60 percent.

29. The e-mail was sent by Ryan McFadyen, who later became known as "Player 41," referring to the number on his lacrosse jersey. The website The Smoking Gun reported the contents of the e-mail on April 5, 2006, after a March 14, 2006, probable cause affidavit from the Durham County Superior Court was unsealed.

30. Stuart Taylor Jr. and KC Johnson, *Until Proven Innocent: Political Correctness and the Shameful Injustices of the Duke Lacrosse Rape Case* (New York: Thomas Dunne Books, 2007).

31. I spent five years at Duke University as a graduate student. I taught for two years at North Carolina Central University. I still have friends and family living in the area, so I paid close attention to the Duke case. I even provided commentary about my experiences at Duke and NCCU during a National Public Radio interview on April 7, 2006. I also provided opinion for an interview with BlackAmericaWeb.com on June 3, 2006.

32. "What does a social disaster sound like?" advertisement, *Chronicle*, April 6, 2006.

33. Ibid., emphasis in original.

34. The exact wording was: "How closely have you followed news about the Duke sexual assault case, in which members of the Duke University lacrosse team were arrested for sexually assaulting a woman at a party? Would you say you have followed it very closely, somewhat closely, not too closely, or not at all?" CBS News Monthly Poll #3, January 2007. This poll, fielded January 18–21, 2007, is a part of a continuing series of monthly surveys that solicits public opinion on the presidency and on a range of other political and social issues. A variation of random-digit dialing using primary sampling units (PSUs) was employed, consisting of blocks of 100 telephone numbers identical through the eighth digit and stratified by geographic region, area code, and size of place. Within households, respondents were selected using a method developed by Leslie Kish and modified by Charles Backstrom and Gerald Hursh. An oversample of black respondents was also conducted for this poll. This data collection was produced by CBS News, New York.

35. Danielle L. McGuire, " 'It Was Like All of Us Had Been Raped': Sexual Violence, Community Mobilization, and the African American Freedom Struggle," *Journal of American History* 91 (2004): 917.

36. Deborah Gray White, *Ar'n't I a Woman: Female Slaves in the Plantation South,* 2nd ed. (New York: W. W. Norton, 1988).

37. Tera W. Hunter, *To Joy My Freedom: Southern Black Women's Lives and Labors After the Civil War* (Cambridge, MA: Harvard University Press, 1997).

38. Darlene Clark Hine, "Rape and the Inner Lives of Black Women in the Middle West," *Signs* 14 (1989): 912–920.

39. This incident is recounted in Taylor and Johnson, *Until Proven Innocent,* 73. Taylor and Johnson have a decidedly different tone in their recounting of this event because they use it as evidence that the black community vastly overreacted to the charges. Rather than indicting the black women engaged in this action, I am interested in understanding the historical context of the Duke rape charges in a way that helps us understand why black Durham assumed the players' guilt in this case.

40. Patricia J. Williams, *The Alchemy of Race and Rights: Diary of a Law Professor* (Cambridge, MA: Harvard University Press, 1992), 174.

41. George K. Jennison, "The View of a Lacrosse Parent (2)," *Duke Magazine,* May–June 2006.

42. Joseph W. Bellacosa, "Duke Faculty Should Be Shunned by Students," *Newsday,* August 23, 2007.

43. Charlotte Allen, "Duke's Tenured Vigilantes: The Scandalous Rush to Judgment in the Lacrosse 'Rape' Case," *Weekly Standard,* January 29, 2007; Karla FC Holloway, "Coda: Bodies of Evidence," *Scholar and Feminist Online* 4, no. 3 (2006).

44. Phillip Dray, *At the Hands of Persons Unknown: The Lynching of Black America* (New York: Random House, 2007).

45. Taylor and Johnson, *Until Proven Innocent,* 338, 116, 112.

46. Peter H. Wood's award-winning book is *Black Majority: Negroes in Colonial South Carolina from 1670 Through the Stono Rebellion* (1973; New York: W. W. Norton, 1996).

47. William H. Chafe is the cofounder of the Duke-UNC Center for Research on Women, the Duke Center for the Study of Civil Rights and Race Relations, and the Duke Center for Documentary Studies. His books include *Civilities and Civil Rights: Greensboro, North Carolina, and the Black Struggle for Freedom* (New York: Oxford University Press, 1981) and *Never Stop Running: Allard Lowenstein and the Struggle to Save American Liberalism* (Princeton, NJ: Princeton University Press, 1998), and he is coeditor of *Remembering Jim Crow: African Americans Tell About Life in the Segregated South* (New York: New Press, 2001).

48. Taylor and Johnson, *Until Proven Innocent,* 338, 338, 337, 392 (quoting Richard Bernstein, *Dictatorship of Virtue* [1995]). Robyn Wiegman, Wahneema Lubiano, and Michael Hardt, three professors from the original group of eighty-eight, published a personal and analytic response to the trial and its aftermath in 2007. "In the Afterlife of the Duke Case" offers a very different assessment of the events of discussed by Taylor and Johnson. These professors do not tell the story of the university administration bowing to their whims as race scholars. They recall their professional and scholarly expertise being ignored by the university: "The most extreme marginalization was reserved for the faculty whose professional expertise made them most competent to engage the discourses on race and gender unleashed by the inaugurating incident—scholars of African American and women's studies. Instead, administrators, like the bloggers themselves, operated under the assumption that everyone was an expert on matters of race and gender, while actually existing academic expertise was recast as either bias or a commitment to preconceived notions about the legal case." "In the Afterlife of the Duke Case," *Social Text* 25 (2007): 6–7.

49. Patricia Hill Collins, *Black Feminist Thought: Knowledge, Consciousness, and the Politics of Empowerment* (Boston: Unwin Hyman, 1990).

50. Laura Smart Richman and Charles Jonassaint, "The Effects of Race-Related Stress on Cortisol Reactivity in the Laboratory: Implications of the Duke Lacrosse Scandal," *Annals of Behavioral Medicine* 35 (2007): 105–110.

51. Ibid., 109.

52. Drew Westen, *The Political Brain: The Role of Emotion in Deciding the Fate of the Nation* (New York: Public Affairs, 2007).

53. Steven Greene, "Understanding Party Identification: A Social Identity Approach," *Political Psychology* 20 (1999): 393–403.

54. Martha C. Nussbaum, *Hiding from Humanity: Disgust, Shame, and the Law* (Princeton, NJ: Princeton University Press, 2004), 55.

55. Janice Lindsay-Hartz, "Contrasting Experiences of Shame and Guilt," *American Behavioral Scientist* 27 (1984): 702.

56. Nell Painter, *Sojourner Truth: A Life, a Symbol* (New York: W. W. Norton, 1996), 167. We cannot be certain that Sojourner Truth made this speech, but the legend, as written by white journalist Frances Gage in 1863, holds that Truth was responding to the sexist comments of several white men when she argued, "Ar'n't I a Woman."

57. Montana-Leblanc, *Not Just the Levees Broke*, 13.

Chapter 5. Strength

Epigraph: Trudier Harris, *Saints, Sinners, Saviors: Strong Black Women in African American Literature* (New York: Palgrave, 2001), 12.

1. Psychologist Carlene Young describes the strong black woman, writing that she "confronts all trials and tribulations on behalf of those she loves, perseveres with no attention to her needs as an individual or woman, and provides unlimited support and encouragement necessary for her husband/lover." "Psychodynamics of Coping and Survival of the African-American Female in a Changing World," *Journal of Black Studies* 20 (1989): 210.

2. Regina Romero, "The Icon of the Strong Black Woman: The Paradox of Strength," in *Psychotherapy with African American Women: Innovations in Psychodynamic Perspectives and Practice*, ed. Leslie C. Jackson and Beverly Greene (New York: Guilford, 2000), 225–238.

3. Literary critic Trudier Harris argues that African American writers have consistently used strength as the defining virtue of their black women characters. She maintains that "African American writers have assumed that strength was the one unassailable characteristic they could apply in representing black women. . . . Strength was frequently the only virtue available to black women. . . . So, against the backdrop of unwritten taboos and efforts to avoid stereotypes, African American writers inadvertently created another stereotype—that of the black female character who was more suprahuman than human." Harris, *Saints, Sinners, Saviors*, 11.

4. Ibid., 9.

5. Romero, "Icon of the Strong Black Woman."

6. We should expect that the opinions and expectations of other African Americans will have heightened meaning for black women. Criminologist John Braithwaite demonstrates that "proximate groups" such as families or cultural minorities within a country will have greater influence on shame and self-concept

because members are more interdependent in these proximate groups. John Braithwaite, *Crime, Shame and Reintegration* (Melbourne: Cambridge University Press, 1989).

7. Romero, "Icon of the Strong Black Woman."

8. Ibid.

9. Ibid., 227.

10. The story of John Henry originated in 1870 among the miners drilling the Big Bend Tunnel of the Chesapeake and Ohio Railway in West Virginia. Award-winning author Ezra Jack Keats turned John Henry into a well-loved children's book in 1965. For a full treatment of the history of John Henry, see Scott Reynolds Nelson, *Steel Drivin' Man: John Henry, the Untold Story of an American Legend* (New York: Oxford University Press, 2008).

11. Sherman A. James et al., "Socioeconomic Status, John Henryism, and Hypertension in Blacks and Whites," *American Journal of Epidemiology* 126 (1987): 664–673.

12. Melvin Lerner, "The Desire for Justice and Reactions to Victims," in *Altruism and Helping Behavior,* ed. J. Macaulay and L. Berkowitz (New York: Academic Press, 1970); Lerner, "The Justice Motive in Social Behavior: Some Hypotheses as to Its Origins and Forms," *Journal of Personality* 45 (1977): 1–43; Lerner, *The Belief in a Just World: A Fundamental Delusion* (New York: Plenum, 1980).

13. Melvin Lerner's research offers the surprising insight that believing in a just world can actually undermine the commitment to justice. When an innocent person suffers, those who believe in a just world may seek to justify that suffering in order to maintain the belief that outcomes are appropriate to the character and action of the victim. Lerner, *Belief in a Just World.*

14. Later extensions of the work have suggested that those who explicitly report a belief that the world is just have an even greater propensity to distort narratives of innocent victimization in order to maintain the belief that people get what they deserve. Carolyn L. Hafer Laurent Bègue, "Experimental Research on Just-World Theory: Problems, Developments, and Future Challenges," *Psychological Bulletin* 131 (2005): 128–167.

15. Framing effects "refer to changes in judgment engendered by subtle alterations in the definition of judgment or choice problems." Shanto Iyengar, "Television News and Citizens' Explanations of National Affairs," *American Political Science Review* 81 (1987): 815–832.

16. Ibid., 820.

17. Kathleen M. McGraw, "Manipulating Public Opinion with Moral Justification," *Annals of the American Academy of Political and Social Science* 560 (1998): 129–142.

18. Donald Haider-Markel and Mark R. Joslyn, "Gun Policy, Opinion, Tragedy, and Blame Attribution: The Conditional Influence of Issue Frames," *Journal of Politics* 63 (2001): 520–543.

19. Iyengar, "Television News and Citizens' Explanations of National Affairs," 820.

20. Wendy Rahn, "The Role of Partisan Stereotypes in Information Processing About Political Candidates," *American Journal of Political Science* 37 (1993): 472–496.

21. Descriptions of white men showed the second tightest description, with 42 percent of responses accounted for in the most common categories.

22. Linda Dickson, "The Future of Marriage and Family in Black America," *Journal of Black Studies* 23(1993): 480.

23. This is a photograph of Clara Hale, known by many as "Mother Hale." Hale, who died in 1992, was an African American humanitarian and social activist whose work focused on black children and families. In 1969 she founded the Hale House Center in New York City to provide services to at-risk black infants and children. Only one focus group participant, a forty-three-year-old woman in New York, referred to Hale by name. Most seem to think that she was anonymous as were the women in the other photos.

24. "There is a myth that Black women are unshakable, that somehow they are physically and emotionally impervious to life's most challenging events and circumstances. The stereotype of the strong, tough Black woman is pervasive in American society." Charisse Jones and Kumea Shorter-Gooden, *Shifting: The Double Lives of Black Women in America* (New York: Perennial, 2003), 11.

25. Julia A. Boyd, *In the Company of My Sisters: Black Women and Self-Esteem* (New York: Dutton, 1995), 15.

26. More than a century after Sojourner Truth's "Ar'n't I a Woman" defined black womanhood in terms of struggle, Michele Wallace published *Black Macho and the Myth of the Superwoman* (New York: Dial, 1979). This controversial monograph directly addressed the symbol of the strong black woman. Wallace argues that family dynamics lead little black girls to internalize the idea that strength is an imperative. Wallace describes her first reactions to the women in her family whom she thought were "too domineering, too strong, too aggressive, too outspoken, too masculine." Wallace argues that white power sources and sexist black political leaders are invested in perpetuating the myth that black women are endowed with a unique vigor. In Wallace's view these power sources manipulate the idea of black women's strength in order cast them as emasculating and overbearing.

27. James Jackson and David Williams, Detroit Area Study, 1995. Social Influences on Health, Stress, Racism, and Health Protective Resources. ICPSR

version. Ann Arbor, MI: University of Michigan, Department of Sociology, Detroit Area Studies [producer], 2002. Ann Arbor, MI: Inter-university Consortium for Political and Social Research [distributor], 2002. This survey uses a random sampling technique and a large survey questionnaire format to explore how social influences affect physical and mental health. The 1995 DAS includes data on white men and women as well as black men and women. This allows for a comparison across race and gender categories that further illuminate the unique experience of African American women. The 1995 Detroit Area Study includes 401 black women respondents, 309 white women respondents, 185 black men, and 244 white men

28. To test this hypothesis, I modeled a simple linear relationship and estimated it with an ordinary least squares procedure. The model makes overall life satisfaction the dependent variable. Life satisfaction is measured with a single item that asked respondents: "Please think about your life as a whole. How satisfied are you with it—are you completely satisfied, very satisfied, somewhat satisfied, not very satisfied, or not satisfied at all?" This measure is then modeled as a function of several types of variables: Life satisfaction = f: (perceived physical health, self-reliance, socioeconomic status, personal connections, personal stressors, political beliefs).

29. The model tests several possibilities. First, I include an overall physical health self-rating. Previous research suggests that individuals with better health are more satisfied with life overall. I also include socioeconomic status measures such as education, income, household wealth, and a measure of the relative economic position of the family of origin. Each of the measures of socioeconomic status should be positively related to life satisfaction because those with more economic resources tend to have a greater sense of security and mastery and therefore greater overall life satisfaction. The model also includes several measures of personal connection: religiosity, marital status, children, racial identity, and how well the respondent feels loved by family and friends. We should expect that individuals with more secure social networks should also feel more satisfied with life. Higher scores on each of these measures should be positively correlated with life satisfaction because a sense of connection with God and with one's race, family, and friends should contribute to life satisfaction. Several political attitude measures are used as controls in the model. Measures of political and social ideology, partisanship, and patriotism are included to control for any effects that could occur from liberals and Democrats being more satisfied with life in general because a Democratic president was in office in 1995.

The key variables that I want to understand are the self-reliance scale and the personal stressor items. The self-reliance scale is created from the four measures reported. Together they measure a belief that a person is solely responsible for his or her own future and that working harder is the best response to difficult circumstances. Black women report higher overall levels of self-reliance. I want to know if there is a relationship between life satisfaction and sense of self-reliance. It is possible that those who depend mostly on themselves are more satisfied with their lives, but it is also possible that an insistence on independence makes black women feel worse about their lives. This regression will help us determine which of these possibilities is true for the women in this survey. I am also interested in the personal stressor measures. We have already seen that black women feel more burdened by their families than do individuals from other race and gender categories; now we can test whether those burdens influence life satisfaction. Because the DAS asks the same questions of black and white women and men, we can compare how these various ideas and beliefs affect each group.

30. The analysis estimates the same regression equation for each race and gender category separately. This allows us to compare the relative importance of the variables of interest for black women versus other groups.

31. Frank Clemente and William Sauer, "Life Satisfaction in the United States," *Social Forces* 54 (1976): 621–631; James Near, Robert Rice, and Raymond Hunt, "Work and Extra-Work Correlates of Life and Job Satisfaction," *Academy of Management Journal* 21 (1978): 248–264.

32. Although the coefficients are also positive in the equations for black and white men, they fail to reach statistical significance at the level of $p < .05$.

33. Religiosity is measured as a three-item scale from responses to the following questions: "How often do you attend religious services?" "How often do you pray?" and "In general, how important are religious or spiritual beliefs in your day-to-day life?" The scale is constrained to a unit range so that 1 reflects the highest score on all three items.

34. Toinette M. Eugene, "There Is a Balm in Gilead: Black Women and the Black Church as Agents of a Therapeutic Community," *Women and Therapy* 16 (1995): 55–71.

35. Deborah K. Padgett et al., "Ethnic Differences in Use of Inpatient Mental Health Services by Blacks, Whites, and Hispanics in a National Insured Population," *Health Services Research* 29 (1994): 135–153.

36. Douglas Massey and Nancy Denton, *American Apartheid: Segregation and the Making of the Underclass* (Cambridge, MA: Harvard University Press, 1998).

37. Sudhir Venkatesh, *Off the Books: The Underground Economy of the Urban Poor* (Cambridge, MA: Harvard University Press, 2006).

38. I once again estimated simple linear regression models using ordinary least squares on each of the individual race and gender categories.

39. These three items are combined in a single scale measured from 0 to 1 such that 0 represents complete disagreement with all the statements and 1 represents complete agreement with all the statements.

40. Jennifer Hochschild, *Facing Up to the American Dream: Race, Class, and the Soul of the Nation* (Princeton, NJ: Princeton University Press, 1996).

41. Zick Rubin and Anne Perplau, "Who Believes in a Just World?" *Journal of Social Issues* 31 (1975): 65–89.

42. The Chicago African American Attitudes Study was specifically designed to determine the effects of exposure to narratives about strong black women on the political attitudes of African American women. The CAAAS was conducted on November 5–6, 1999, and is a public opinion survey with an embedded experimental manipulation. Graduate student researchers from the University of Chicago entered 15 black beauty salons and barbershops (randomly selected from the entire population of black salons) in three Southside Chicago neighborhoods. The respondents are 194 adult African American individuals who chose to complete a survey instrument while receiving service in the selected businesses. The response rate for this study was exceptionally high. Eighty-seven percent of individuals who were approached by students in the barbershops and beauty salons participated in the study. All the student researchers were African American. Male researchers were assigned to barbershops and female researchers were assigned to beauty salons. Therefore, most respondents were matched by both race and gender to the researchers. There were a few women customers in barbershops and men customers in beauty salons, but the vast majority of the sample was matched.

43. The analysis that follows uses a number of policy attitudes as dependent variables. The main exogenous variables of interest are the experimental manipulations. The central hypothesis is that the treatments have an effect. Maximum likelihood logistical estimations determine significant and important effects on policy attitudes caused by exposure to the various stories about Nikki. The model also includes measures of exposure to various sources of black information: *general black media knowledge,* a five-indicator measure of recognition of black media figures; *black women's information networks,* a four-part measure of recognition of black women popular culture figures; and *hip-hop knowledge,* a three-part measure of recognition of rap artists. These sites of information are sources for images of messages about black women and for development of political attitudes. They are hypothesized to have an effect on political attitudes that is independent of exposure to the experimental manipulations and to have an effect that moderates the impact of exposure to the experimental settings. The most general form of the estimated model is: Political Attitudes = f: (experimental manipulation, black media knowledge, black women's information networks, hip-hop knowledge).

44. I model support or opposition to a policy as a dichotomous choice and estimate all the policy attitudes using maximum likelihood logistic estimation. The decision to convert the likert items to dichotomous variables is indicated because the distribution of responses to the policy questions is bimodal, clustered around strong support and strong opposition, with far fewer individuals falling into the middle ranges. Therefore all policy items are modeled as bimodal processes and estimated with logits.

45. bell hooks, *Sisters of the Yam: Black Women and Self-Recovery* (Boston, MA: South End Press, 1993), 15.

46. Zora Neale Hurston, *Their Eyes Were Watching God* (1937; New York: Harper Perennial Classics, 1998), 16, 192.

Chapter 6. God

Epigraph: Alice Walker, *In Search of Our Mothers' Gardens: Womanist Prose* (San Diego: Harcourt Brace Jovanovich, 1983), xi.

1. C. Eric Lincoln and Lawrence H. Mamiya, *The Black Church in the African American Experience* (Durham, NC: Duke University Press, 1990), 8.

2. Eugene D. Genovese, *Roll, Jordan, Roll: The World the Slaves Made* (New York: Vintage, 1976), 4; Aldon D. Morris, *The Origins of the Civil Rights Movement: Black Communities Organizing for Change* (New York: Free Press, 1984); Katherine Tate, *From Protest to Politics: The New Black Voters in American Elections* (New York: Russell Sage Foundation, 1993).

3. Joseph R. Washington Jr., *Black Religion: The Negro and Christianity in the United States* (Boston: Beacon, 1964).

4. Some portions of this chapter are taken from my chapter "Liberation to Mutual Fund: The Political Consequences of Differing Conceptions of Christ in the African American Church," in *From Pews to Polling Places: Political Mobilization in the American Religious Mosaic,* ed. J. Matthew Wilson (Washington, DC: Georgetown University Press, 2007).

5. James H. Cone and Gayraud S. Wilmore, eds., *Black Theology: A Documentary History,* Vol. 1: *1966–1979* (Maryknoll, NY: Orbis Books, 1993), 16.

6. J. Deotis Roberts Sr., "Black Theological Ethics: A Bibliographical Essay," *Journal of Religious Ethics* 3, no. 1 (1975): 69–109.

7. Dwight N. Hopkins, *Introducing a Black Theology of Liberation* (New York: Orbis Books, 1999).

8. Delores S. Williams, *Sisters in the Wilderness: The Challenge of Womanist God-Talk* (Maryknoll, NY: Orbis Books, 1993), 5.

9. Hopkins, *Introducing a Black Theology of Liberation.*

10. Jacquelyn Grant, *White Women's Christ and Black Women's Jesus: Feminist Christology and the Womanist Response* (Atlanta, GA: Scholars Press, 1989); Katie G. Cannon, *Black Womanist Ethics* (Atlanta, GA: Scholars Press, 1988); Cannon, *Katie's Canon: Womanism and the Soul of the Black Community* (New York: Continuum, 1995); Renita J. Weems, *Just a Sister Away: A Womanist Vision of Women's Relationships in the Bible* (San Diego, CA: LuraMedia, 1988); Williams, *Sisters in the Wilderness.*

11. Cannon, *Katie's Canon,* 126.

12. Williams, *Sisters in the Wilderness;* Grant, *White Women's Christ and Black Women's Jesus.*

13. Frederick C. Harris, *Something Within: Religion in African-American Political Activism* (New York: Oxford University Press, 1999), 157.

14. Cheryl J. Sanders, *Saints in Exile: The Holiness-Pentecostal Experience in African American Religion and Culture* (New York: Oxford University Press, 1999).

15. Bettye Collier-Thomas, *Daughters of Thunder: Black Women Preachers and Their Sermons, 1850–1979* (San Francisco: Jossey-Bass, 1997).

16. Cheryl Townsend Gilkes, *"If It Wasn't for the Women": Black Women's Experience and Womanist Culture in Church and Community* (Maryknoll, NY: Orbis Books, 2001).

17. Lincoln and Mamiya make a distinction between the denominations on one hand and the black sacred cosmos on the other. Delores Williams marks this division, writing, "This book makes a distinction between the black church as invisible and rooted in the soul of community memory and the African-American denomination churches as visible." *Sisters in the Wilderness,* 206.

18. Williams, *Sisters in the Wilderness.*

19. Grant, *White Women's Christ and Black Women's Jesus.*

20. Diana L. Hayes, "And When We Speak: To Be Black, Catholic, and Womanist," in *Taking Down Our Harps: Black Catholics in the United States,* ed. Diana L. Hayes and Cyprian Davis (Maryknoll, NY: Orbis Books, 1998), 102–118.

21. Karen Fraser Wyche, "African American Muslim Women: An Invisible Group," *Sex Roles: A Journal of Research* 51 (2004): 319–328; Carolyn Moxley Rouse, *Engaged Surrender: African American Women and Islam* (Berkeley: University of California Press, 2004); Rouse, "Shopping with Sister Zubayda: African American Sunni Muslim Rituals of Consumption and Belonging," in *Women and Religion in the African Diaspora: Knowledge, Power, and Performance,* ed. R. Marie Griffith and Barbara Dianne Savage (Baltimore: Johns Hopkins University Press, 2006), 245–264; Linda E. Thomas, ed., *Living Stones on the Household of God: The Legacy and Future of Black Theology* (Minneapolis, MN: Augsburg Fortress, 2004).

22. Emilie M. Townes, *Womanist Ethics and the Cultural Production of Evil* (New York: Palgrave Macmillan, 2006).

23. There is still vigorous debate in social scientific scholarship as to whether the church is truly an agent of political change for African Americans. Scholars writing in the traditions that perceive the black church as a tool of assimilation, isolation, or compensation argue that black churches function as an opiate, directing the energy of their congregants toward salvation and otherworldly rewards rather than focusing them on political struggle against injustice. See E. Franklin Frazier, *The Negro Church in America* (New York: Schocken Books, 1974); and Gary T. Marx, *Protest and Prejudice: A Study of Belief in the Black Community* (New York: Harper and Row, 1969). Even scholars who argue that the church is a site of political inspiration recognize the diversity among black churches and acknowledge that some do little to encourage and sometimes actively discourage political engagement by their members. Harris, *Something Within*.

24. Henry E. Brady, Sidney Verba, and Kay Lehman Schlozman, "Beyond SES: A Resource Model of Political Participation," *American Political Science Review* 89 (1995): 271–294; Doug McAdam, *Political Process and the Development of Black Insurgency* (Chicago: University of Chicago Press, 1984); Morris, *Origins of the Civil Rights Movement;* Harris, *Something Within;* Allison Calhoun-Brown, "African American Churches and Political Mobilization: The Psychological Impact of Organizational Resources," *Journal of Politics* 58 (1996): 935–953; Christopher G. Ellison, "Religious Involvement and Self-Perception Among Black Americans," *Social Forces* 71 (1993): 1027–1055; Mary Pattillo-McCoy, "Church Culture as a Strategy of Action in the Black Community," *American Sociological Review* 63 (1998): 767–784.

25. Sociologist Cheryl Townsend Gilkes reminds us, "The tendency to view black churches only as agencies of sociopolitical change led by black male pastors obscures the central and critical roles of black women. Throughout all varieties of black religious activity, black women represent from 75 to 90 percent of the participants; yet there is little documentation or analysis of their role in the development of this oldest and most autonomous aspect of black community life." Gilkes, " 'Together and in Harness': Women's Traditions in the Sanctified Church," *Signs* 10 (1985): 679.

26. Evelyn Brooks Higginbotham, *Righteous Discontent: The Women's Movement in the Black Baptist Church, 1880–1920* (Cambridge, MA: Harvard University Press, 1993).

27. "These women were as militantly pro-black, pro-woman, and pro-uplift as their Baptist and Methodist sisters were, and their political consciousness was fueled by spiritual zeal. They were somewhat more successful than Baptist and Methodist women in gaining access to the pulpit or lectern. . . . In some cases,

Baptist and Methodist women defected to the Sanctified Church in order to exercise their gifts." Gilkes, " 'Together and in Harness,' " 682.

28. Judith Weisenfeld, *African American Women and Christian Activism: New York's Black YWCA, 1905–1945* (Cambridge, MA: Harvard University Press, 1997).

29. Paula Giddings, *When and Where I Enter: The Impact of Black Women on Race and Sex in America* (New York: Harper and Row, 1984).

30. Cheryl Townsend Gilkes, "Plenty Good Room: Adaptation in a Changing Black Church," *Annals of the American Academy of Political and Social Science* 558 (1998): 101–121.

31. Barbara Dianne Savage, "W. E. B. Du Bois and 'The Negro Church,' " *Annals of the American Academy of Political and Social Science* 568 (2000): 235–249.

32. Grant, *White Women's Christ and Black Women's Jesus,* 325.

33. Gilkes, "Plenty Good Room," 114.

34. Harris, *Something Within,* 167–168.

35. Clyde Wilcox, "Race, Gender Role Attitudes, and Support for Feminism," *Western Political Quarterly* 43 (1990): 113–121.

36. Brady, Verba, and Scholzman, "Beyond SES."

37. Melissa Victoria Harris-Lacewell, *Barbershops, Bibles, and BET: Everyday Talk and Black Political Thought* (Princeton, NJ: Princeton University Press, 2004).

38. Philip Converse, "The Nature of Belief Systems in Mass Publics," in *Ideology and Discontent,* ed. David E. Apter (New York: Free Press of Glencoe, 1964), 206–261.

39. Grant, *White Women's Christ and Black Women's Jesus;* Judylyn S. Ryan, "Spirituality and/as Ideology in Black Women's Literature: The Preaching of Maria W. Stewart and Baby Suggs, Holy," in *Women Preachers and Prophets Through Two Millennia of Christianity,* ed. Beverly Mayne Kienzle and Pamela J. Walker (Berkeley: University of California Press, 1998), 267–287; A. Elaine Brown Crawford, *Hope in the Holler: A Womanist Theology* (Louisville, KY: Westminster John Knox Press, 2002); Cannon, *Katie's Canon;* Thomas, *Daughters of Thunder.*

40. The General Social Surveys (GSS) have been conducted by the National Opinion Research Center annually since 1972, except for the years 1979, 1981, and 1992 (a supplement was added in 1992), and biennially beginning in 1994. For each round of surveys, the Roper Center for Public Opinion Research prepares a cumulative data set that merges previous years of the GSS into a single file, with each year or survey constituting a subfile. The content of each survey changes slightly as some items are added to or deleted from the interview schedule. Main

areas covered in the GSS include socioeconomic status, social mobility, social control, the family, race relations, sex relations, civil liberties, and morality. Topical modules designed to investigate new issues or to expand the coverage of an existing subject have been part of the GSS since 1977, when the first module on race, abortion, and feminism appeared. The topical modules for 1998 focused on the themes of medical care, medical ethics, religion, religion and health, culture, job experiences, and interracial friendships. In 1994, two major innovations were introduced to the GSS. First, the traditional core set of questions was substantially reduced to allow for the creation of mini-modules (small to medium-sized supplements). The mini-modules permit greater flexibility to incorporate innovations and to include important items proposed by the social science community. Second, a new biennial, split-sample design was instituted, consisting of two parallel subsamples of approximately 1,500 cases each. The two subsamples contain identical cores and different topical ISSP modules.

41. The "forgiveness" variable is a factor composed of three indicators: (1) I have forgiven myself for things I have done wrong; (2) I have forgiven those who hurt me; and (3) I know that God has forgiven me. The second variable, "overall sense of connection with a divine presence," is a factor composed of four indicators when respondents were asked, "To what extent can you say you experience the following?" (1) I feel God's presence; (2) I find strength and comfort in my religion; (3) I feel deep inner peace or harmony; and (4) I desire to be closer to or in union with God. The third area of religious belief is a single item asking respondents the level of agreement with the statement, "I try hard to carry my religious beliefs over into all my other dealings in life." Finally, respondents gave a self-rating of their level of religious fundamentalism, ranking themselves as fundamentalist, moderate, or liberal. Each item is constrained to a unit scale so that numbers approaching 1 indicate the highest level of agreement with the measure.

42. Albert B. Cleage Jr., *The Black Messiah: The Religious Roots of Black Power* (New York: Sheed and Ward, 1969).

43. James H. Cone, *Black Theology and Black Power* (New York: Harper and Row, 1969).

44. Anna Case-Winters, *God's Power: Traditional Understandings and Contemporary Challenges* (Louisville, KY: Westminster John Knox Press, 1990), 173.

45. Albert Cleage writes, "Put down this white Jesus who has been tearing you to pieces. Forget your white God. Remember that we are worshipping a Black Jesus who was a Black Messiah. God must be black if he created us in his own image. You can't build dignity in black people if they go down on their knees everyday worshipping a white Jesus." Cleage, *Black Messiah*, 98.

46. Grant, *White Women's Christ and Black Women's Jesus*, 212.

47. No other pairwise comparison produces a statistically significant result.

48. These data are gathered from the cumulative data file of the General Social Surveys, 1980–1998.

49. Karen Lincoln and Linda Chatters, "Keeping the Faith: Religion, Stress, and Psychological Well-Being Among African American Women, in *In and Out of Our Right Minds: The Mental Health of African American Women,* ed. Diane R. Brown and Verna M Keith (New York: Columbia University Press, 2003), 223–241.

50. "This myth . . . facilitates the silence around abuse and violence in the black community. Black women have been expected to bear all and tell nothing. . . . The demand for silence around abuse and violence also has roots in the black community, which has, for decades, been forced to fight for voice regarding its oppression by the dominant society. The unity of the black community has centered around standing together, supporting one another, and a kind of understood loyalty that does not allow one to air 'dirty laundry.' " Crawford, *Hope in the Holler,* 74.

51. A moving memoir from Meri Nana-Ama Danquah, chronicles one woman's lifetime of experiences with clinical depression. Danquah writes, "Out of nowhere and for no reason—or so it seemed—I started feeling strong sensations of grief. I don't remember the step-by-step progression of the illness. What I can recall is that my life disintegrated; first, into a cobweb of fatigue. I gradually lost my ability to function." *Willow Weep for Me: A Black Women's Journey Through Depression* (New York: Ballantine, 1998), 27.

52. Research shows that depression among African American women is correlated with socioeconomic status and with support networks. See I. C. Scarinci et al., "Depression, Socioeconomic Status, Age, and Marital Status in Black Women: A National Study," *Ethnicity and Disease* 12 (2002): 421–428.

53. The connections between the imperative of strength and the various psychological burdens experienced by black women are described by the contributing authors to Brown and Keith, *In and Out of Our Right Minds.*

54. The studies and stories from Brown and Keith's volume, *In and Out of Our Right Minds,* call into question a symbol many believe to be empowering. Author Joan Morgan discusses the difficulty of challenging a myth that allowed her to believe "that the ability to kick adversity's ass is a birthright." In her text, Morgan chooses to retire her strong black woman badge which assumed, "that by sole virtues of my race and gender I was supposed to be the consummate professional, handle any life crisis, be the dependable rock for every soul who needed me, and, yes, the classic—require less from my lovers than they did from me." Joan Morgan, *When Chickenheads Come Home to Roost: My Life as a Hip-Hop Feminist* (New York: Simon and Schuster, 1999), 87.

55. Tamara Beauboeuf-Lafontant, *Behind the Mask of the Strong Black Woman: Voice and the Embodiment of a Costly Performance* (Philadelphia: Temple University Press, 2009), 64.

56. Kevin M. Malone et al., "Protective Factors Against Suicidal Acts in Major Depression: Reasons for Living," *American Journal of Psychiatry* 157 (2000): 1084–1088.

57. Monica A. Coleman, *Making a Way Out of No Way: A Womanist Theology* (Minnesota, MN: Fortress Press, 2008).

58. Ibid., 26.

59. Raquel A. St. Clair, *Call and Consequences: A Womanist Reading of Mark* (Minneapolis, MN: Fortress Press, 2008).

60. The dependent variable is a scale of negative mental and emotional self-reports by black women respondents on the 1998 GSS. Respondents were asked how frequently they felt (1) so sad that nothing could cheer you up, (2) nervous, (3) restless, (4) hopeless, (5) that everything was an effort, and (6) worthless. These measures are combined in a single indicator and constrained to a unit scale, so that 0 means the respondent never felt any of these negative emotions and 1 means that the respondent felt all of these negative emotions all of the time. This scale is used as the dependent variable and modeled as a function of a self-report of physical health in the four areas of religious belief explored in the section above, the images of God discussed in the section above, religious coping mechanism, religious practice, and a variety of demographic variables. An overall physical health self-rating is included in the model because there is substantial previous research establishing the empirical connection between individuals' assessment of their physical well-being and their mental and emotional well-being. Religious practice is operationalized through two separate measures: (1) self-report of frequency of prayer and (2) self-report of church attendance.

61. Kristine M. Rankka, *Women and the Value of Suffering: An Aw(e)ful Rowing Toward God* (Collegeville, MN: Liturgical Press, 1988), 54.

62. Womanist theologian Delores Williams writes, "Black women should never be encouraged to believe that they can be united with God through this kind of suffering. There are quite enough black women bearing the cross by rearing children alone, struggling on welfare, suffering through poverty, experiencing inadequate health care, domestic violence and various forms of sexism and racism." Williams, *Sisters in the Wilderness,* 169.

63. Karen Baker-Fletcher, *Dancing with God: A Womanist Perspective on the Trinity* (St. Louis, MO: Chalice Press, 2006).

64. Barbara E. Reid, *Taking Up the Cross: New Testament Interpretations Through Latina and Feminist Eyes* (Minneapolis, MN: Fortress Press, 2007).

65. Harris, *Something Within.*

66. Ellison, "Religious Involvement and Self-Perception Among Black Americans."

67. Calhoun-Brown, "African American Churches and Political Mobilization."

68. Under the direction of Michael Dawson, Ronald Brown, and James S. Jackson, the National Black Politics Study (NBPS) was designed to provide information on attitudes and opinions regarding a number of issues of importance to black Americans. Topics included the performance of President Bill Clinton, the economic condition of black Americans, and what respondents thought ought to be done to improve the condition of black people. Questions regarding black women and their role in the black community were also asked. In addition, the role and extent of religion in black politics was investigated. Respondents also provided information about their political self-identification and their community and political involvement, as well as their feelings toward various political leaders, political groups, and national policies. Demographic information on respondents included sex, age, education, marital status, income, and occupation and industry. The data come from a probability sample of all African American households, yielding 1,206 respondents who are African Americans eighteen years or older. The survey was conducted between November 20, 1993 and February 20, 1994, with a response rate of 65 percent. National Black Politics Study, 1993 (computer file), ICPSR02018-v2 (Ann Arbor, MI: Inter-university Consortium for Political and Social Research, 2008-12-03).

69. To model political action, I constructed a scale of political participation from responses to the following questions: (1) Did you vote in the last presidential election; and in the past five years have you (2) contacted a public official; (3) attended a protest meeting or demonstration; (4) taken part in a neighborhood march; (5) signed a petition in support of or against something? This scale is coded on a unit range so that 0 means that the respondent did not engage in any of these political activities and 1 indicates that the respondent engaged in all of the political activities.

70. For religious beliefs, I modeled the flexibility of divine imagery through a measure that asks respondents: "When you speak or think of Christ, do you imagine Christ as being black or white?" This measure is an unambiguous indication of belief in a black Christ, a central tenet of black theology, but it also represents a broader capacity to envision the divine beyond the limitations of normative American Christian understandings. Unfortunately, the richer imaging variables in the GSS are not available in this data set, but the image of a black Christ stands as at least one indicator of a flexible divine imagination. I also in-

cluded a measure of denomination to capture some of the variation in religious teachings across denominations and a measure of whether religion provides guidance in day-to-day living. This variable is coded on a unit range where higher values indicate that religion is more important as a daily guide.

Using the measures available in the NBPS, it is possible to model participation in politicized churches. These measures are combined into additive scales of church-based political discussion and church-based political action, and are included to account for earlier findings about the centrality of politicized black churches. I also model how politicized a church is. The models also include an independent measure of self-reported activity within the church. This question asked respondents how active they are in church-sponsored charitable and social activities.

The models also include two important measures of racial attitudes. Political scientists Michael Dawson (*Behind the Mule: Race and Class in African-American Politics* [Princeton, NJ: Princeton University Press, 1994]) and Katherine Tate (*From Protest to Politics: The New Black Voters in American Elections* [New York: Russell Sage Foundation, 1993]) show that individuals who perceive their own fate as linked to the fate of the race are more likely to participate politically. The NBPS asks respondents if "what happens to black people affects what happens in my own life." This measure of black-linked fate is coded on a unit range where higher values indicate stronger connection with the fate of the race. The model also includes a measure of support for racial self-reliance. Black liberation theology emerged from black nationalist projects of the late 1960s. It is possible that those who believe Christ is black are more likely to be black nationalists and that any differences in political participation will be due to nationalist disposition rather than the religious beliefs. A measure of support for black self-reliance is coded from agreement with the statement, "Black people should rely on themselves not on others." This measure is included to control for the effect of black nationalist sentiment.

Finally, the models include controls for demographic variables: age, education, income, and urban dwelling. Age is coded in years, with forty-three the average age of the sample. Education is measured as the highest grade completed, with high school diploma as the modal response category. Income is annual household income measured in nine income categories ranging from under $10,000 to over $75,000. Urbanity is a dichotomous variable where those who report living in a city are coded as 1.

71. Pattillo-McCoy, "Church Culture as a Strategy of Action in the Black Community."

72. Sandra L. Barnes, "Black Church Culture and Community Action," *Social Forces* 84 (2005): 967–994.

73. Harris, *Something Within.*

74. Courtney Young, "Tyler Perry's Gender Problem," *Nation,* August 31, 2009.

75. Ntozake Shange, *for colored girls who've considered suicide / when the rainbow is enuf* (New York: Scribner, 2010), 11.

76. According to the 1998 *Statistical Abstract of the United States,* black women have the lowest suicide rate of any race or either gender. However, suicide rates have been climbing among African Americans, particularly among young blacks. Unlike white suicide patterns, which peak in middle age, black suicide rates peak in young adulthood: 47 percent of black suicides occur in people aged 20–34. Black men, however, are still far more likely to commit suicide than black women. For more on this, see George Howe Colt, *The Enigma of Suicide: A Timely Investigation into the Causes, the Possibilities for Prevention, and the Paths to Healing* (New York: Summit Books, 1991).

77. Courtney Young, "For Colored Girls, Is Tyler Perry's Film Enuf?" *Nation,* November 12, 2010.

78. Salamishah Tillet, "Black Feminism, Tyler Perry Style," *theRoot.com,* November 11, 2010.

79. Combahee River Collective, 1974, reprinted in *Words of Fire: An Anthology of African-American Feminist Thought,* ed. Beverly Guy-Sheftall (New York: New Press, 1995), 236.

80. Crawford, *Hope in the Holler,* 117.

81. Toni Morrison, *Beloved* (1987; New York: Plume, 1998), 88.

Chapter 7. Michelle

1. "Remarks of President-Elect Barack Obama," November 4, 2008, Chicago; available at: http://my.barackobama.com/page/community/post/stateupdates/gGx3Kc.

2. Anna Julia Cooper, *A Voice from the South* (1892; New York: Oxford University Press, 1990).

3. Liza Mundy, *Michelle: A Biography* (New York: Simon and Schuster, 2008); David Colbert, *Michelle Obama: An American Story* (New York: Houghton Mifflin Harcourt, 2009); Elizabeth Lightfoot, *Michelle Obama: First Lady of Hope* (Guilford, CT: Globe Pequot Press, 2008).

4. For a similar argument about Barack Obama's strategy of building identity coalitions, see David Remnick, *The Bridge: The Life and Rise of Barack Obama* (New York: Alfred A. Knopf, 2010).

5. Rosalind Rossi, "The Woman Behind Obama," *Chicago Sun-Times,* January 20, 2007.

6. Shailagh Murray, "A Family Tree Rooted in American Soil: Michelle Obama Learns About Her Slave Ancestors, Herself and Her Country," *Washington Post,* October 2, 2008.

7. James Bone, "From Slave Cabin to White House: A Family Rooted in Black America," *Times* (London), November 6, 2008. See also Rachel L. Swarns and Jodi Kantor, "In First Lady's Roots, a Complex Path from Slavery," *New York Times,* October 7, 2009.

8. "Fox Refers to Michelle Obama as 'Baby Mama,'" MSNBC, June 12, 2008, http://today.msnbc.msn.com/id/25129598/ns/today-entertainment/.

9. Jim Rutenberg, "Fox Forced to Address Michelle Obama Headline," The Caucus, June 12, 2008, http://thecaucus.blogs.nytimes.com/2008/06/12/fox-apol ogizes-for-michelle-obama-headline/.

10. During the "Obama Chronicles" segment of the September 16, 2008, edition of Fox News's *The O'Reilly Factor,* host Bill O'Reilly stated of Michelle Obama: "Now I have a lot of people who call me on the radio and say she looks angry. And I have to say there's some validity to that. She looks like an angry woman." During the segment, O'Reilly asked *Vogue* magazine contributing editor Rebecca Johnson: "The perception is that she's angry in some quarters. Valid?" Johnson began her response by stating: "Well—they say she looks angry because of maybe of the cast of her eyebrows or something like that. But, no, I don't find her to be angry. I think what happens is that we expect women to be cheerful and happy all the time in that kind of television personality kind of way. And she's not like that. She's a thoughtful person." He later asked *Human Events* columnist Michelle Oddis: "Now, did you find out about the angry woman thing, Rebecca? I'm sorry, Michelle? Did you—is there any validity to that? Or is that an urban myth?" Oddis responded: "I wouldn't say it's an urban myth. I think we all can tell just by appearances and speeches and the way that Michelle has personified herself that she's not warm and fuzzy. We know that about her."

11. Michelle LaVaughn Robinson, "Princeton Educated Blacks and the Black Community" (Senior thesis, Princeton University, 1985).

12. Evan Thomas, "Alienated in the U.S.A.," *Newsweek,* March 13, 2008.

13. Mike Allen, "Obama Slams *New Yorker* Portrayal," *Politico,* July 13, 2010, http://www.politico.com/news/stories/0708/11719.html.

14. CBS News/New York Times monthly polls, February 2008–April 2009 (June 2008 and March 2009 polls conducted by ABC News/Washington Post). Overall, favorable opinions of Michelle Obama increased by 30 percentage points or more between February 2008 and April 2009 among all subgroups analyzed. All subgroups reported a drop in favorable opinions in April 2008. However, since the February 2008 survey included only a very small number of observations, the smaller percentages in April 2008 may not represent true decreases in favorable

opinion. The seemingly unusual spikes in favorable opinions in June 2008 and March 2009 may be due to differences in question wording and format (these two are the ABC News/Washington Post surveys). Overall, however, whites, men, and women all exhibit increasingly favorable opinions of Michelle Obama from October 2008, immediately preceding the general election, through April 2009 (excluding March 2009). African Americans' opinions appear more variable, and it is hard to know whether this variation represents actual opinion change or is a function of different sampling procedures among the surveys. Only the June 2008 and April 2009 surveys used oversamples of African Americans, interviewing 201 and 212 black respondents, respectively.

15. Erin Aubry Kaplan, "First Lady Got Back," *Salon.com,* November 18, 2008.

16. See Latoya Peterson, "Salon: "First Lady Got Back," *Racialicious.com,* November 18, 2008.

17. Maureen Dowd, "Should Michelle Cover Up?" *New York Times,* March 7, 2009.

18. Courtney Young, "Tyler Perry's Gender Problem," *Nation,* August 31, 2009.

19. See Sander Gilman, "Black Bodies, White Bodies: Toward an Iconography of Female Sexuality in Late Nineteenth-Century Art, Medicine and Literature," *Critical Inquiry* 12 (1985): 212; and E. Frances White, *Dark Continent of Our Bodies: Black Feminism and the Politics of Respectability* (Philadelphia: Temple University Press, 2001).

20. For historical accounts of the still controversial relationship between Thomas Jefferson and Sally Hemings, see two books by legal historian Annette Gordon-Reed: *Thomas Jefferson and Sally Hemings: An American Controversy* (Charlottesville: University of Virginia Press, 1998), and *The Hemingses of Monticello: An American Family* (New York: W. W. Norton, 2008).

21. In response to her shameless sleevelessness, Michelle Obama's arms have become iconic and even profitable. American women can now buy exercise programs promising "Michelle Obama Arms in 21 Days." Rylan Duggan, *Totally Toned Arms: Get Michelle Obama Arms in 21 Days* (Wellness Central).

22. Dorothy Roberts, *Killing the Black Body: Race, Reproduction and the Meaning of Liberty* (New York: Vintage, 1998).

23. Susan J. Douglas and Meredith W. Michaels, *The Mommy Myth: The Idealization of Motherhood and How It Has Undermined All Women* (New York: Free Press, 2004), 160–161.

24. Barack Obama, *The Audacity of Hope: Thoughts on Reclaiming the American Dream* (New York: Crown, 2006), 359.

25. Interview with Tonya Lewis Lee, "Your Next First Lady?" *Glamour,* September 2007.

26. Richard Wolffe, "Barack's Rock," *Newsweek,* February 25, 2008.

27. James T. Patterson, *Freedom Is Not Enough: The Moynihan Report and America's Struggle over Black Family Life from LBJ to Obama* (New York: Basic Books, 2010).

28. Chris Rock interview, *Rolling Stone Magazine,* April 2008.

29. Overall, African Americans were victimized by intimate partners at significantly higher rates than persons of any other race between 1993 and 1998. Black females experienced intimate partner violence at a rate 35 percent higher than that of white females, and about twenty-two times the rate of women of other races. Black males experienced intimate partner violence at a rate about 62 percent higher than that of white males and about twenty-two times the rate of men of other races. Callie Marie Rennison and Sarah Welchans, *Intimate Partner Violence,* US Department of Justice, NCJ 178247, 2000.

30. Beth E. Richie, *Compelled to Crime: The Gender Entrapment of Battered Black Women* (New York: Routledge, 1996).

31. Joanne Bamberger, "A Softer, Gentler Michelle Obama?" *Huffington Post,* June 18, 2008, http://www.huffingtonpost.com/joanne-bamberger/a-softer-gentler-michelle_b_107829.html.

32. Bart Landry, *Black Working Wives: Pioneers of the American Family Revolution* (Berkeley: University of California Press, 2000).

33. Hill Harper, *The Conversation: How Black Men and Women Can Build Loving, Trusting Relationships* (New York: Gotham Books, 2009); Steve Harvey, *Act Like a Lady, Think Like a Man: What Men Really Think About Love, Relationships, Intimacy, and Commitment* (New York: HarperCollins, 2009); and Jimi Izrael, *The Denzel Principle: Why Black Women Can't Find Good Black Men* (New York: St. Martin's, 2010).

34. Allison Samuels, "What Michelle Means to Us," *Newsweek,* November 22, 2008.

Index

Page numbers in *italics* indicate illustrations.